Most of the world's population and the vast majority of the world's poor live and work in villages. Their activities are usually centered in households, but interactions among households shape the impacts of policy, market, and environmental changes on rural production, incomes, employment, and migration. This book presents a new generation of villagewide economic modeling designed to capture these interactions when assessing the impacts of policy, market, and environmental changes on rural economies in less developed countries.

J. Edward Taylor and Irma Adelman present a general framework for modeling village economies based on computable general-equilibrium techniques, estimate models for villages and a village-town in five different countries, and use these models to conduct a series of comparative experiments. The findings offer explanations for some paradoxical outcomes of exogenous shocks as their influence wends its way through rural economies, and they underline the importance of adopting a local economywide perspective when designing development policies.

T0312109

Village economies

Village economies

The design, estimation, and use
of villagewide economic models

J. EDWARD TAYLOR
University of California, Davis

IRMA ADELMAN
University of California, Berkeley

with contributions from
Elise H. Golan, Blane D. Lewis,
Katherine Ralston, Shankar
Subramanian, and Erik Thorbecke

CAMBRIDGE
UNIVERSITY PRESS

CAMBRIDGE UNIVERSITY PRESS
Cambridge, New York, Melbourne, Madrid, Cape Town, Singapore, São Paulo

Cambridge University Press
The Edinburgh Building, Cambridge CB2 2RU, UK

Published in the United States of America by Cambridge University Press, New York

www.cambridge.org
Information on this title: www.cambridge.org/9780521550123

First published 1996
This digitally printed first paperback version 2006

A catalogue record for this publication is available from the British Library

Library of Congress Cataloguing in Publication data
Taylor, J. Edward.
Village economies : the design, estimation, and use of villagewide
economic models / J. Edward Taylor, Irma Adelman with contributions
from Elise H. Golan . . . [et al.].
p. cm.
Includes bibliographical references.
ISBN 0-521-55012-2 (hc)
1. Villages. 2. Rural development. I. Adelman, Irma.
II. Title.
HT431.T39 1996
307.76′2 – dc20   95–43030

ISBN-13 978-0-521-55012-3 hardback
ISBN-10 0-521-55012-2 hardback

ISBN-13 978-0-521-03229-2 paperback
ISBN-10 0-521-03229-6 paperback

For Peri, Sebastian, and Julian

For my colleagues

CONTENTS

ACKNOWLEDGMENTS

The research leading to this book spans nearly a decade, and many people who played a role in it deserve thanks. Above all, we are greatly indebted to our five colleagues and friends who contributed chapters to this book; without their dedication to villagewide modeling this book would not have been possible. Catherine Taylor provided extensive writing and editorial assistance. Peri Fletcher provided us with helpful suggestions and anthropological insights throughout this project and played a key role in gathering data used for the Mexican village model. We are also indebted to Antonio Yúñez, Sherman Robinson, Jaime de Melo, Alain de Janvry, and Bekele Shiferaw for their comments and suggestions at various stages of the project, and to Scott Parris and three anonymous referees whose insights were instrumental in guiding our revisions of the original draft. Pauline Griego provided extraordinary word processing support. Finally, we have benefited from the reactions and ideas of participants in numerous seminars and conferences in which we have presented portions of this research. We would especially like to thank participants in the University of California, Davis, Agricultural Economics Development and Trade Policy Seminar Series and the OECD Development Centre. Taylor's research on this project was supported by grants from the National Science Foundation, the Hewlett Foundation, the Pacific Rim Research Institute, the Mexican CONACYT, and the University of California Consortium for Mexico and the United States (UC MEXUS).

1

Introduction

More than half of humanity and the overwhelming majority of the world's poor live and work in villages. Their production and consumption activities take place within small units, usually households. Yet these units do not behave in isolation from one another. Interactions among village households in factor and commodity markets create local income linkages and general-equilibrium feedbacks. Village institutions shape these interactions. Economic linkages and feedbacks alter the impacts of policy, market, and environmental changes on rural economies quantitatively, and they may shape them qualitatively as well.

In the past, the study of village economies and institutions was primarily the domain of anthropologists. Ethnographic research has provided a window into the structure and workings of village economic, social, and cultural institutions. For the most part, however, these insights have not made their way into quantitative economic modeling.

This book is motivated by our conviction that modeling village economies in diverse economic, social, and cultural settings is critical for understanding the likely impacts of rural development policies. Policymakers and researchers concerned about economic welfare and rural and urban economic growth need to recognize the central role of villages in economic development and in alleviating poverty. Quantitative models of village economic activity are required to analyze the complex impacts of government policies and other exogenous influences on production, incomes, poverty, and inequality in LDC (less developed country) rural areas.

Agriculture and development

When we started work on village economic modeling, there was a growing awareness in development economics that governments should pay close attention to the rural sector of LDCs when designing development policies. The 1980s and 1990s witnessed an appreciation among researchers and policymakers of the multifaceted role that agriculture plays in economic development. Agriculture's major contributions to development have been recognized for some time (Johnston and Mellor, 1961). Increasing productivity in the food and other primary-goods sectors is critical in order to avoid bottlenecks in national development (Morris and Adelman, 1988; Timmer, 1988; Johnston and Mellor, 1961). The need for agricultural development became acute in the 1980s, as binding foreign exchange constraints put a premium on promoting agro exports while limiting LDCs' ability to rely on imports as substitutes for improving agricultural productivity and increasing marketed surplus. Squatter problems and unemployment, fed by accelerating migration into urban areas, created a mandate to expand productive employment in the countryside (Todaro, 1980). As the most labor-intensive sector of LDC economies, agriculture was a prime candidate to play this employment-generating role. Furthermore, development economists recognized the potential for rural consumption demand to create a mass market for domestically produced goods, both agricultural and manufactured (Mellor, 1976; Adelman, 1984).

Econometric analysis based on household expenditure surveys has demonstrated repeatedly that rural expenditure patterns favor domestically produced goods over imports, goods with a high labor content over capital-intensive goods, and goods whose production relies on domestic inputs rather than imported inputs (e.g., Haggblade, Hazell, and Brown, 1988). These considerations, together with the sheer numbers of people living in rural areas, make a strong case for agricultural-development-led industrialization (Adelman, 1984). Recent research suggests that there is a more fundamental symbiotic relationship between agriculture and other sectors, to such an extent that when agriculture does well, so does the rest of the economy, and vice versa (Timmer, 1988). Promoting agricultural development appears to be a prerequisite to promoting national economic development.

How to promote agricultural development, however, is a subject of debate in the development economics literature and among development practitioners. The often disastrous performance of centrally planned economies and inward-looking development strategies, and the success of export-led growth strategies making selective use of markets (and controls) in the "Asian Tiger" economies turned the focus of development economists away from planning and toward markets in the 1980s (e.g., World Bank, 1986). The effectiveness of markets in allocating resources, however, depends critically on the existence of these markets, on the ability of markets to convey information to producers and consumers, and on the costs of using markets for everyday transactions.

Understanding the likely impacts of policy, market, and environmental changes on rural incomes requires understanding microresponses in household-farms, the complex linkages among household-farms within villages, and the linkages between villages and the outside world.

From household-farm to villagewide models

Most recent economic research on the impacts of policy changes on rural economies has followed one of two paths: microeconomic household-farm modeling and a nascent effort to develop village social accounting matrix (SAM) multiplier models. The models in this book represent a further advance over village SAM multiplier models in exploring village or local economywide impacts of policy and market changes.

We propose a village (or micro) computable general-equilibrium (CGE) approach. Micro-CGE models occupy a middle ground between household-farm models and aggregate (national) CGE models for policy analysis. Like household-farm models, they are rooted in the microeconomy and constructed "from the bottom up" using household-farm survey data. However, in the micro-CGE approach, models of household-farm activity are incorporated into a local general-equilibrium framework. This makes it possible to capture the complex linkages and general-equilibrium feedbacks among household-farms that shape the effects of exogenous shocks on local economies. Simulations using villagewide models are unique in their ground-level view of the likely impacts of exogenous policy and market changes on local economies, a view critical for designing rural development policies.

To understand the usefulness of this new generation of economic models, it is helpful first to consider the contributions of the household-farm and village SAM approaches.

The extensive literature on household-farm modeling (e.g., Barnum and Squire, 1979; Singh, Squire, and Strauss, 1986) reflects a concern for how agricultural price policies affect the marketed surplus of food available for urban areas. The first-round impacts of policy changes on rural economies are usually found in agricultural households. Household-farm models examine these first-round impacts and elucidate the dual character of agricultural households as producers and consumers interacting with regional markets for outputs, inputs, and consumption. These models explain the sometimes paradoxical responses of small farmers to price policies. For example, they advance the theoretical possibility of a positive own-price demand elasticity (upward-sloping demand curve) for food in farm households. Empirical findings reveal that this theoretical possibility often is borne out in the real world and has an important effect on marketed surplus. Variations of agricultural household models have been used to explore the impacts of market imperfections on household-farm behavior (de Janvry, Fafchamps, and Sadoulet, 1991; Singh, Squire, and Strauss, 1986).

By treating the household as a small economy and incorporating both production and consumption into the same modeling framework, agricultural household models are, in reality, very small economywide models. This is most apparent in the case of household-farm models with missing markets, in which the family strikes an internal equilibrium between its supply and demand for nontradables. In the case of a missing market for labor, the agricultural household faces the internal general-equilibrium constraint that the sum of leisure and work demands for family time equals the family's fixed time endowment. In the case of a missing market for staples, the household's consumption equals its own output (plus stocks minus storage). Net marketed surplus (transactions with markets) ensures that all markets for tradables clear within the household. Both quantities and "virtual" or "shadow" prices (which reflect the family's subjective valuation of nontradables, like time or subsistence crops) adjust to ensure that the household economy is in equilibrium when markets for commodities or factors are missing.

Applications of agricultural household models confirm that the household needs to be treated as a whole microeconomy if there is any hope of understanding the complex impacts of exogenous policy and market shocks on household-farm economies.

The shortcoming of microeconomic household-farm models is that they do not examine interactions among households. Because of this, an analysis that treats individual households as whole economies is incomplete: Where economic linkages among households are important, microeconomic household (or household-farm) models may produce misleading findings, including biased estimates of the impacts of policy and market changes on the rural economy.

Consider a simple example. Suppose that a 10 percent price support stimulates a 6.1 percent increase in staple production in village household-farms. Higher profits from staple production raise staple-producing households' incomes and their demand for normal goods, including staples. The result is a 6.6 percent increase in the marketed surplus of staples. (These production and marketed surplus changes correspond to elasticities for Malaysia presented in Barnum and Squire, 1979.) The policy analyst, who is no doubt concerned with securing food supplies for urban consumers, concludes that the price policy is an effective tool for increasing the marketed surplus of staples.

However, income linkages and local general-equilibrium feedbacks within the local economy may alter the impact of the price change on marketed surplus. Most likely, they will dampen the marketed surplus effect, and they may reverse it. Staple producers purchase inputs (e.g., labor) from other households in the village. Their increased consumption expenditures usually include a demand for goods produced in the village, including local nontradables. Increased demand drives up the price of nontradable goods and factors. If the affected goods or factors are inputs in staple production, the higher prices will dampen the staple-supply response. In the extreme case, where some village factors are fixed and there are no substitutes for these factors in the staple-production function, the supply response may be nil. Nevertheless, the higher staple-price increases farm profits from existing (baseline) production and is likely to stimulate a flow of value-added into nonstaple-producing households.

Staples are usually a normal good for village households. Increased income in nonstaple-producing households boosts the village demand for staples. The combination of a smaller output elasticity and an increase in local staple demand reduces the availability of staples for consumers outside the village. It may even create a backward-bending village marketed surplus response, akin to the well-known backward-bending labor supply curve in microeconomics.

Microeconomic household-farm models do not capture the income linkages and the general-equilibrium effects that can profoundly influence the outcomes of policy changes, as in the preceding example. Village SAM multiplier models have demonstrated that linkages within villages are important in shaping the effects of policies and other exogenous changes on production and incomes (Adelman, Taylor, and Vogel, 1988; Subramanian and Sadoulet, 1990; Lewis and Thorbecke, 1992; Parikh and Thorbecke, 1994; Ralston, 1992; Golan, 1990). Exogenous changes that do not directly affect marketed surplus or agricultural production may have indirect effects as their impacts work their way through the village. Migrant remittances, particularly in the presence of imperfect or missing markets, are a case in point (Taylor, 1995).

Another shortcoming of household-farm models is that the household as basic unit of economic decision making is not universal and fixed; it must sometimes be recast from one village context to another, and production and consumption decisions may take place in different economic units (e.g., households and compounds) within the same village. Anthropological debates about households point to the complexity and flexibility of household arrangements and structures, to alternatives to households as basic units of production and consumption in some villages, and to the diversity of village institutions that influence interhousehold relationships (e.g., Yanagisako, 1979).

Taking rural income linkages and general-equilibrium feedbacks into account requires studying microeconomic household-farms as part of a rural economic community and explicitly modeling their unique institutions and interactions. It is entirely possible that the most important impacts of a policy change on production, marketed surplus, or incomes will not be found within the households seemingly most affected by the policy, but in the ways that one household transfers the impacts of policy changes to another. Ignoring villagewide economic effects may give a quantitatively if not qualitatively distorted view of policy outcomes.

Village SAMs and SAM multiplier models

The SAM approach is ideal for analyzing village economies in diverse social and cultural settings. Village SAMs provide a snapshot of the structure of village economies, village institutions, and village interactions with the outside world. They also provide an accounting framework that can serve as a basis for modeling village production activities and institutions in response to changes in economic, policy, and environmental variables. The village and village-town applications in Chapters 3 through 7 of this book illustrate the flexibility of the SAM framework in distinct economic, social, and cultural settings as well as the diversity of analytical uses to which SAMs neatly lend themselves.

SAM-based village models are restrictive, however. The linearity of SAM multipliers, their assumption of a Keynesian, demand-driven village economy without resource constraints, and their absence of prices limit their usefulness for many types of policy analysis. Creative efforts have been made to overcome some of these limitations by modifying SAM models (see Chapter 2). However, the basic structure of SAM multipliers limits the extent to which these problems can be addressed within the SAM framework.

Village CGEs

In this book, we propose and develop a CGE framework that combines the strengths of microeconomic household-farm models with those of SAM-based, villagewide models. At the heart of the village CGE is the household-farm, which is both producer and consumer. The CGE links household-farms together into a village general-equilibrium model, incorporating resource constraints on household-farm decisions, nonlinearities, and price effects and capturing economic linkages among household-farms within the village as well as between the village and the outside world. It takes into account general-equilibrium feedbacks of household-farm responses to policy, market, and environmental changes in markets where villages are cut off from the outside world or where local markets do not exist (e.g., family labor).

Our policy experiments using villagewide economic models based on CGE methods explore the impacts of price policies, technological change, ecological decline, income transfers, factor market changes, and macrovariables on production, incomes, employment, migration, and demand linkages inside and outside four villages and a village-town. Our findings offer insights into the workings of village economies that sometimes defy conventional economic wisdom, and they suggest explanations for development policy paradoxes: Why are policies to increase food supplies through price incentives effective in some cases but ineffective in others? Why are attempts to raise rural incomes and alleviate poverty through income programs often unsuccessful and even counterproductive, and why do they sometimes trigger more migration, not less? Why does economic research reveal such contrasting findings about the impact of migration on development in migrant-sending economies? What are the implications of environmental degradation for incomes, poverty, and inequality in developing countries, and why are the economic incentives to preserve environments so small?

Organization of this book

The primary goal of this book is to provide readers with theoretical and empirical insights into the structure of village economies. A second objective is to compare the impacts of changes in government policies, commodity and factor markets, and environmental variables on villages in different economic, social, and cultural milieux. Along the way, we provide readers with examples of how to design and construct villagewide models. The study of villages requires a combination of economic and anthropological research tools, as is demonstrated by the variety of village institutions and economic structures portrayed in Chapters 3 through 7.

The book is organized as follows. Chapter 2 introduces the village SAM, which is the analytical and empirical starting point for villagewide modeling. Chapters 3 through 7 present contextual information and estimated SAMs for villages in the Peanut Basin of Senegal, a cotton-producing zone in Maharashtra in Western India, and a migrant-sending region in central Mexico; for a market-oriented village in West Java, Indonesia; and for a village-town in the Kutus region of Kenya. Surveys of these villages and village-town were originally designed to address an array of policy questions: land tenure in Senegal, agricultural production constraints in India, migration in Mexico, rural–urban linkages in Kenya, and calorie intake in Indonesia. With the exception of the India model, all of the data for these models were collected by the contributors of Chapters 3 through 7. In the India case, supplemental fieldwork was carried out to complement existing survey data.

The five village SAMs are the basis for designing and estimating village general-equilibrium models. The basic structure of the village CGE models is presented in Chapter 8, together with a comparison of model parameters across villages and a description of the computer program we developed to estimate the models and conduct our policy experiments. In Chapter 9, we use the five estimated village models to analyze villagewide effects of exogenous changes in policy, market, and environmental variables. Our policy simulations illustrate differences in villagewide responses to change, and they offer a basis for designing policy interventions to accomplish objectives related to production, incomes, poverty, and environmental sustainability in diverse LDC rural settings. Chapter 10 presents our conclusions.

2

Modeling village economies

Villages in less developed countries often are very complex in their social, cultural, and political structures, yet the structure of their economic activities can be reasonably simple. Agricultural production forms the core of economic activity for the villages in this book. Some of this production is consumed by the production units themselves, and thus does not enter the exchange economy inside or outside the village. Many of the inputs used in production are supplied by the same production units, in the form of family factors (labor, draft animal power) or intermediate inputs produced by the household (e.g., saved seeds). Nevertheless, as Chapters 3 through 7 illustrate, economic activity varies strikingly among villages, often in ways that reflect villages' integration with outside markets.

Village economic linkages and market development

If all agricultural households were self-sufficient and supplied their own inputs – that is, if all goods were household nontradables – production and expenditure linkages among village households would be nonexistent. At the other extreme, if all households were perfectly integrated with goods and factor markets outside the village and all goods and factors were village tradables (i.e., in a perfectly neoclassical world), production and expenditure linkages among village households would again be nonexistent. All input and output prices would be exogenous, fixed by markets outside the village. An increase in a village household's demand for goods produced in the village would simply decrease the availability of these goods for sale outside the village (i.e., village-marketed surplus).

There would be little rationale for village economic models in either of

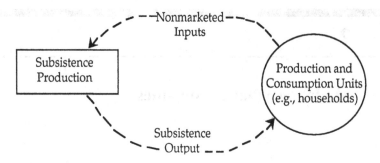

Figure 2.1. Basic economic flows in village economies at low level of market development.

these extremes. In a world of nontradables, there would be little scope for policy intervention (except perhaps for market development to promote trade). In a perfectly neoclassical world, a villagewide economic model would not be needed to understand the impacts of exogenous policy on village production, consumption, or marketed surplus to outside markets. Microeconomic household-farm models, estimated separately for different household-farm groups (e.g., net-surplus-producer and net-purchaser households), would suffice.

Most villages are not characterized by either of these extremes. Typically, some goods are household nontradables, supplied and demanded by the same production–consumption unit. Others are village nontradables, exchanged among households within the village but not between the village and the outside world. Still others are village tradables, for which all households and the village as a whole are price takers.

In short, market interactions among village households at different levels of market integration between households and the outside world are characterized by a U-shaped relationship. They are weakest in subsistence agricultural household economies and also when the village economy is perfectly integrated with outside product and factor markets. They are strongest when all goods are village nontradables.

Figures 2.1 through 2.3 illustrate economic linkages in villages at different levels of market development. The broken lines in these figures denote nonmarket interactions (household nontradables); the solid lines denote market transactions. Market transactions may involve either village tradables or village nontradables.

Subsistence village economies

Figure 2.1 illustrates the extreme of an isolated, closed household economy. Agricultural households supply all of their inputs and consume all of their output. There are no interactions among production units or between the village and the rest of the world. Opportunity costs within households in terms of families' subjective valuation of time and production shape resource allocations. One could characterize these subjective valuations in terms of household-specific shadow prices. However, it is only when some possibilities exist for trade and for substituting market for family-supplied goods and factors (ruled out in Figure 2.1) that shadow prices become useful for economic analysis.

The absence of market exchange does not preclude rich social interactions in consumption and production. Some of these may appear to be market interactions; for example, it might be argued that labor exchanges – a major type of factor interaction among households in traditional economies – represent a form of market exchange. However, labor exchanges have individualized prices; there may be as many prices as there are individual agreements. A defining attribute of a market – a single price – is missing in this case.

The structure of production and consumption tends to be simplest in the poorest and least developed subsistence-village settings. Poverty imposes constraints on diversity in both production and consumption, while limiting village market transactions.

Village economies at intermediate levels of market development

Most villages support some marketing of surplus production (e.g., in weekly markets) and some participation in labor markets inside and outside the village. It is often surprising to find a large share of labor from seemingly isolated villages in Africa, Latin America, and Asia allocated to internal migration or to far-flung international migration. Income remitted by migrants permits new forms of market interactions inside villages as well as between villages and the outside world.

With increased income growth, a village economy's production side initially tends to become more complex. Patterns of village economic growth vary greatly from one context to another and are shaped by both endogenous and exogenous forces. Even in the poorest villages in our study, the subsistence food economy coexists with a food or nonfood commercial agricultural sector, whose product is mostly "exported" from the village. The existence of a handicraft sector is an important feature of many village economies. Like migration, commercial production stimulates exchange relationships inside the village and between the village and the rest of the world. Modern inputs may be "imported" into the village, labor may be purchased, and markets play an increasingly important role in supplying village consumption. Village resource allocation becomes more complex. Land, labor, and financial resources are distributed among subsistence production, commercial production, and wage labor according to generally accepted local allocation rules.

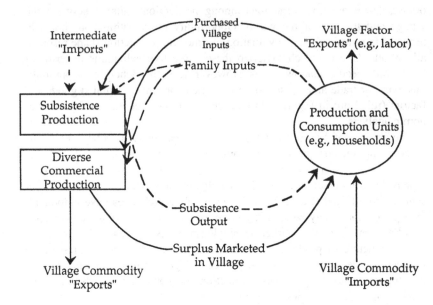

Figure 2.2. Basic economic flows in village economies at intermediate level of market development.

Figure 2.2 illustrates a typical village at a low-to-intermediate level of integration with outside markets and represents the broad category into which the villages in our study fall. In this prototype village, interactions appear among production–consumption units on the input side. Hiring and exchange of labor and various land-use arrangements emerge among production–consumption units. Production is more diversified and oriented toward outside markets on both the input and the output sides. Some village and outside factor markets, especially in labor, become integrated. Nevertheless, the list of goods and factors supplied and demanded by village households includes a mixture of household nontradables, village nontradables, and village tradables. Costs of transacting with outside markets, together with local supply and demand, determine whether the village is a net exporter or a net importer of a good or factor or whether the village is self-sufficient. They, together with transactions costs within the village, determine whether individual households participate in village and outside markets. Outside institutions – governments, marketing institutions, outside employers such as plantations or capitalist farms, and migrants – have varying degrees of impact on the village economy. National policies, including terms-of-trade and exchange rate policies, become increasingly important.

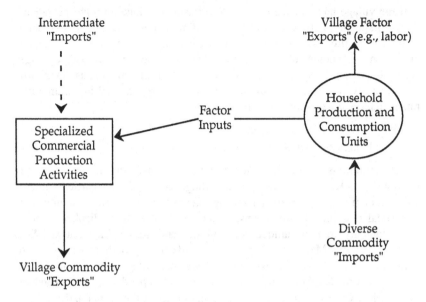

Figure 2.3. Basic economic flows in villlage economies at high level of market development with everything tradable.

Specialized village economies

Contact with outside markets permits specialization in village production for export to regional or sometimes international markets. Usually, this type of production specialization occurs at relatively high levels of village integration with regional, national, or international commodity and labor markets. Specialization reflects villages' comparative advantage in production for regional markets, and it is accompanied by a diversity in village consumption supported by those markets. Specialization may also be imposed on village economies by colonial or national policies, for example, those that flood the market with cheap substitutes for local handicrafts, as occurred in the case of Burmese and Indian textiles in the second half of the nineteenth century.

At a high level of integration with the outside, linkages within villages are increasingly replaced by linkages between village households and the outside world (Figure 2.3). As regional trade centers emerge to supply clusters of villages with production inputs and consumer goods, diversity in consumption is decoupled from local production. At the same time, village production becomes increasingly specialized, commercialized, and directed toward regional, national, and possibly international markets. Households may buy and sell tradables within the village, but this is largely irrelevant to the analysis. Because prices are exogenously determined, village demands have no effect on the village production of tradables.

If the village has no clear comparative trade advantage through specialization, village production may generate a diminishing share of total village income over time, and wage labor activities outside the village (including migration) may contribute an increasing share. In the extreme case, a village may specialize in "exporting" labor. By contrast, if the village has developed a comparative advantage in production, this will be reflected in commodity, rather than factor-market, specialization.

Village institutions

Local institutions set the rules for production, consumption, and exchange relationships. Resource allocation in village economies is carried out by socioeconomic groups characterized by internally hierarchical structures and reciprocal relations. These groups, structures, and relations display tremendous diversity in their unique sociocultural and geographic contexts. For example, in the Mexican village, households act as both production and consumption units. By contrast, in the Senegalese village, farm production is organized at the level of compounds composed of dependent and independent households. Consumption, however, occurs either at the compound level, in the case of dependent households, or at the household level, in the case of independent households.

Exchange relations among village households are both market and nonmarket. In our highly monetized Mexican village, labor used in household-farm production is either supplied by the household itself or is hired wage labor, and labor substitutes (tractors, chemical weed control) are increasingly common. (Ten years ago labor exchanges were more common in this village.) In the Senegalese village, households and individuals have labor obligations to the compound in its production of millet, the staple crop. These obligations are based on linked reciprocal relations in production and consumption between compound and household. There is also lending of land across compounds.

A complex system of tenurial relationships provides village production units (households, compounds, etc.) with access to land, thereby generating one of the central forms of economic interaction in villages. These, too, vary tremendously among and within villages. For example, security of tenure in the Senegalese village varies even within compounds. The right to use land does not necessarily imply a right to decide on cropping patterns or the right to sell land, and the right to inherit land is not uniquely related to security of tenure in production. Until recently, the Mexican *ejido* land right precluded sale or rental of ejido lands but permitted inheritance to a designated family member (*sucesor*). Nevertheless, various sharecropping arrangements, including some interlinking of land and credit, exist.

The diversity of village institutions is instrumental in how government policies and economic and environmental changes affect village economic activities and incomes.

The village SAM framework

Village social accounting matrices (SAMs) are designed to capture the complex interlinkages among village production activities, village institutions, and the outside world. SAMs are a useful starting point for villagewide economic analysis. In Chapters 3 through 7 they serve as an expository device to portray the structure of village economies. They also provide the basic data input for our village general-equilibrium modeling in Chapters 8 and 9. Village SAMs summarize and neatly illustrate the flows of inputs, outputs, and income between food production and other productive sectors in the village, the flows of income between production activities and village households, the channeling of household incomes into consumption and investments, and the exchange of goods and factors between the village and the rest of the world.

The SAM approach was originally developed by Stone (1978) to reconcile national income and product accounts with input–output analysis. It has been used to model widely diverse national economies for purposes of policy analysis and planning. (For a bibliography and examples, see Pyatt and Round, 1979.) The first application of SAMs to village economic analysis appears in Adelman, Taylor, and Vogel (1988).

The social accounting matrix framework is a form of double-entry accounting. The SAM presents income and product accounts and input–output production accounts as debit and credit entries in income balance sheets of institutions and activities. Activities may include farm and nonfarm production (or any disaggregation of the two). Institutions in SAMs typically include different household groups, government, and the rest of the world. In economics, the term "institutions" is generally used to characterize structured rules of the game for interactions among economic entities. In the context of villagewide modeling, this term has a somewhat different meaning: Institutions are categories of economic actors. It is assumed, of course, that all members of a given category of actors interact in a similar manner with the other categories and activities in the village. In this sense, the two concepts of institution overlap.

Entries in a SAM include intermediate input demands between production sectors; income (value-added) paid by production sectors to different types of labor (male or female, educated or uneducated, or different ethnic groups) or attributable to land or capital; the distribution of labor, land, and capital value-added across different household groups; and the distribution of household groups' expenditures across savings, consumption of domestically produced goods and services, and imports. A government account collects taxes from activities and households and redirects this income within the system (to government demand for goods and services, transfers to production activities, or household groups), saves it, or uses it to pay foreigners (for imported goods and services or repayment of debt).

The total product of each activity must be allocated to some use inside or outside the economy (intermediate demand, consumption, investment, government demand, or exports). Total (gross) receipts of each activity must be allocated to some entity inside or outside the system (purchases of inputs from other activities, payments to labor and capital, imports, taxes, and savings). A fundamental characteristic of SAMs, derived from double-entry accounting, is that equality must be maintained between the sum of expenditures (column total) and the sum of revenues (row total) for every account in the system. The SAM accounts to which incomes and expenditures are assigned are the same on the revenue and expenditure side; that is, the SAM is a square matrix.

The great strengths of the SAM are its comprehensiveness and its flexibility in adapting to diverse institutional settings and economic structures and in providing an accounting framework to address diverse policy and planning issues. The flexibility of the SAM framework is demonstrated by the richness of activities, village institutions, and rest-of-the-world accounts included in the village SAMs in this volume.

Village SAMs have the same overall conceptual framework as national SAMs, but they depart from national SAMs in specific ways to reflect the unique nature of village economies and institutions. One departure from the national SAM is that specific rest-of-the-world subaccounts of village SAMs do not necessarily balance. For example, a regional or national government may be a net surplus appropriator or a net subsidizer of a village. Remittances to village households from migrants abroad (a foreign account) may not necessarily be used to purchase goods from abroad; they may be used to purchase goods produced in the village or imported into the village from regional or national markets. Methodologically, these inconsistencies are addressed through the use of entries representing payments between rest-of-world accounts or through aggregation – for example, by combining some rest-of-world accounts, the sum of whose transactions with the village must balance.

Another departure is that in national SAMs all transactions are monetized, whereas in village SAMs nonmonetary transactions typically are important. These nonmonetary transactions include production for own consumption, labor exchanges or labor lending, interlinked factor markets, interlinked factor- and nonfactor-input markets, and access to the commons.

A simple prototype village SAM appears in Table 2.1. The rows of the SAM contain receipts of different village activities, village factors, village institutions, village capital accounts, and the rest of the world. The columns contain the expenditures made by these accounts. Consistency of the SAM requires that the totals of these rows and columns match.

The northwest corner of the SAM contains village production activity accounts – that is, it is the village input–output (Leontief) submatrix (denoted A). This submatrix may consist of any combination of accounts at any level of aggregation, provided that it includes all village production. In the Mexico village SAM, for example, the production submatrix consists of five sectors: farming (principally maize and bean production for own consumption, i.e., the *milpa*), livestock (primarily for export), renewable resource extraction (fishing and wood gathering), construction, and village retail activities.

Village production activities result in income payments to capital and labor. The intersections of activity columns with factor rows (F) reveal the distribution of village production value-added across factors. The village factor accounts typically include land and physical (machinery or animal) capital, family or compound labor, and hired labor.

Payments to capital, or capital value-added, include explicit payments ranging from land rents to hired ox-and-plow and tractor services. They also include imputed returns to capital when no explicit payment occurs or when transactions are linked. Both types of payment are included in the capital factor account. Labor value-added accounts include explicit payments to hired labor and implicit payments to family or compound labor, valued at the market prices for these services or as a residual of production value over other explicit and implicit costs. Modern inputs into village production are "imported" from the rest of the world (AM).

Village value-added, in turn, is distributed across institutional (e.g., household or compound) accounts. Submatrix D, the intersection of the factor columns with the institution rows, summarizes this village value-added distribution. In a closed economy, this submatrix would summarize the distribution of total village income across institutions. By contrast, in the open village economy, village production value-added is supplemented by income from the rest of the world, for example, migrant remittances (R) and government transfers (T). In some villages there may in fact be a low correlation between the distribution of village production value-added and the distribution of total village income. Total institutional income is the sum of receipts across the institution rows.

Institutions' incomes are allocated across consumption expenditures (C), savings (S), and taxes (HT). Savings are allocated to investment demand, including private human capital investments. Government tax receipts may or may not be injected back into the village as demand for village goods (G), as income transfers (T), education and health expenditures, or production subsidies (AT, i.e., a "negative" indirect tax). If government is a net village surplus extractor, this will be reflected in a positive entry in the government-

Table 2.1 *Outline of village social accounting matrix framework*

Receipts	Expenditures						
	1. Activities	2. Factors	3. Institutions	4. Capital	5. Human capital	6. Rest of the world	7. Total
1. *Activities*	A (Village input-output table)		C,G	I	HKI (Human capital investment)	X	Total sales
a. Farming							
b. Livestock							
c. Renewable resources							
d. Construction							
e. Retail							
2. *Factors*	F (Value-added in village production)						Total capital and labor value–added
a. Capital							
b. Family labor							
Hired labor							
3. *Institutions*		D (Payments to households for labor & capital services used in production)	T,HT (Payment to households for migrant labor services; government transfers)			R (Migrant remittances)	Total migrant remittances
a. Migrants							
b. Landless							
c. Smallholder households							Total household income
d. Largeholder households							
e. Government	AT (Taxes)						Total government receipts

	Total payments to capital and labor	Total institutional expenditures	Total physical capital investment	Total human capital investment	Exports to rest of the world	Total receipts/expenditures
4. *Capital*		S (Household and government savings)				Total savings
5. *Human capital*		HKS (Household human capital savings)				Total human capital savings
6. *Rest of the world*	AM (Imports)					Total imports from rest of the world
7. *Total*	Total payments	Total institutional expenditures	Total physical capital investment	Total human capital investment	Exports to rest of the world	Total receipts/expenditures

to-rest-of-nation entry (the intersection of the government column with the rest-of-the-nation row).

Some output of village production activities may be exported to local or national markets outside the village or to government or private national marketing institutions in the form of marketed surplus. (Exports of village production to the world market normally are channeled through these institutions.) These "exports" from the village are contained in submatrix X.

The village SAMs in this book depict a diversity of production activities, institutions, and rest-of-world accounts. Examples of production activities include subsistence food production (all villages), export crop production (Senegal, Kenya), traditional health services (a healer in Java), and religious activity (a Hindu temple and a mosque in India). Village institutions include households grouped by base-period calorie intake, compounds grouped by compound landholdings, and village schools. Examples of rest-of-world accounts include marketing cooperatives, a plantation, weekly markets, a nearby "central place" or town, and domestic and foreign migrant labor markets.

Estimating village SAMs

Estimation of a village SAM involves designing a specific SAM framework, collecting data, and blowing up sample results to the village universe.

Designing the village SAM

The task of designing a village SAM includes identifying the major production activities in the village; factors used in village production; village institutions for production, consumption, and marketing; and exogenous institutions and capital accounts. The design must be based on a thorough prior understanding of the structure of village production, markets, institutions, and interactions with the outside world. Here, economists must learn from anthropologists. Typically, a significant amount of time in the village is required before the researcher actually gathers SAM data. This is not merely a matter of establishing trust between researcher and villagers. To avoid possible inaccuracies or omissions in the survey, the researcher first needs to obtain a feel for the workings of the village economy and society. This includes a knowledge of any limiting factors and institutions, conditions specifying access to resources, village hierarchies, patron–client relations, gender relations, nonmarket exchanges, exchange obligations, linked transactions, and traditional distribution entitlements with regard to both the consumption of village output and the factors in village production.

The design of a village SAM must reflect not only village realities but also the purposes of the research. For example, if the focus is migration's impact on the village economy, the village SAM institutions should include migration institutions (as in the Mexican village SAM). If the focus is on nutrition, a categorization of household institutions by calorie intake is appropriate, as in the Indonesian village SAM. And if the focus is on the effects of transforming traditional land rights to modern ones, a categorization of institutions according to where traditional land rights reside is in order, as in the Senegalese village SAM. A focus on regional economic development may call for the inclusion of both town and farm households, as in the Kenyan (Kutus) SAM. However the village SAM design reflects research goals, it must at the same time be true to the structure of the village economy, society, and institutions.

Data collection

The raw data to estimate village SAMs are generated from farm budget surveys. In these surveys, production–consumption units (usually household-farms) are asked about the types of production they carry out; the uses to which this production is put, both inside and outside the village; the types of inputs and their sources (including imported inputs); the quantities or values of inputs and outputs; and prices. The inputs include all nonpurchased (e.g., family) inputs. A family time-use module therefore is an important part of these surveys. Detailed information is also gathered on the production–consumption units' income from activities other than farm production. This income includes income from wage labor, cottage industries, and transfers from migrants and government. The distribution of value-added from production in the village across consumption units and indirect taxes must also be obtained.

On the expenditure side, the budget survey elicits detailed information on the allocation of consumption units' income to consumption demand for various types of goods produced in the village and for imports; savings, both in money and in in-kind; interhousehold transfers; and direct taxes.

With the exception of the Indian village and the Kenyan village-town, the farm surveys used to construct the village SAMs in this volume were based on sample sizes of fewer than 100 units.[1] The farm survey teams varied from one surveyor (Taylor) in the Mexican village case to the researcher plus a half dozen local enumerators in the case of the Indonesian and Senegalese villages. Typically, a year of fieldwork was necessary to familiarize researchers with the village and to collect, verify, and code the data used to construct the village SAM. In many of these cases, the data to construct the village

---

1. Depending upon the level of detail (i.e., number of accounts) the researcher wishes to include in the SAM, the survey design may require stratification. However, a stratified sample design was not used for any of the studies reported in this book.

SAM were gathered in conjunction with the collection of data for other research purposes (e.g., micromodeling of household-farm decisions or intra-household food allocations).

From survey data to village SAMs

To go from farm budget surveys to the village SAM, surveys first have to be "cleaned." That is, the original data have to be checked for internal consistency and coding errors. Typically, this process requires several months, and perhaps a return trip to the field site, regardless of how carefully the data were collected and cross-checked in the field.

Second, to obtain consistent generalizations, survey sample results must be blown up to represent the whole village. To ensure accuracy, all production activities in the village must be included in the survey sample. There is no intrinsic reason why, in the village sample, income and expenditure accounts aggregated across production–consumption units should balance. The selection of units surveyed may miss some important aspects, even sectors, of village production, unless great care is taken in sample design. The researcher must make sure that all purchases from village sources appearing on the expenditure side of the survey are also captured on the production side.

"Exports" from the village (some units inside or outside the sample may produce partially or entirely for markets outside the village) must also be taken into account, or else production by units picked up in the sample may exaggerate village demand for partially exported goods or services. For example, in the Indonesian village, one villager ran a small transportation operation that provided services both to residents in the village and to residents in an adjacent village. The same was true for a milling operator in this village. Had these partial-export activities been missed, villagers' expenditures on transport and milling picked up by the budget surveys would mistakenly have been allocated to imports (on the assumption that someone outside the village had supplied the services). Had the miller and transport operator been part of the survey sample but information on their sales to residents outside the sample not obtained, they would have been recorded as exports only. In this case, the supply of the services (estimated from the production side of the surveys of the miller and the transport operator) would exceed the demand for these services (estimated from the expenditure side of household-farms in the sample).

Generalizing from the sample to the village universe also requires allocating the output of surveyed units between demand inside the sample and demand outside the sample but inside the village. For example, suppose the village contains one corner store. A preliminary understanding of the village enables us to make certain that store sales are picked up in the survey. But sales by this store inevitably will include sales to units outside the sample, which are missed by the survey, as well as sales to units inside the sample, which are picked up by the survey. By eliciting the origins of purchases by consumption units, the survey should enable the researcher to determine what share of the store's output is sold to units covered by the survey. Similarly, by eliciting the destination of sales by the store, sales to nonvillage production or consumption entities can be netted out of estimates of village demand for store output. Otherwise, if researchers purchase American soft drinks from the store, they may produce a "Heisenberg effect" on village demand! Weekly markets are another example of the same sort of problem.

The difficulties encountered in the transition from sample data to a consistent village SAM described here illustrate the importance of obtaining detailed origin and destination information for transactions on both the revenue and expenditure sides of units included in the sample. They also reemphasize the need to obtain a thorough knowledge of the economic structure of the village, markets, and institutions prior to designing and carrying out the survey.

Village models

To move from the village SAM as an accounting framework to a village model first requires making assumptions about the behavior of village actors (institutions) and the specification of production functions. The SAM summarizes transaction flows among economic actors in the village. In designing village models, the simplest assumption is that the responses of village actors to income changes are strictly proportional to the total level of activity in each account (i.e., the column totals in the SAM). This means that, on the expenditure side, marginal expenditures by village institutions equal average shares derived from the SAM and that, on the production side, there is a fixed input–output technology. These assumptions are restrictive, but they are necessary to estimate fixed-price, village SAM multipliers (described later), which are analogous to the Leontief multiplier in input–output analysis. These multipliers are the basis for the SAM policy experiments in Adelman, Taylor, and Vogel (1988); Subramanian and Sadoulet (1990); Lewis and Thorbecke (1992); Parikh and Thorbecke (1994); Ralston (1992); and Golan (1990).

Constructing a village model also requires specifying which accounts in the village SAM are endogenous and which are exogenous. Choosing exogenous and endogenous accounts is critical in modeling the impact of change on village economies, because, strictly speaking, the modeler is free to change only exogenous variables and model parameters. The endogenous accounts in the model capture the responses of village economic actors to changes in the exogenous accounts or in parameters. In village models, the logical choices for exogenous accounts are government, capital, and the rest of the world. The simulations presented in Chapter 9 illustrate the ways in which changes in a wide range of policy, market, and environmental variables affect the village economy through changes in exogenous accounts or model parameters.

SAM multipliers

For a SAM multiplier analysis, the village SAM transaction matrix is converted into a matrix of average expenditure propensities by dividing each element in the SAM by its respective column total. This normalization produces a matrix of average shares, S. Let X denote the exogenous income flows into the rows corresponding to the endogenous accounts of the SAM. Deleting the exogenous rows and columns from S yields a submatrix of endogenous shares, A. The village SAM multiplier matrix, a square matrix denoted M, is easily derived as:

$$M = (I - A)^{-1}$$

Given some exogenous change in X, the effect on endogenous accounts in the village, Y, is determined by this village multiplier matrix:

$$Y = M * X$$

The matrix M is called the village multiplier matrix because it contains estimated total direct and indirect effects of exogenous income injections on the endogenous accounts in the village SAM. The village Leontief (input–output) multiplier is one component of the village SAM multiplier. In addition to capturing Leontief production linkages, the SAM multiplier also captures expenditure linkages induced by changes in production activities through their effect on incomes in the village. These expenditure linkages typically are stronger than production linkages in village SAM models.

Linkages between production and factors, between factors and households, and between households and production shape the impact of exogenous changes on the village economy. To illustrate, consider an exogenous increase in the demand for village exports. The initial, direct impact of this change is felt on the production side of the village SAM, as the affected sector and Leontief-type production linkages increase the output of village production activities. A Leontief village multiplier analysis would stop here. The increase in village production, however, generates increases in value-added, resulting in increased incomes for village institutions. Part of this income is spent on goods and services produced in the village, and some of it leaks out of the village through village "imports." Increased demand for production unleashes a new round of income changes in the village.

The village multiplier consists of multiple rounds of feedback among subaccounts in the village SAM. Each new injection of income into a SAM subaccount first swirls around the local subsystem of accounts and then is transmitted to other subsystems of the SAM. This process continues as part of the new income generates a derived demand for goods and services or induces a redistribution of income flows within the village, while part leaks out. Formal derivations of this decomposition for national SAM multipliers are available in Pyatt and Round (1979) and Stone (1978).

Limitations of village SAM multiplier models

The village SAM multiplier has the same basic limitations as its national counterpart, although some of these are less important in the village context. First, prices are absent. In a perfect neoclassical village economy, production and consumption decisions are shaped by prices determined by markets outside the village. In a village characterized by market imperfections, shadow prices on village resources (e.g., family labor) may diverge from market prices (e.g., wages) outside the village. In simulations using village SAMs, the critical question is whether prices vary in response to exogenous changes and whether variations in price induce changes in the SAM share matrix. Because the village economy is small, when the cost of transacting with outside markets is low, the village is likely to be a price taker for most goods and factors. However, where markets for goods or production factors are missing or imperfect, shadow prices take the place of exogenous market prices in guiding resource allocation decisions by village household-farms. The extreme case is the completely isolated, self-sufficient village, in which all prices are endogenous. The village acts much like a Chayanovian family farm, using village resources to produce for local subsistence demands. The isolated Chayanovian village is rare. However, high transaction costs of participating in outside markets and imperfect substitutability between family and hired factors of production may result in endogenous prices for some village goods and factors, as depicted in Figure 2.2.

A second limitation of SAM multiplier models is their implicit assumption that supply is perfectly elastic. That is, SAM models assume a Keynesian, demand-driven system without resource constraints. If constraints on village resources such as land or seeds (e.g., as a result of market imperfections) are binding, they should be taken into account when modeling the impacts of exogenous changes on village economies. Subramanian and Sadoulet (1990) and Lewis and Thorbecke (1992) attempt to do this in village SAM multiplier models by imposing constraints on production in the form of a perfectly inelastic supply response in some sectors, and Parikh and Thorbecke (1994) allow for the possibility of inelastic supply response beyond predetermined output levels. In real life, however, resource constraints generate high shadow prices on the resources whose supply is fixed. These high shadow prices guide the scarce resources to their most productive use inside or (as in the case of family labor) outside the village (e.g., in migration work). They also generate rents for owners of these resources, with important expenditure-linkage effects in the village. These complex price effects cannot be captured in fixed-price, SAM models.

Third, SAM multiplier models assume that production utilizes linear, fixed-proportion technologies and that average and marginal expenditure propensities are the same. The second assumption can be somewhat relaxed by incorporating marginal rather than average shares into the SAM expenditure shares matrix prior to calculating the multiplier M (see, e.g., Pyatt and Round, 1979; Adelman and Taylor, 1990; and Lewis and Thorbecke, 1992). Linearity on the production side, which implies constant marginal productivities of factor inputs, however, poses more difficult problems.

A village general-equilibrium model

The village computable general-equilibrium (CGE) model presented in Chapter 8 of this volume represents an effort to overcome the limitations of linear, fixed-price models while utilizing village SAMs as a basis to explore village responses to a variety of policy, market, and environmental changes.

The general equilibrium approach retains the major strengths of the SAM-based village models with respect to consistency across all production, household, and capital accounts and with respect to the diversity of factors and institutions that reflect villages' unique social, cultural, and economic settings.

However, it offers several advantages over a village SAM model. First, it permits us to introduce nonlinearities into the model. On the production side, fixed inputs and production technologies generate decreasing returns to variable inputs, which have an important influence on how factors are allocated across production and leisure activities. Second, constraints on the availability of resources for village production are incorporated directly into the village CGE. In the case of land and physical capital, this is accomplished by making the short-run assumption that factor inputs are fixed. In the case of family labor, factor supplies to diverse village production activities, migration, and leisure demand are influenced by the family wage or opportunity cost of family time, which equals the marginal utility of leisure. The returns to family labor in migration work typically exert an important influence on the family wage and hence on village production.

A third major advantage of the general-equilibrium approach is the explicit role played by prices. Exogenous or, in the case of imperfect or missing markets (e.g., for family labor), endogenous village shadow prices guide the allocation of family resources toward their utility-maximizing use. Prices add an important element to village models. Where prices for goods and production factors are set by government policy or determined in regional or national markets, the CGE framework makes it possible to explore the effects of changes in these exogenous prices on village economic activity. Where prices are endogenous to the village, they transmit policy, market, and other income shocks through the village economy. The choice of which prices are exogenous and which are endogenous to the village is largely empirical. To ensure consistency across experiments, and because the villages studied in this volume are relatively well integrated into regional markets for goods, we assume that all prices are determined exogenously, with the exception of family labor, land, and capital. At the same time, we explore the sensitivity of our results to the assumption of a fixed wage for hired labor and a fixed price for staples.

Village SAM, household-farm, and CGE models compared

Policy simulations using village SAM, neoclassical household-farm, and village CGE models may yield vastly different results, both qualitatively and quantitatively. Consider, for example, the impact of a 10 percent change in migrant remittances on village production, value-added, and trade linkages with the outside world (as in the "Migration and Development" experiment in Chapter 9). Table 2.2 summarizes the results of this experiment for the Mexican village described in Chapter 5 using (1) a village SAM model; (2) a neoclassical household-farm model with all goods and factors tradable (as in Barnum and Squire, 1979; Singh, Squire, and Strauss, 1986); and (3) two versions of CGE models of a Mexican village. In the first CGE model, all goods are tradable, but not all labor is tradable: Family labor is nontradable at the household level, and hired labor is tradable among households but not between the village and the outside world. In the second CGE model, all labor and staples are village nontradables.

Remittances stimulate village production in the SAM model. The increase in remittances first increases migrant households' demand for goods and services inside and outside the village. Given the SAM model's assumption of perfectly elastic supply responses, increases in demand translate into equivalent increases in supply. This generates new rounds of income increases in the village, as village production activities demand inputs from one another and factors from village households. Basic grains production increases by 2.2 percent, and output from other sectors rises by 1.3 to 2.8 percent (column 1). Gross village product rises by 1.8 percent, and trade linkages between the village and the outside world, as represented by the village demand for manufactures, rise substantially (3.6 percent). In short, a

Table 2.2. *Impacts of migrant remittances in village SAM, household-farm, and village CGE models*

Sector	Village SAM (1)	Household-farm (2)	Village CGE — Missing labor market (3)	Village CGE — Missing labor and staples market (4)
Production (prices)				
Basic grains	2.19	0.00	− 1.31	0.23
				(1.80)
Livestock	1.31	0.00	0.05	0.06
Resource extraction	2.76	0.00	− 5.78	− 5.87
Services	1.91	0.00	− 5.41	− 5.45
Value-added				
Family labor	2.32	− 37.04	− 2.81	− 2.77
Hired labor	2.40	440.29	− 4.11	− 4.32
Capital	1.96	0.00	− 1.08	− 0.98
Land	1.47	0.00	− 0.30	− 0.16
Gross village product	1.82	0.00	− 1.21	− 1.09
Income (real)	3.71	7.43	3.45	3.67
Migration	N.A.	18.55	6.82	6.48
Marketed surplus	0.00	− 0.31	− 1.59	N.A.
Manufactures	3.59	7.91	6.54	7.31

Note: The numbers represent the effects of a 10 percent increase in international migrant remittances in the four models.

village SAM model would lead one to the conclusion that migrant remittances stimulate both village production and rural–urban trade linkages.[2]

The household-farm and village CGE models give strikingly different results. In the neoclassical household-farm model, production is unaffected by migration or remittances. Although higher returns to migration may induce families to allocate more of their members' time to migration,[3] family and

2. The migration response to the increased returns to migration cannot be ascertained in a SAM model, because migration is exogenous: Remittances are an exogenous payment to village households by the rest of the world. This is, in essence, an income transfer experiment in the SAM framework.
3. The migration response, like the labor-supply response, is not necessarily positive in a household-farm model (e.g., see Singh, Squire, and Strauss, 1986, on labor-supply elasticities in household-farm models).

hired labor are, by assumption, perfect substitutes in production. This eliminates the trade-offs between migration and production and also between income activities and leisure: Migrant households substitute hired labor for family labor in their production activities. Higher remittances increase migrant households' income, and the incomes of families supplying labor to migrant households also rise.[4] However, instead of stimulating production in the village, higher incomes increase the demand for village tradables; that is, they affect the village marketed surplus but not the village supply. Local prices do not change, so higher remittances do not alter the conditions for profit maximization that determine households' supply response.

Column 2 in Table 2.2 reveals no effect of higher remittances on village production and hence on gross village product. The only impact of higher remittances on value-added in the household-farm model is on the distribution of value-added between family and hired labor. There is a very large increase in migration (a migration elasticity of 1.9), because migrant households can replace family members who migrate with perfect hired substitutes in household-farm production. The demand for tradables produced outside the village rises by nearly 8 percent.

The production effects are negative in the two village CGE models (columns 3 and 4). Here, migration competes with local production activities for scarce family time. In the first village model, output decreases by 1.3 percent in staples and by more than 5 percent in nonagricultural activities. This results in decreases of 2 to 4 percent in labor value-added and a drop by more than 1 percent in gross village product. The only production activity that benefits from remittances in both CGE models is livestock, which uses very little labor. Households respond to the increased migration and leisure demand for family time by switching from more labor-intensive activities to livestock production. Staple production increases only in the second model, where the village is constrained to be self-sufficient in staples (i.e., staples are a nontradable). Because of family time constraints and an imperfect substitutability between family and hired labor, the migration response is lower in the village CGEs (between 6 and 7 percent) than in the neoclassical model. The combination of this and the negative production effects means that higher remittances lead to smaller total-income changes in the two CGE models.

Summary

This chapter presented a basic social accounting matrix (SAM) framework for studying the economies of villages in diverse social, cultural, and market settings. Chapters 3 through 7 utilize this village SAM framework to portray

---

4. We take account of these cross-income effects between migrant and nonmigrant households in the household-farm experiment in Table 2.2. This is actually a step beyond a conventional household-farm model toward a CGE.

the structures of five village economies, to explore linkages among production activities and institutions within those villages, and to identify economic linkages between the villages and the outside world. In Chapter 8, the village SAMs are used as the basic data input to design and estimate five village CGEs. These village CGEs are the basis for simulating the villagewide effects of exogenous policy, market, and environmental changes in Chapter 9.

3

The village economy and tenure security in West Africa: A Senegalese village SAM

ELISE H. GOLAN

The bulk of Senegal's population lives and farms in the Peanut Basin. This region extends southward from Louga to Kaolack and eastward from Thies to Tiaf and broadly follows the historical and current distribution of peanut production in Senegal. It is also the area that has suffered the most from environmental degradation. Overworked soil, deforestation, overgrazing, wind erosion, a falling water table, and salinization are all weakening the economic base of the Peanut Basin farmers.

A hypothesis frequently advanced to explain environmental degradation in the Peanut Basin is that the insecurity of traditional landholdings discourages investment in soil conservation. The legal land tenure system in Senegal is complex. A Law of National Domain passed in 1964 granted the state ownership rights in previously unregistered land. With this law, approximately 98 percent of all Senegalese land became part of the national domain and consequently fell under state control. However, due to incomplete and uneven application of the law, usufruct or ownership rights over most agricultural land are still determined through traditional practice.

This chapter has two main objectives. The first is to use a village social accounting matrix to explore the role of secure and insecure landholdings and the role of the institutions (compounds) that govern their use in two villages in the Senegalese Peanut Basin. The second is to compare income flows and soil conservation practices between the two villages, which have differing degrees of soil insecurity. This research sheds light on the possible consequences that enforcing the Law of National Domain would have on economic activity and environmental degradation in the Peanut Basin.

Elise H. Golan is a Visiting Researcher, Department of Agricultural and Resource Economics, University of California, Berkeley.

31

The Peanut Basin

Like all of Senegal, the Peanut Basin has a late summer rainy season (about four months) and an extended dry season (about eight months). Rain levels in the basin range from approximately 800 millimeters in the south to approximately 475 millimeters in the north, with rains becoming more variable as one moves north. The most common soil types in the basin are desaturated ferruginous tropical soils, and the natural vegetation ranges from wooded savanna in the south to sparsely wooded, shrubby steppe in the north. Giant baobab trees are prevalent throughout the area.

In the basin, the Wolof and then the Serer ethnic groups predominate, though Peul, Lebou, Malinke, Toucouleur, Nouminda, and Bambara are scattered throughout the region. As of 1980, population densities in the basin ranged from thirty to forty people per square kilometer in the north and east, to approximately a hundred people per square kilometer in the south-center districts. These densities are high for a desert region like the Sahel.

Historically, land in the basin was claimed by the first settlers by right of having cleared it by fire. These men became known as the "masters of fire" or the *borom daye* (wolof). They usually claimed vast areas of land with up to six days of burning. Being unable to cultivate the totality of their holdings themselves, these men accorded use rights or "rights of hatchet" to men who could cultivate the land. Once given use rights, the "master of hatchet" or *borom n'gadio* (wolof) had incontestable, irrevocable rights to that land as long as he paid a yearly homage to the master of fire. Usually, this annual payment was symbolic (e.g., an ear of millet), but in different areas and at different times in the basin's history, the homage payment became a substantial portion of the year's harvest. Rights of fire and hatchet were (and still are) passed from father to son. In the area of the basin where this study was conducted, farmers reported that the right of fire had died out during French colonial rule and that, at present, only the right of hatchet remained.

Farm production is organized at the compound level. The compound comprises any number of households. The nucleus of the compound typically consists of one male who has right of hatchet and his household (wives, children, older parents, aunts, sisters, unmarried male relatives, etc.). This male with rights of hatchet is not only the head of his household, but also the head of the compound. Other households in the compound are headed by male relatives of the compound head (brothers, sons, or cousins). These secondary households are broken into two categories: independent and dependent households. The primary distinction is that independent households prepare their own meals and are responsible for meeting their own millet needs. The position of head of the compound, along with the right of hatchet, is passed from father to oldest son. If the oldest son is unable or unwilling to assume control, responsibility is passed to the most appropriate male (or occasionally female) relative. If male children have access to job opportunities or land outside of their father's land, they can leave their natal compound to form one of their own.

The compound head is responsible for distributing compound land between millet and peanut crops. He oversees the compound's millet fields and has the ultimate responsibility for meeting the food needs of the compound. If there is an independent household in the compound, the head of that household will oversee a millet field in order to supply his household's grain needs. The millet flow between the compound and independent member households seems to be fluid, with transfers taking place in both directions.

After allocating enough land to millet production, the compound head distributes the remaining land among the various compound members for cultivation. Occasionally, land is set aside for manioc, vegetables, and condiments. Wives, unmarried older members (called *sourga*), older male children, heads of households, brothers, cousins, aunts, uncles, and others can all be allocated land to cultivate for their personal benefit (peanuts are usually the crop of choice). The compound head also cultivates a peanut field for his own cash needs. All compound members donate labor to the compound's millet fields, but assuring enough labor for the peanut fields is usually the responsibility of each field manager, and labor swaps are arranged on an individual basis. Peanut and millet fields are usually rotated on a yearly basis; thus, from one year to the next many compound members do not know which fields they will be allocated for their personal peanut crops.

Two types of hired labor are common in the Peanut Basin. One type is the *firdou*. The firdou travel around the basin supplying supplemental labor as needed. They are usually paid in cash and are given food and lodging for the duration of the labor contract. *Navetanes* are the second type of common hired labor. These men hire out their labor in return for the loan of peanut seeds and a parcel of land. Traditionally, navetanes work on the compound fields in the mornings and on their personal peanut field in the afternoon. At the end of the season, they repay the peanut seed loan with interest. Navetanes live and eat with their host compounds during the growing season and then return home during the dry season. Navetanes usually have ongoing relationships with a compound, returning year after year to the same place.

Inputs such as seeds, pesticides, and fertilizer are acquired by the compound in a number of ways. Up to and including 1986, the year of this study, farmers had access to government-provided peanut seed (and pesticide), which was distributed on credit through the farmers' cooperative. With this system, farmers received the peanut seed and pesticide at the beginning of the season, and after harvest they were responsible for reimbursement with interest. Heads of compounds and sometimes independent heads of house-holds were the only compound members with access to peanut seed credit; thus, it was their responsibility to determine the allocation of this seed and of pesticide among the other compound members who wished to plant peanut fields. Peanut seed is also available for sale on the open market. Some farmers reserve seed from the previous year's crop, though this prac-tice cannot be continued over a long period of time due to the eventual deterioration of seed quality. Pesticide and fertilizer are both sold on the open market, although fertilizer is extremely expensive and relatively difficult to obtain.

Tool use in the basin is restricted primarily to horse- or donkey-pulled plows and small hand-held implements. The *iler,* a metal arrow-shaped piece attached to a long stick, appears to be the most popular tool in the area. It is principally used for weeding, but has many other uses, from field preparation to seeding and harvesting.

Compounds and land rights

The agricultural land-management focus of this study requires that careful attention be given to the structure of the farming system in the basin. In light of this, the survey questionnaire emphasized two issues often neglected in the agricultural development literature: first, the organization of the farming unit or compound and, second, the tenure rights of the compound as a whole and the rights of each individual member of the compound.

The farming unit. Faulty or incomplete characterization of the Afri-can farming unit has led economists astray in many land management studies. Economists and other development planners must be careful to go beyond the compound head (who usually is the easiest person to interview) and identify the role of each member of the compound. Most development studies reduce the African farming unit to "the farmer." References to "the farmer" allude to an owner-operator and, in some studies, "the farmer" comes to stand for the compound-household as a whole, making of it an amorphous entity. In almost all cases, "the farmer" ends up meaning the compound head, and he is accorded owner-operator status.

This is a costly reduction. In the African setting, compound heads, wives, children, cousins, uncles, nephews, and others can all be "field managers" responsible for cultivating compound land. Each one of them is "the farmer," and each is subject to a different set of constraints and a different set of motivations. By persisting to model rural Africa using only the constraints and motivations of the compound head and excluding those of other farmers in the compound, economists cannot hope to develop successful agricultural programs. In this study, each compound member responsible for the cultivation of a field was interviewed. Likewise, the constraints and incentives of each field manager were evaluated.

Tenure rights. There are many rights associated with land ownership, and these rights must be detailed individually to accurately describe a system of tenure and to provide a basis for comparison with other systems. In the words of S. R. Simpson (1976):

> The collection of rights pertaining to any one land parcel may be likened to a bundle of sticks. From time to time the sticks may vary in number (representing the number of rights), in thickness (representing the size or "quantum" of each right), and in length (representing the duration of each right). Sometimes the whole bundle may be held by one person or it may be held by a group of persons such as a company or a family or clan or tribe, but very often separate sticks are held by different people. Sticks out of the bundle can be acquired in many different ways and held for different periods, but the ownership of the land is not itself one of the sticks; it must be regarded as a vessel or container for the bundle, the owner being the person (individual or corporate) who has the "right of disposal" as it can be called.

The sticks in the bundle can be determined in any number of ways. They can be determined according to ecological use, which might specify seasonal rights to fish, hunt, gather, or graze over a virtually unbounded area of land. Or they can be determined according to market or production specifications, which might delineate rights over trees and plants, minerals or water, as well as alienability or mortgageability.

A list of the sticks that might appear in the African tenurial bundle is given below. This list was composed with production and allocation questions in mind.

a. Right of access to land: The owner of this right has the right of access to group (either compound or village or tribal) land. The parcel of land is not specified and could be changed from season to season by the group authority.

b. Right of access to a particular parcel: These are use rights to a specified piece of land. They are relatively secure, meaning that they are not likely to be shifted on a seasonal basis.

c. Root rights: With root rights, the planter of a tree, bush, tuber, peanut plant, and the like has rights over the fruits of the plant as long as the roots remain alive. This is particularly important in the case of trees or bushes that are useful over a long period of time.

d. Right to decide on crop: Whether a farmer has the right to grow crops on a piece of land, the right to decide on what crops to grow could be vested in another party such as the group authority or even the government cooperative or marketing board.

e. Water rights: This specifies whether a farmer has the right of access to irrigation water.

f. Right to determine heirs: This right specifies whether a landowner has the right to specify who will inherit his or her land.

g. Right to sell: This denotes the right to alienate land permanently.[1]

h. Right to lend (rent): Here it is important to indicate what kind of rent (if any) is paid for the use of the land.

i. Right to mortgage: This determines whether the farmer's land parcel can be mortgaged to obtain credit.

j. Right to product: This is the right to determine what happens to the harvest or revenue generated by a particular field.

For Western economists and development planners, the idea of land rights being likened to a bundle of sticks is appealing, and Simpson is quoted or referred to in a number of tenure studies. Many scholars understand that the bundle of rights the African farmer possesses might contain different sorts of rights than those possessed by American or European farmers. What most studies fail to do is to untie the bundle of rights: They identify all rights as those of "the farmer," or the compound head. This is a mistake. Even though the compound head is usually allocated the lion's share of land rights, other compound members also possess solid rights over compound land. These rights are recognized by the whole community and often limit those possessed by the compound head.

In this study, considerable effort went into determining not only the rights of the compound as a whole over land, but also the individual compound members' rights to land, that is, the individual sticks. In this way, the tenure security and incentive structure operating on every field manager within the compound, as well as on the compound as a whole, can be reconstructed. By dissecting the compound farming organization, the true costs and benefits of land reform can be evaluated. By focusing on the compound's land rights as perceived by its members, this study is able to separate fact from theory. Many tenure laws or reforms adopted at the national level, such as the Law of National Domain, have scant impact on the perceptions and actions of the population at large. By carefully analyzing the bundle of rights that each field manager claims to possess, erroneous conclusions about a land reform that was never successfully implemented can be avoided. Here, it was not assumed that the Law of National Domain had been adopted by the rural

---

1. S. R. Simpson contends that this is the right that defines land ownership. This is also the right that characterizes many African tenure systems in that it does not exist. But African farmers, compounds, villages, and ethnic groups most definitely own their land; they cannot be dispossessed.

Table 3.1. *Outline of Senegal village SAMs*

	I. Activities	II. Factors	III. Institutions	IV. Savings	V. Rest of world
I. *Activities* Peanuts Millet Other crops Animals Service Commerce	Village input–output table	Empty	Village produced consumption	Seed stock investment	Exports from village
II. *Factors* Manager labor Household labor Compound labor Village labor Imported labor Nonagricultural labor Secure fields Moderately secure fields Insecure fields Borrowed fields Grazing rights	Factor value-added	Empty	Empty	Empty	Empty
III. *Institutions* Large compounds Medium compounds Small compounds	Inputs supplied by other compounds	Distribution of value-added	Empty	Empty	Remittances and salaries
IV. *Capital/Savings*	Empty	Empty	Savings	Empty	Empty
V. *Rest of world* Cooperatives Weekly market Other Senegal	Imported inputs	Imported labor	Imported consumption	Imported investments	Empty

population. Instead, all compound members were asked to enumerate their
rights over compound land.

Village SAM framework and estimation

A social-accounting matrix framework guided the collection of village data
for this study. An outline of the village SAMs appears in Table 3.1. The

SAMs are the conceptual basis for the two village SAMs presented in this chapter. They consist of twenty-one endogenous accounts: six activities; six labor factors, designated by labor type and source; five land factors, distinguished by security of tenure and rights of access; three compound institutions, designated by compound size; and an endogenous capital account. The exogenous accounts consist of three rest-of-world accounts: cooperatives, a weekly market, and the world beyond the weekly market. The twenty-four village SAM accounts are described in some detail below.

Sample area and survey methods

Every region in Senegal is broken into administrative units called village sections, each of which is governed by a rural council. Depending on the population density of an area, these sections are composed of one or more villages. At the village section level, land disputes and inheritance are decided by a democratically elected rural council.

Two village sections in the Peanut Basin were chosen for the study sample, primarily based on logistical criteria. These sections both consist of single villages. Each section is less than an hour's drive from the huge daily market at the regional capital of Kaolack, and each section is within walking distance of a large weekly market. Sections with a number of marketing opportunities readily available to farmers were selected. The proximity to Kaolack also facilitated site visits and transportation for the enumerators. The sample sections (villages), Keur Marie and Keur Magaye,[2] were chosen also because they reflect the variation in population density in the Peanut Basin. Keur Marie is located to the west of Kaolack, where population densities are highest, whereas Keur Magaye lies to the east, where population densities are at their lowest.

Three enumerators were hired for study. Each had extensive experience doing agricultural survey work for the Institut Senegalais de Recherches Agricoles. Their input was invaluable. Enumerators lived in the study villages during the week and returned to Kaolack and their families on the weekends. The length and depth of the interviews required that the enumerators be on call from morning until late evening in order to take advantage of the spare moments of the various compound members.

A list of compound heads for each village was acquired from government extension agents. Compounds were then chosen randomly from the list, with approximately one-third of each section's compounds chosen for the study. In Keur Marie, twenty-two compounds were interviewed, and in Keur Magaye, twenty-six compounds were interviewed. Interviewing was conducted from

---

2. Three compounds from the adjoining section of Keur Ismaila are included with the compounds of Keur Magaye.

January 1987 to May 1987, the agriculturally slow period in the Peanut Basin. The study therefore relies almost solely on recall data concerning the 1986 agricultural season. These data were collected as soon after harvest as was feasible, given the time constraints of the compound and the availability of enumerators.

The data were collected as part of a study on African tenure and land management conducted by the United States Agency for International Development, the World Bank, and the Land Tenure Center at the University of Wisconsin (Golan, 1990). Data were collected on every aspect of the farming system in order to provide information about the constraints and incentive structure bearing on land managers and landowners in the study area.

The interviews for the Peanut Basin study were carried out at four different levels. The first level was conducted with the compound head to elicit a general description of the compound, including human characteristics, capital stock, extra-agricultural income, food grain purchases and gifts, and the compound head's impression of the Law of National Domain. To avoid biased answers on tenure claims, the questions concerning the National Domain Law were kept for the last day of interviewing.

The second level of interviewing was again conducted with the compound head and focused on mapping compound landholdings. The compound's parcels were enumerated and the tenure history of each parcel was constructed. In the sense used here, *parcel* denotes a continuous landholding bordered by someone else's land. If the parcel was fallow, length of and reason for fallow period were recorded. The number and size of each field were also established and the name of each crop and field manager noted for the next round of interviewing. In the present research, *field* refers to a separate crop area or separate management area within a parcel. For example, a large parcel that is only planted in peanuts might in actuality contain three different fields: one area of the parcel might be managed by the compound head, another by his first wife, and another by his second wife. Or a single parcel might be broken into millet and peanut fields, both managed by the compound head. The total number of fields in the sample thus exceeds the number of parcels. The title of *manager* denotes the compound member who owns or has responsibility for distributing the product of a field. In all cases, the compound head readily identified the field managers.

The third round of interviews was directed at the field manager, who, besides controlling the distribution of the product of a field, was usually responsible for the actual management of inputs for the field. When the field manager did not oversee field management, the true field overseer was identified and interviewed jointly with the field manager. During this round of interviewing, questions were asked concerning crop and input management, and the tenurial rights of the manager over the field were determined.

The fourth and final round of interviews involved both field managers and

Table 3.2. *Parcels and hectares by village: Keur Marie and Keur Magaye*

	No. of parcels		Hectares		% of hectares	
	Marie	Magaye	Marie	Magaye	Marie	Magaye
Total	138	213	190.56	546.20	100	100
Owned and operated	98	150	151.97	412.05	80	76
Borrowed	25	24	25.23	40.61	13	7
Lent	15	39	13.36	90.75	7	17
Borrowed and lent	0	1	0	.10		
Fallow	34	74	35.21	208.97	18	39
Fallow: Owned and operated	30	71	31.36	203.62		
Borrowed	3	3	3.23	5.35		
Lent	1	0	.62	0		

other compound members. Each manager was asked how the portion of each crop or the revenue gained from each crop that he or she controlled was distributed. Once the income of each compound member was established, each member was asked how he or she spent that income. Information on expenditures was collected for general categories of investment or consumption goods and services (each orange or scoop of tomato paste was not enumerated). Managers were also asked about the source and cost of seeds, pesticide, and fertilizer.

To examine thoroughly the rights and responsibilities of each field manager required lengthy individual interviews. In the Peanut Basin sample, 136 different field managers, supervising a total of 262 fields, were identified. (Some managers supervised numerous fields.)

To gauge the tenurial rights of the field managers, managers of fields were asked questions concerning how they obtained the field or right to work the field, years of experience managing the field, security of right to the field, rights of disposal, and management rights.

Land tenure in the survey area

The forty-eight compounds in the sample owned or operated a total of 734.07 hectares of land which included 351 parcels. Of this total, 65.84 hectares were borrowed, 104.11 were lent, and 0.10 was borrowed and then lent. During the 1986 season, 244.18 hectares, or approximately one-third of the total, were left fallow. Statistics on size and number of parcels are presented in Table 3.2, where they are disaggregated by village.

The land areas held by the two villages are quite different. Keur Marie is located in a more densely populated area. The twenty-six compounds in Keur

Table 3.3. *Average distance between compound and parcel (meters)*

	Keur Marie	Keur Magaye
All parcels	441	1,632
Owned and operated	489	1,465
Lent	272	2,163
Borrowed	356	1,879
Fallow	584	1,679

Magaye control almost three times the amount of land controlled by the twenty-two compounds in Keur Marie. They also have twice the amount of land in fallow as the Keur Marie sample.

Owned land area per compound in Keur Magaye ranged from 0.13 hectare to 59.66 hectares, whereas that in Keur Marie ranged from 0 to 18.10. The average owned land area per compound in Keur Marie was 7.5 hectares (standard deviation [sd] = 5.01), as compared with an average owned land area of 19.34 hectares (sd = 15.79) in Keur Magaye. The average amount of land to which each compound had access during the previous year (i.e., owned [including fallow] + borrowed − lent) was 8.05 hectares for Keur Marie (sd = 5.10) and 17.41 hectares for Keur Magaye (sd = 12.98). The average amount of operated land per compound (i.e., owned land + borrowed − lent − fallow) was 6.48 hectares for Keur Marie and 9.37 hectares for Keur Magaye. The ratios of land per compound in the two villages become more similar once borrowing and lending are considered, and closer still once fallow lands (particularly the huge tracts of fallow in Keur Magaye) are removed from the calculations.

The average distance between a compound and one of its parcels was approximately 1 kilometer (sd = 1,312 meters). Compound members usually walk this distance, although horse or donkey carts are sometimes employed for long treks, which range up to 6 kilometers. Small huts are built on the most distant parcels for overnight stays by compound members. Average distances for each village and for each type of parcel are given in Table 3.3. Given the size of the holdings in Keur Magaye, it is not surprising to find that, on average, they lie almost four times farther from the compound than those in Keur Marie.

The 262 fields owned by the various compounds can be classified according to the bundle of tenurial rights possessed by their field managers, based on the managers' responses during the fourth round of the survey. In the village social accounting matrices, the fields are grouped into three classes: those managed by managers possessing secure tenure rights, those

Table 3.4. *Relationship of manager to compound head and degree of security*

Relationship to compound head	Total (number of people)	Total number of fields			
		Secure	Moderately secure	Insecure	Borrowed
Wife	31	3	7	14	5
Son	24	4	12	10	2
Brother	13	11	3	2	5
Sister-in-law or daughter-in-law	10	0	1	3	2
Mother	4	0	1	3	0
Nephew	2	1	1	4	0
Aunt	1	0	0	1	0
Father	1	0	0	0	1
Cousin	1	0	0	0	1
Sister	1	0	0	0	1
Brother-in-law	1	0	1	0	0
Unknown	1			2	

managed by managers possessing moderately secure rights, and those managed by managers with insecure tenure rights. Table 3.4 summarizes the security of land rights according to the relationship of field managers to compound heads.

Managers with the most secure rights over a field are those who stated that no one could take the field from them, that they would work the field next year, and that their children would someday manage the field. These managers determined what crops they planted, the amount of seeds planted, and the amount of pesticide used. There are 126 fields with secure rights in the sample. Of these 126 fields, 31 had managers who enjoyed the added rights of determining who would inherit the field and stated that they had the unconditional power to give the field away. Most, however, insisted that they would never give a field away, even if they could. All of the secure managers stated that their children would someday operate the field in question.

The fields in the moderately secure classification are under managers who stated that no one could take the field away from them, but they either did not determine the crop, seed, or pesticide use, or else did not know if they would be working the field next year or if their children would work the field. Only 30 fields fall into this category.

The insecure classification includes 75 fields managed by individuals who felt that someone had the right to take the land away from them. Sixty of these field managers said that the compound head could take the field from them, eight said the village chief, one said the rural council, one said another relative, and three said someone else. Also included in this classification are two managers who did not know if someone could take the land away from them.

A category for borrowed fields was added to the three already given. The inclusion of the borrowed fields brings the total number of fields to 262: 126 with secure tenure, 30 with managers possessing moderately secure rights, 75 with managers possessing insecure rights, and 41 borrowed fields. The field portfolios of the mangers can be diverse, with some managing 1 field and others managing several. For example, a single manager could be responsible for 3 fields: one over which he or she has secure tenure rights, another over which he or she has insecure rights, and another that is borrowed. Of course, the tenurial security of every field manager is conditioned by the tenure rights and security of the compound as a whole.

The survey reveals sharp differences between the two villages with respect to insecurity of land tenure. In response to population pressure on the land tenure system, the villagers in Keur Marie express strong reservations about lending land outside of the compound. The Keur Marie villagers are far more knowledgeable about the Law of National Domain, and this knowledge has made them fearful of losing compound land. In addition, the incidence of land disputes is much higher in Keur Marie. The survey data make it possible to compare economic structures and conservation practices in villages with different levels of land-tenure insecurity.

The social accounting matrices and models

Two SAMs were constructed using the Peanut Basin data, one for the village section of Keur Marie and the other for the village section of Keur Magaye. The accounts within each SAM are identical to those presented in Table 3.1. All entries in the SAMs are in CFA (Communauté Française Africaine) values. At the time of the study, 1,000 CFA were the equivalent of approximately three dollars.

The village-economy structures and institutions

The estimated village SAMs for Keur Marie and Keur Magaye are presented in Tables 3.5 and 3.6, respectively. Viewed from the perspective of SAMs, the basic structures of the two village economies are similar. Both villages have single cash-crop and single staple-crop economies that revolve around peanuts and millet. The income and expenditure patterns are not complicated. The majority of purchased inputs and consumption items are imported into the village, and the majority of cash crops are exported from the village. There is relatively little interaction between compounds within each village, and neither village has a store or market.

Table 3.5. *Senegal village social accounting matrix: Keur Marie*

	Activities						Factors						
	1. Peanuts	2. Millet	3. Other crops	4. Animals	5. Service	6. Commerce	7. Manager labor	8. Household labor	9. Compound labor	10. Village labor	11. Imported labor	12. Nonagricultural labor	13. Secure fields
Activities													
1. Peanuts	223,176												
2. Millet		26,669											
3. Other crops			3,165			40,000							
4. Animals	218,500	218,000	22,500										
5. Service													
6. Commerce													
Factors													
7. Manager labor	105,920	269,875	28,550										
8. Household labor	265,143	455,125	22,938										
9. Compound labor	81,875	79,500	20,500										
10. Village labor	31,000	100,875	3,000	12,000									
11. Imported labor	4,875	11,750	250										
12. Nonagricultural labor				396,750	124,500	296,750							
13. Secure fields	808,613	1,423,700	31,513										
14. Moderately secure	119,875	32,650	72,300										
15. Insecure fields	346,775	11,500	63,550										
16. Borrowed fields	292,875	222,300	-9,150										
17. Grazing rights				50,250									
Institutions													
18. Large compounds	19,817		125				109,000	338,875	54,750	46,500		186,500	999,575
19. Medium compounds	19,817						169,233	224,393	125,625	56,375		447,750	1,051,500
20. Small compounds	19,817						126,113	179,938	1,500	44,000		183,750	212,750
Capital/savings													
21.													
Rest of world													
22. Cooperatives	343,439	125	4,760			197,500							
23. Weekly markets	39,884	2,381	1,000		500								
24. Other Senegal						1,725,000					16,875		
Total	2,941,400	2,854,450	265,000	459,000	125,000	2,259,250	404,345	743,205	181,875	146,875	16,875	818,000	2,263,825

Table 3.5. (cont.)

	Factors				Institutions			Investment	Rest of world			
	14. Moderately secure	15. Insecure	16. Borrowed	17. Grazing rights	18. Large compounds	19. Medium compounds	20. Small compounds	21. Capital/ savings	22. Cooper-atives	23. Weekly markets	24. Other Senegal	Total
Activities												
1. Peanuts					109,313	78,811	3,480	113,407	2,413,213			2,941,400
2. Millet					1,079,073	1,093,983	654,725					2,854,450
3. Other crops					79,920	29,680	25,835				86,400	265,000
4. Animals												459,000
5. Service					68,750	42,500	13,750					125,000
6. Commerce					159,088	98,345	31,817			625,000	1,345,000	2,259,250
Factors												
7. Manager Labor												404,345
8. HH labor												743,205
9. Compound labor												181,875
10. Village labor												146,875
11. Imported labor												16,875
12. Non-ag labor												818,000
13. Secure fields												2,263,825
14. Moderately secure												224,825
15. Insecure fields												421,825
16. Borrowed fields												506,025
17. Grazing rights												50,250
Institutions												
18. Large compounds	176,225	114,175	248,850	25,125							2,360,700	4,680,217
19. Medium compounds	48,600	307,650	91,500	17,587							303,820	2,863,849
20. Small compounds			165,675	7,538							5,000	946,080
21. Capital/savings					194,015	113,416	13,476					320,907
Rest of world												
22. Cooperatives					2,990,058	1,407,114	202,997	107,500				343,564
23. Weekly markets								100,000				4,952,694
24. Other Senegal												1,842,875
Total	224,825	421,825	506,025	50,250	4,680,217	2,863,849	946,080	320,907	2,413,213	625,000	4,100,920	

Table 3.6. *Senegal village social accounting matrix: Keur Magaye*

	Activities						Factors						
	1. Peanuts	2. Millet	3. Other crops	4. Animals	5. Service	6. Commerce	7. Manager labor	8. Household labor	9. Compound labor	10. Village labor	11. Imported labor	12. Non-agricultural labor	13. Secure fields
Activities													
1. Peanuts	649,977												
2. Millet		33,264	3,355										
3. Other crops													
4. Animals	375,000	187,000	25,000										
5. Service													
6. Commerce													
Factors													
7. Manager labor	376,875	261,963	43,100										
8. Household labor	577,200	363,813	17,063										
9. Compound labor	238,250	90,388	3,675										
10. Village labor	38,000	26,438	3,125	81,000									
11. Imported labor	119,625	72,500	1,250										
12. Nonagricultural				192,225	428,000	197,500							
13. Secure fields	3,905,762	1,957,462	362,462										
14. Moderately secure	1,398,363	23,138	131,425										
15. Insecure fields	1,990,626	190,075	226,000										
16. Borrowed fields	1,438,675	-43,775	73,525										
17. Grazing rights				313,775									
Institutions													
18. Large compounds	8,031	250	1,120			200,000	259,438	423,888	193,250	89,375		99,625	2,666,325
19. Medium compounds	8,030	249	1,120			100,000	205,125	270,813	116,313	19,250		354,350	2,396,875
20. Small compounds	8,030	249	1,120			50,000	217,375	263,375	22,750	39,938		363,750	1,162,486
21. Capital/savings					162,000	125,000							
Rest of world													
22. Cooperatives	1,418,513	47,367											
23. Weekly markets	108,743	1,822	5,361										
24. Other Senegal											193,375		
Total	12,659,700	3,212,200	898,700	587,000	590,000	672,500	681,938	958,075	332,313	148,563	193,375	817,725	6,225,686

Table 3.6. (cont.)

	Factors				Institutions			Investment		Rest of world		
	14. Moderately secure	15. Insecure	16. Borrowed	17. Grazing rights	18. Large compounds	19. Medium compounds	20. Small compounds	21. Capital/ savings	22. Coop- eratives	23. Weekly markets	24. Other Senegal	Total
Activities												
1. Peanuts					231,219	62,128	5,508	94,372	8,480,042		3,136,454	12,659,700
2. Millet					925,126	1,622,040	588,050	2,199		23,252	18,269	3,212,200
3. Other crops					298,660	94,935	60,600	17,145		170,502	253,503	898,700
4. Animals												587,000
5. Service					289,100	182,900	118,000					590,000
6. Commerce					79,625	50,375	32,500			510,000		672,500
Factors												
7. Manager Labor												681,938
8. HH labor												958,075
9. Compound labor												332,313
10. Village labor												148,563
11. Imported labor												193,375
12. Non-ag labor												817,725
13. Secure fields												6,225,686
14. Moderately secure												1,552,926
15. Insecure fields												2,406,701
16. Borrowed fields												1,468,425
17. Grazing rights												313,775
Institutions												
18. Large compounds	1,328,838	1,188,963	656,300	125,510							455,500	7,696,412
19. Medium compounds	15,138	1,022,238	260,800	109,821							65,000	4,945,121
20. Small compounds	208,950	195,500	551,325	78,444							18,800	3,182,092
21. *Capital/savings*					296,093	103,860	272,958					672,911
Rest of world												
22. Cooperatives					5,576,589	2,824,883	2,104,474	15,000				1,480,880
23. Weekly markets						4,000		374,195				11,283,065
24. Other Senegal								170,000				367,375
Total	1,552,926	2,406,701	1,468,425	313,775	7,696,412	4,945,121	3,182,090	672,911	8,480,042	703,754	3,947,526	

Table 3.7. *Retained seeds: Percentage of total seeds planted in 1986*

	Keur Marie	Keur Magaye
Peanut seeds retained	34	31
Millet seeds retained	93	89
Other crop seeds retained	39	29

Examination of the flows into and out of the villages makes clear the cash-crop–staple-crop dichotomy in the two village economies. Peanut seeds and pesticides are primarily purchased from the government cooperative. The peanut crop is then sold to the cooperative. Millet seeds are almost exclusively selected from previous harvests, and most millet production is consumed by the compound. Very little seed, consumption stocks, pesticide, or fertilizer is traded between compounds.

Percentage breakdowns of the amount of seed that village compounds retained for their own use are given in Table 3.7. In both villages, almost all of the compounds' millet seed needs are met by retained stocks. The small amount of peanut seed retained by the compounds from one year to the next can be explained by three facts. First, peanut seed is supplied by the government cooperative on credit, an important consideration for an area with a "hungry season." Second, peanut seed storage can prove quite costly. Whereas on average it requires only three kilograms of seed to plant a hectare of millet, it requires about eighty-five kilograms of peanut seed to plant the same area. Third, the quality of peanut seed generated from continuous plantings deteriorates from one year to the next, and farmers must periodically supplement retained stocks with higher quality seeds. The retained seed table also shows that in both villages the largest portion of other crop "seed" is purchased, either from village neighbors, the weekly market, or elsewhere in Senegal. This is because in Keur Magaye, manioc is a booming crop, with farmers currently planting first-time plantations, and in Keur Marie, the vegetable and melon market is organized by Lebanese merchants from Dakar who supply seeds, fertilizer, and pesticide on credit.

It is interesting to note that in both villages the amount of peanut seed retained for cultivation in 1987 exceeded that in 1986. In Keur Marie, 50 percent more seeds were saved and in Keur Magaye, 14 percent more. The large increase in retained seeds in Keur Marie probably reflects the uneasiness that Keur Marie farmers were experiencing over expected changes in the government's peanut seed distribution policy. The relatively small increase in Keur Magaye may reflect the confidence that farmers in Keur Magaye re-

Table 3.8. *Percentage of harvest retained for compound consumption*

	Keur Marie	Keur Magaye
Peanuts	6.5	2.4
Millet	99	98
Other crops	51	50

vealed to us in the ability of their cooperative president to assure them of a continued supply of government peanut seed.

Neither village substantially increased its retained millet seed: 0 percent for Keur Marie and 7 percent for Keur Magaye. The increase in Keur Magaye is too small to indicate confidently that farmers in this section anticipated expanding millet production in 1987. But the increase in other crop seeds retained in Keur Magaye reflects a definite trend; farmers are allocating more and more land to manioc production. From 1986 to 1987, more than five times more seed was retained for this purpose, and, indeed, through conversations with farmers it became clear that a manioc craze was sweeping this village section. No similar craze has hit the vegetable and melon farmers in Keur Marie, and manioc is not popular in this area.

The distinction between cash crop and staple is clearly drawn in consumption as well. Table 3.8 shows the percentage of harvest retained for compound consumption. Very few peanuts are kept for compound consumption, and very little millet is sold. In both villages, the other crop, primarily melons and vegetables in Keur Marie and manioc in Keur Magaye, is almost equally sold and consumed by the compounds. Not one farmer in either village listed a neighbor as the purchaser of peanuts, millet, or other crops, and, conversely, in the consumption questionnaire, not one farmer reported purchasing any of these crops from a neighbor for consumption. This implies that a village market for consumption crops does not exist, and the consumption of these goods by village compounds represents a compound's own production exclusively.

In both villages, the primary village-produced consumption good is a compound's own millet. The vast majority of all other consumption goods is imported. Village consumption goods consist primarily of clothes, foodstuffs (sugar, tea, coffee, condiments, fish, etc.), and small manufactured goods (matches, pots, utensils, etc.).

The amount and type of village-produced goods and services exported to markets outside the village again reflect the millet–peanut dichotomy: Peanuts are sold outside the village, and millet is grown for own consumption.

As can be seen from the SAMs, the organization of the peanut market is a bit different in the two villages. Keur Marie farmers sold their peanuts exclusively to the government-sponsored cooperative, whereas farmers in Keur Magaye sold 27 percent of their marketed surplus to peanut merchants from the rest of Senegal. As for millet, the farmers in Keur Marie did not sell any of their harvest to the outside world (or to anyone), whereas in Keur Magaye, a paltry 1 percent was sold at the weekly market or to merchants from the rest of Senegal. In Keur Magaye, the manioc crop was sold at the weekly market and to other points in Senegal, while in Keur Marie all of the "exported" vegetables and melons were sold to the Lebanese merchants from Dakar who were responsible for initiating these crops. In neither village section were any services sold to the rest of Senegal, but more than 75 percent of the commerce activities (76 percent in Keur Marie and 87 percent in Keur Magaye) were completed in locations other than the village.

The main economic interaction within the villages takes place on the factor side: There is borrowing and lending of fields among compounds, and compounds use not only household and compound labor but also labor from other compounds. The complexity of these SAMs is generated through the grouping of compounds according to landholding size and through the identification and classification of each compound land manager by degree of tenure security. The Senegalese SAMs trace out not only the interactions among village compounds but also the interactions within each compound. The importance of intervillage and intercompound interaction is illustrated in the factor value-added calculations. Here, the percentage of farm income due to labor and land transactions is evident. Table 3.9 presents the percentage of farm income derived from the various factors of production. Labor value-added shares across labor types and compound types are comparable, with all compounds deriving most labor value-added from household, manager, compound, and village labor in descending order. But, although the distribution across labor types is similar, small compounds had almost twice the labor value-added share of large compounds. This means that, relative to the income gained, small compounds expended about twice the labor time on agriculture as large and medium compounds. Animal use across compounds is not strikingly different between the two villages. Secure fields account for most of the land value-added, although in Keur Magaye smaller compounds relied most heavily on borrowed land.

A clear understanding of land value-added in the SAMs can be obtained by calculating the value of land services per hectare for the four categories of fields. First, the value of land services by field type is obtained by summing across compound types. This amount is then divided by the total number of hectares of each field type to obtain the value of land service per hectare for secure, moderately secure, insecure, and borrowed fields. The results of this calculation are presented in Table 3.10.

Table 3.9. *Factor value-added as a percentage of farm income*

	Large compounds	Medium compounds	Small compounds
Keur Marie			
Manager labor	6	7	15.4
Household labor	15	10	22
Compound labor	2	6	.2
Village labor	2	2	5
Secure fields	44	46	26
Moderately secure fields	8	2	0
Insecure fields	5	14	0
Borrowed fields	11	4	20
Animals	7	9	11
Keur Magaye			
Manager labor	3.4	5	13
Household labor	6	66	15
Compound labor	3	2	1
Village labor	.6	.2	1
Secure fields	38	53.5	9
Moderately secure fields	19	.3	12
Insecure fields	17	23	11
Borrowed fields	9	6	32
Animals	4	4	6

Table 3.10. *Value of land services per hectare (in CFA)*

	Secure fields	Moderately secure	Insecure	Borrowed
Keur Marie	25,880	33,558	70,851	22,719
Keur Magaye	54,598	65,401	65,023	56,743

Excluding for a moment the Keur Marie entry for insecure fields, the fields in Keur Magaye have about twice the value of land services as those in Keur Marie. Because earlier investigation showed that land management practices in the two villages are fundamentally the same, the difference in the value of land services can only be explained by higher-quality land in Keur Magaye as compared with that in Keur Marie. This may be because Keur Magaye is a younger, less populated village section. Moreover, farmers in Keur Marie are not as strict about following a peanut–millet rotation schedule as those in Keur Magaye. This could have led to greater soil deterioration in Keur Marie. Comparison of the value of land services for different field types in the same village reveals little variation in Keur Magaye; however, in Keur Marie the difference between insecure fields and secure fields is quite large. An explanation for this finding could lie in the fact that insecure fields tend to be peanut fields managed by younger compound members or wives for their personal consumption expenditure, whereas secure fields tend to be millet fields managed by the compound head for general compound consumption. The managers of the insecure fields have strong incentives to plant extensively, knowing that they will benefit directly from this practice and that, in most cases, they will not cultivate the same field the next year. The compound head, as manager of the millet field, has an incentive to plant carefully and wisely, knowing that the compound depends on millet. However, he or she also has an interest in the long-term quality of the soil, which militates against planting too extensively.

What is most striking about the two village SAMs is that they describe two economies that are fundamentally identical. They are single cash-crop and single staple-crop economies that revolve around peanuts and millet. There is very little economic interaction between compounds within each village section. The flow patterns described by these SAMs are uncomplicated. The majority of purchased inputs and consumption items are imported. The majority of the cash crops is exported. Compounds consume most of their own millet production. Neither village has a store or market.

Nevertheless, one important difference between the two villages does emerge from the portrait drawn by the SAMs. Remittance, salary, and extra-agricultural income play a much more important role in Keur Marie than in Keur Magaye. The twenty-two compounds in Keur Marie earn 2,669,520 CFA (31 percent of income) from remittances or salaries originating in "Other Senegal," whereas the twenty-six compounds in Keur Magaye earn only 539,300 (3 percent of income) from those sources. These numbers are somewhat misleading because a large portion of the amount earned by Keur Marie households (1,800,000 CFA) is earned by one compound with a member who works as a trained bookkeeper in Kaolack. Even if this individual's salary is excluded from the total, however, remittance and salary income in Keur Marie is still 869,520 CFA, or 10 percent of the total. There is also a large difference in the shares of income from village-based extra-agricultural activities. In Keur Marie, 818,000 CFA of compound income (or 10 percent) is acquired from service or commerce activities, while in Keur Magaye this number is 817,725 CFA (5 percent of total income).

Two facts explain the relative importance of salary, remittance, and extra-agricultural income in Keur Marie compared with that in Keur Magaye. First, due to greater population pressure and a stronger application of the Law of National Domain, farmers in Keur Marie are less secure in their landholdings than those in Keur Magaye. Second, because of the structure of the government cooperative in Keur Marie, farmers in Keur Marie are less secure in

Table 3.11. *Land improvements (no. of fields)*

	Keur Marie	Keur Magaye
No improvements	75	133
Trees	66	70
Fences	8	14
Pasturage	2	1
Manure	0	1
Wells	8	0
No response	0	3

their continued access to government-supplied peanut seeds. Finally, soils in densely populated Keur Marie are more worked than in Keur Magaye. As a result of these sources of insecurity and low productivity, farmers in Keur Marie have had a greater incentive to diversify away from agriculture into income-earning activities that augment farm incomes and help insure against a potential scarcity of peanut seed and the possibility of land being reallocated by the state.

Tenure insecurity and soil conservation

The comparison of village SAMs reveals patterns consistent with institutional and economic adaptations to land-tenure insecurity, soil degradation, and population pressure. However, there is no evidence that any technical responses to population growth and soil degradation are being implemented to a greater extent in the more heavily populated village. Aggressive measures to prevent soil degradation have not been undertaken in either Keur Marie or Keur Magaye. Few improvements have been made to land in either village (no bunding, contour planting, etc.), and fallow land is not being managed. For the most part, rotation schedules are adhered to. This is a simple, inexpensive soil-saving technology.

Table 3.11 presents statistics on land stewardship. The most common type of improvement in both villages is tree planting, and the number of real investments in land maintenance found here is probably inflated because scrubby bushes were often defined as trees. The fences in both villages were primarily around small fields of vegetables, melon, and manioc. The wells in Keur Marie were built to provide water for the vegetable and melon fields. No wells were found in Keur Magaye because the water table is too low. The information presented in Table 3.11 corresponds to 80 fields with one or more improvements in Keur Magaye and 63 fields with one or more improvements in Keur Marie. This translates to 38 percent of Keur Magaye's 213 fields and

Table 3.12. *Reason parcels were left fallow (%)*

	Keur Marie	Keur Magaye
Lack of peanut seed	65	66
Lack of seeds other than peanut	0	3
Lack of labor	3	3
Give land a rest	23	22
Too far from compound	0	1
Poor quality land (insect holes, etc.)	9	3
No response	0	3

Table 3.13. *Incidence of no rotation*

	Keur Marie	% of fields	Keur Magaye	% of fields
For three years				
Peanuts	1	1	0	0
Millet	2	2	11	7
For two years				
Peanuts	2	2	2	1
Millet	12	12	8	5

46 percent of Keur Marie's 138 fields. The quality and quantity of land improvements in both villages are minimal.

Fallow land is not being actively managed for soil conservation. The Peanut Basin study found that in almost every case, compounds had more land in fallow than they would have preferred, and aside from deciding which parcels to leave fallow, very little strategy went into determining the amount of fallow; compounds left land fallow because of resource constraints. Out of the 108 parcels that were left fallow in the two village sections, 76 were fallow due to lack of seeds or labor, 6 because they were too far from the compound or were of exceptionally low quality (insect holes or perpetual harassment by animals), and 2 had no response given. Only 24 of the 108 parcels were left fallow "in order to give the land a rest" (Table 3.12). Despite the differences in land insecurity reported here, the percentage of land left in fallow for productive reasons is almost exactly the same for the two villages: 23 percent in Keur Marie and 22 percent in Keur Magaye.

An alternative soil-saving practice is field rotation. For the most part, an every-other-year rotation schedule between peanuts and millet is closely maintained throughout the Peanut Basin. Farmers recognize the benefits of crop rotation for soil quality and hence for productivity. Most compounds in the sample have enough parcels to rotate between millet and peanuts. Table

3.13 reports the number of fields that were left in peanuts or millet for three years in a row and the number planted in peanuts or millet for two years in a row. Data were collected for the three-year period from 1984 through 1986. The sample size is 103 fields in Keur Marie and 151 fields in Keur Magaye.

On average, farmers in land-scarce Keur Marie are not as meticulous about following rotation schedules as those in Keur Magaye. In particular, they are more likely to designate a field as the compound's millet field and cultivate millet there for consecutive years. This is a surprising observation given the well-known cost-effectiveness of crop rotation in the area.

Conclusions

The two Senegalese village SAMs in this chapter present a portrait of villages with different levels of land-tenure insecurity, population pressure, and soil degradation. The production structure of these two villages is similar. However, the SAMs reveal differences in the responses of these villages to environmental and demographic constraints. These differences are particularly evident in the structure of income receipts. Remittances are a considerably larger source of income in the poor-land, small-parcel, and densely populated village of Keur Marie.

The paucity of technical packages to support agriculture while at the same time reversing or at least staying the decertification process in the Sahel has led many experts to conclude that migration and regional diversification are necessary steps to combat soil degradation and support rural incomes. Reduced cultivation caused by migration and diversification, however, will not necessarily lead to improvements in the environment unless it is accompanied by agroforestry innovations or other conservation projects. Reductions in the agricultural labor force through migration could actually reduce the possibility for labor-intensive soil conservation (weeding, land preparation, contouring, walling, intercropping, etc.). More generally, in diversified village economies, noncrop activities compete with the environment for scarce family resources.

Efforts to establish complementary conservation practices and foster active participation of the rural community in Senegal are complicated by the complexity of the compound farming system. The diversity of field managers in the compound and the possible splintering of incentive structures make it very difficult to encourage conservation through subsidies or other means. All subsidies, fines, and taxes must be tailored to the incentives of the individual field managers. As an alternative to such an involved subsidy scheme, tree cultivation (or other conservation practices) could be encouraged through changes in the current usufruct laws (Golan, 1990).

In theory, individualization of land tenure could be an effective means to internalize the benefits of conservation. Evidence from this study and else-

where, however, suggests that the environmental benefits from private registered land ownership as contrasted to traditional ownership have yet to
materialize. It appears that other constraints to efficient land management
(environmental, infrastructure, market, etc.) are currently more binding than
any constraints that traditional tenure might pose. In addition, due to the
economic, social, and cultural complexity of the compound system, caution
must be exercised when devising land or resource privatization schemes.

Appendix: Accounts in the Senegal village SAMs

I. Endogenous accounts
  a. Activities
    1. *Peanuts* – Peanut farming. Approximately 36 percent of all cultivated land
       in the two villages.
    2. *Millet* – Millet farming. Approximately 53 percent of all cultivated land in
       the two villages.
    3. *Other crops* – Includes mango, sorghum, beans, corn, melon, vegetables,
       manioc, and byssap. These crops account for approximately 11 percent of
       all cultivated land in the two villages.
    4. *Animal services* – Registers the use of animal traction (cattle, horse, don-
       key) in the villages. The value of the use of animal traction services on a
       field was calculated at 2,500 CFA for the use of a horse or a bullock, and
       2,000 CFA for the use of a donkey. These two rates were observed.
    5. *Services* – Well digging, construction, teaching, and tea making.
    6. *Commerce* – Consists exclusively of petty trade. The merchants bought
       oranges, fish, condiments, and miscellaneous commodities at relatively
       large markets and then sold their wares at smaller markets or in front of
       their compounds.
  b. Factors
    7. *Manager labor* – The amount of time, valued at the agricultural wage rate,
       that the field managers spent working on their own fields. The agricultural
       wage rate was calculated at 500 CFA per day for planting, the first weeding,
       and for harvest, and at 250 CFA per day for field preparation and the
       second weeding. These were the prices for each of these tasks in the
       villages. By convention, the labor time of children (under fifteen years old)
       was valued at half that of adults. At the exchange rates that were in effect
       at the time of the study, 500 CFA translated into $1.50 per day and 250
       CFA into $.75 per day.
    8. *Household labor* – The amount of time, valued at the agricultural wage
       rate, that members of the field manager's immediate household spent
       working on the manager's fields.
    9. *Compound labor* – The amount of time, valued at the agricultural wage
       rate, that members of the field manager's compound (not including his or
       her immediate household) spent working on the manager's fields.
    10. *Village labor* – The amount of time, valued at the agricultural wage rate,
        that members of the village spent working on the manager's fields.

11. *Imported labor* – The amount of time, valued at the agricultural wage rate, that workers from outside the village spent working on the manager's fields.

12. *Nonagricultural labor-value of labor time spent on nonagricultural activities* – Time spent watching animals calculated at 250 CFA per day to correspond to the agricultural opportunity cost of labor. The lower wage rate was used because herders are often marginal laborers.

13. *Secure fields* – The value of the land services of those fields supervised by managers possessing secure tenure rights. The value of land services was calculated by subtracting the value of labor time, seeds, pesticide, and fertilizer from the value of the crop in question.

14. *Moderately secure fields* – The value of the land services of those fields supervised by managers possessing moderately secure tenure rights.

15. *Insecure fields* – The value of the land services of those fields supervised by managers possessing insecure tenure rights.

16. *Borrowed fields* – The value of the land services of borrowed fields.

17. *Grazing rights* – The value of animal grazing land services. Like other land services, this is a residual calculation. It was calculated by subtracting the value of labor time spent watching the traction animals from the total value of animal services.

c. *Institutions*

18. *Large compounds* – Repository of land value-added and managerial, household, compound, and nonagricultural labor value-added. It is the basic unit of consumption and the recipient of remittances and salaries from outside the village. The compounds in the sample have been divided into three categories: those with large landholdings, those with medium-sized landholdings, and those with small landholdings. Because of the large variation in average holding size in the two villages, these categories correspond to very different hectarage breakdowns. In Keur Marie, the six big landholders have areas ranging from 10 to 20 hectares, while in Keur Magaye the eight big landholders have areas ranging from 20 to 60 hectares.

19. *Medium compounds* – In Keur Marie, the nine medium-sized landholdings range from 5 to 10 hectares, and in Keur Magaye, the nine medium landholdings are 10 to 20 hectares.

20. *Small compounds* – In Keur Marie, the seven small compounds have holdings ranging from 0 to 5 hectares, while the nine small compounds in Keur Magaye have holdings ranging from 0 to 10 hectares.

d. *Savings*

21. *Capital/savings/investment* – The compound's "purchases" of investment goods such as animals, seed stock, equipment, or construction.

II. Exogenous accounts

22. *Cooperatives* – All government-sponsored peanut marketing services. These services supply peanut seed and pesticide (often on credit) at the beginning of the season and then purchase most of the farmers' peanut production at the end of the season. In Keur Magaye, these cooperatives also purchase some millet.

23. *Weekly market* – The primary sources of purchased consumption goods. Both the villages of Keur Magaye and Keur Marie are within walking distance of a major weekly market (the markets of Birklane and Gandiaye respectively). Neither Keur Magaye nor Keur Marie has village markets or village stores.

24. *Other Senegal* – The world farther away than the weekly market. This includes the daily market at Kaolack, which is about an hour's drive from each of the villages. Also included in this account are all other points in Senegal, including the capital, Dakar. Salaries and remittances originate in this account.

4

Production and distribution in a dry-land village economy

SHANKAR SUBRAMANIAN

India's agricultural performance in the post–Green Revolution years has been adjudged moderately successful by many quarters, but rapid and sustained growth has been confined only to a few crops, notably rice and wheat, and to regions of assured rainfall or good irrigation. Nor has the Green Revolution had much of an impact on the extent of rural poverty. Thirty-nine percent of the population was below the poverty line in the 1950s, and, according to the latest estimates, 39 percent of the population was still below the poverty line in 1977–1978. Much of this poverty is concentrated in regions with little irrigation and poor rainfall, areas of unstable agriculture that have benefited little from the Green Revolution.

This study is a departure from traditional macrolevel analyses of poverty and income distribution. Instead of examining these issues at a national or regional level, the focus here is on the village economy: the structure of village production, labor supply and use, income generation and distribution, and commodity, labor, and financial flows between the village and the outside world. The social accounting matrix (SAM) provides a unifying framework for such an analysis. This chapter presents a SAM for Kanzara, a village in Akola district, a region of predominantly rain-fed and highly commercialized agriculture in western India. The SAM is used to delineate the structure of the village economy, its links with the outside world, and production and expenditure linkages within the village.

This village SAM has also been used to model several issues of relevance to the persistent rural poverty observed in the semiarid tropical areas of India.

Shankar Subramanian is Assistant Professor in the Department of Economics at Cornell University.

These include the transmission of weather-induced fluctuations in crop output through the village economy, the impact of investment in agriculture, and the effects of antipoverty programs that can create assets for the landless. These efforts at modeling require the introduction of supply constraints into the traditional SAM multiplier model. The results of SAM multiplier exercises appear elsewhere (Subramanian and Sadoulet, 1990).

This chapter examines three topics: the village and the surrounding region; the data for the SAM and the procedure used to estimate various elements of the SAM; and the use of the SAM to examine the structure of the village economy.

The setting

Kanzara is in Murtizapur *taluka*[1] of Akola district in the western Indian state of Maharashtra. The village was one of several studied for more than a decade by the International Crops Research Institute for the Semi-Arid Tropics (ICRISAT) as part of their Village-Level Studies. These villages were chosen to represent the major agroclimatic zones in semiarid tropical (SAT) India.[2] As a result, the findings of this chapter should be applicable to a larger region than would otherwise be expected. In each village, ICRISAT took a sample of forty households, ten of them noncultivating households and ten from each of three equal groups of cultivators stratified by size of operational landholding. Households that disappeared because of migration or subdivision or became uncooperative were replaced with similar households. Since the sample excluded all households whose primary and secondary sources of income were not agricultural, additional data were collected during April and June 1985 on nonagricultural activities, the incomes of nonagricultural households, all salaries, the income and expenditure of a temple in the village, and bank credit for 1984. The SAM presented here is for the crop year 1984, that is, July 1983–June 1984.

Kanzara is in a region with scarce groundwater, no large perennial rivers, and little irrigation. Rainfall is more stable than in other SAT regions nearby, but most of the land is single-cropped, and the average cropping intensity for the households in the sample was only 105 percent over 1980–1984 (Table 4.2). The average rainfall is 817 millimeters. The soils in the region around Kanzara are medium- to deep-black soils. The chief crops are cotton, sorghum, pulses, and groundnut. In addition, wheat, vegetables, and chilies are grown on land irrigated from wells. The main crop is the *kharif* crop, sown in late June and early July soon after the arrival of the southwest monsoon and harvested from September to December.

1. Indian states are divided into districts, which are further divided into talukas, which are typically the smallest administrative units.
2. For details, see Jodha, Asokan, and Ryan, 1977.

Kanzara is relatively well connected to the outside world. A gravel road leads from Kanzara to the highway. The nearest town, Murtizapur, is eight kilometers away. It is a market town, located on a major rail line to Bombay that was laid in the 1860s. A regular bus service runs between Murtizapur and Kanzara. Kanzara has five retail shops, a ration shop dealing in subsidized oil, sugar, and cereals, a middle school, and a primary-health center. The village is electrified, and electricity is used to run agricultural machinery, such as water pumps and threshers. Most of the marketed surplus is sold in the regulated market in Murtizapur. Bullocks are the primary source of power for agricultural operations. The villagers also keep buffalos, cows, and goats. Milk production was unimportant in the past, but milk output for the sample households more than quadrupled between 1981 and 1984. Behind this increase were two factors: the setting up of a milk cooperative in Murtizapur and the provision of subsidized credit for livestock purchases by government antipoverty programs. Other activities include retail trade, two flour mills, the hiring out of threshers and a fodder cutter, and the activities of a potter, two carpenters, two basket makers, two graziers, seven barbers, and three tailors.

Akola and the surrounding districts form part of what was once known as the province of Berar. An 1870 gazetteer (Berar, 1870) provides a detailed account of the political and administrative history of the region, but little is known of its economic history prior to the early seventeenth century, when it was part of the Nizamshahi kingdom of Ahmednagar. After Akbar defeated the Nizamshahis, it became part of the Moghul dominions, only to revert to the Nizamshahis after Akbar's death. The Nizamshahi minister, Malik Amber, is said to have instituted a land revenue system based on surveys by eye, a system later adopted by the Marathas; to have curbed the revenue-collecting powers of the local chiefs, the *deshmukhs* and the *deshpandes*; and perhaps even to have recognized a kind of private property in land. After Amber's death, Berar returned to Moghul rule. After the death of the Moghul emperor Aurangzeb, the weakened Moghuls granted the Marathas the rights to six-tenths of the revenues of Berar. Soon after, in 1724, the Moghul viceroy in the Deccan rebelled and broke away to found the kingdom of Hyderabad, while continuing to claim sovereignty over Berar. Berar was then fought over by the Nizam of Hyderabad and the Marathas, both claiming a right to its revenues and territory. In 1804, after the defeat of the Marathas in Berar by the British, Berar was returned to the Nizam, only to be handed over to the British in 1853 to pay for various debts said to have been incurred by the Nizam.

The extension of direct rule by the British brought with it several changes. The granting of land by the Moghuls or the Marathas to local magnates in exchange for the provision of troops was brought to an end by the British. The system of land revenue determination and collection developed in Bombay Presidency (bordering Berar on the west) was extended to Berar. Under this system, each plot of land was surveyed and its ownership reçorded. The registered owner or *khatedar* paid revenue directly to the state and not through an intermediary. The tax rate was supposed to be fixed in each taluka, taking into account such factors as land quality and yields. Once fixed, the rates were left unchanged for thirty years, based on the underlying notion that a land revenue that did not vary in the short run with the productive capacity of the land would provide a greater incentive to investment and land improvement.

The 1860s saw the extension of the rail line from Bombay and a surge in cotton prices and exports caused by the cessation of cotton exports from the United States as a result of the U.S. Civil War. At their peak in 1865–1866, India's cotton exports stood at almost four times the average of the entire decade of the 1860s (Harnetty, 1971). The older view was that the increase in cotton production had been at the expense of food crops and had caused a decrease in food production that was responsible for the famines that ravaged India at the turn of the century.[3] But Harnetty found that in Berar, long a major cotton-producing tract, the area under cotton had increased but so had total area cultivated, the latter by 75 percent between 1860–1861 and 1869–1870, so that the area under food crops did not decrease.

Unlike other parts of India, Berar was remarkably free of famine until 1896. That year, total rainfall was adequate, but it was concentrated in June and July instead of being spread out over the months of June to October, as would have been normal. Although there was widespread distress, only in one taluka was famine declared.[4] In 1899, the monsoon failed all over India and famines were declared everywhere. Berar was no exception. Total rainfall in Akola was slightly over a third of normal. Total agricultural production fell by 97.5 percent (Berar, 1901 1: para. 9). Despite relief efforts, mortality rates started to climb once food stocks were exhausted. A year after the rains failed, from June to September 1900, mortality rates two to three times higher than normal were recorded (Berar, 1901, app. 4). Though famines recurred until the 1920s in the neighboring province of Bombay, parts of which have agroclimatic conditions and soils similar to those in Berar, the 1899 famine was the last to affect Berar.

Population, land, and caste

As Table 4.1 shows, after an unexplained dip between 1941 and 1951, Kanzara's population increased steadily, almost doubling between 1951 and 1981. The accompanying data for Murtizapur taluka are more complete,

---

3. For a well-argued but not totally convincing refutation of this view, see McAlpin, 1983.
4. The declaration of famine obliged the government to fund relief works.

Table 4.1. *Population (1867–1981)*

	Kanzara			Murtizapur Taluka		
	Total	Male	Female	Total	Male	Female
1867				104,658		
1881				110,573		
1891				121,657		
1901				118,022		
1911				121,986	62,536	59,450
1921				119,893	62,075	57,818
1931				116,621	6,339	56,282
1941	702	348	358	136,350	70,652	65,698
1951	591	299	202	144,233	74,147	70,086
1961	763	401	362	174,488	90,166	84,322
1971	915	466	449	207,297	106,814	100,483
1981	1,144	590	554			

Source: For Kanzara: Census of India (1941, 1951a, 1961a, 1971a, 1981). For Murtizapur Taluka: Census of India (1941, 1951b, 1961b, 1971b).

going back to 1867 when the first census was held. The taluka population increased very little between 1867 and 1931 because population growth was checked by the famine of 1899 and the influenza epidemic of 1918. More detailed censuses of the village were conducted by ICRISAT in 1975 and 1985 at the beginning and end of their village studies project. Key indicators from these censuses are presented in Table 4.2. Between 1975 and 1985 the population increased by a third and the number of households by slightly less than half, while the average household size dropped from 5.5 to 5. The size of the average operational holding fell from 6.1 to 4.67 hectares, and the fraction of area irrigated rose from 4.45 percent to 9.81 percent. The fraction of households renting out all their land appears to have more than tripled from 1975 to 1985. However, the 1975 census took place during a state of emergency, when landowners were reluctant to admit to renting out land (Walker and Ryan, 1990, p. 9). The distribution of land operated is less equitable than that of land owned. Land rental in Kanzara does not follow the once traditional pattern whereby large landlords rented out land to small cultivators (*cf.* Jodha, 1981). Of the twenty-eight households renting out more than half their land, only three own (and rent out) more than twenty acres of land, and a fourth owns and rents out twelve acres. The rest account for more than half the land rented out and own four acres each on average. Today, the renting out of land is largely a result of changing household strategies over the life cycle.

According to the census of September 1985, the population of Kanzara

Table 4.2. *Village statistics from ICRISAT censuses*

	1975[a]	1985
Area (sq km)	5.96	5.88[b]
Cultivable area (ha)	539.61	52,952[b]
Population	930	1,251
Population density (per sq km)	156	213
Households	169	242
Average household size	5.5	5
Literacy rate (%)	42.7	45.2[b]
Average landholding (ha)	6.10	4.67
Landless households (%)	32.5	30.2
Land-operating households (%)	64.5	63.5
Households renting out all land (%)	3.5	5
Extent of irrigation[c] (%)	4.45	9.81
Cropping intensity[c] (%)	106.86	105.14
Family workers per ha[c]	0.91	
Bullocks per ha	0.25	0.35

[a] Jodha, Asokan, and Ryan, 1977.
[b] Census of India, 1981.
[c] Averages for 1975–1979 and 1980–1984.
For 1985, computed from ICRISAT census household-level data.
Source: ICRISAT censuses.

was 637 males and 614 females in 242 households. Eighty-four households owned no land and 87 cultivated no land. The households were divided into five groups, essentially along the lines of ICRISAT's sampling scheme, except that the 87 noncultivating households were divided into two groups, one of 8 households whose primary source of income was government employment (group I), the other of households who were not employed by the government (group II). The households in group I could be separated from the rest because supplementary data on salaries and on their incomes and consumption were available. The 155 cultivating households were divided into three groups of 53, 50, and 52 households (groups III, IV, and V), based on size of operational landholdings. The average operational landholding (see Table 4.9) ranges from 2.52 acres (1.02 hectares) for group III to 24 acres (9.74 hectares) for group V.

Caste is another factor influencing landownership and access to land. Table 4.3 shows the castes in Kanzara, their traditional occupations, and the number of households belonging to and land owned and operated by each caste. The castes are listed in order of decreasing status as generally acknowledged by the villagers (Walker and Ryan, 1990, p. 47). At present, the dominant castes both in number and by landownership are the deshmukhs and jiremalis. The

Table 4.3. *Caste and landownership (September 1985)*

Caste	Social rank	Land (acres)		Landless households		Farming households			
		Owned	Operated	Salaried	Un-salaried	Small	Medium	Large	Total
Deshmukh	1	437.8	526.3	3	6	4	16	13	42
Patil	2	137.5	137.5					4	4
Gosavi	3	148	128.6		2		2	7	11
Jiremali	4	679.8	598	1	41	22	17	19	100
Muslim	5	91.6	69.6		6	3	4	3	16
Suvamakar (goldsmith)	6	27	7		1	2		1	4
Kumhar (potter)	5.5	5.5				1		1	
Navhi (barber)	8	61.3	71.2		2	1	2	2	7
Dhobi (sasherman)	9	12	12		1	1	1		3
Kaikali	10	9	3		1		1		2
Navbudh	11	157.3	107.2	4	11	11	8	3	37
Matang	12	14.5	7.5		5	4	1		10
Muslim[a]		3	3		3	1			4
Sutar[a]		4	4			1			1

[a] Not ranked (ranks are from Walker and Ryan, 1990).

last two castes, the *navbudhs* (who were known as the *mahars* before their mass conversion to Buddhism in the 1950s) and the *matangs* (or *mangs*) were outcastes or untouchables.

The link between caste and landownership in this region can be traced back to the seventeenth century, before which little is known about the region's agrarian social structure (Fukuzawa, 1982, p. 249). In the seventeenth and eighteenth centuries, the village ideally consisted of a headman (*patil*), usually a member of the *kunbi* peasant caste, the accountant (*kulkarni* or *patwari,* as the 1870 gazetteer terms him), proprietary peasants (*mirasdars*), peasants and artisans temporarily residing in the village (*uparis*), and the village menials and artisans (the *bara* [twelve] *balutedars*). The village land was divided into ordinary owned or *miras* land, *inam* land exempt from land revenue, land owned by the state, and land owned by village families that had died out. Miras land was owned by the village officials and the permanent residents of the village and was subject to land revenue. Both village office and miras land were heritable and salable. Inam or tax-free land was held by village officials and other notables. Often, entire villages or groups of villages were held in inam by hereditary officials such as the deshmukhs and deshpandes, and were given by local rulers in inam to temples and mosques. The upari peasants were temporary residents renting in and cultivating village and state land owned by the richer mirasdars.

The balutedars were similarly divided into uparis (or strangers) and mirasdars (or residents). The balutedars were remunerated in kind at harvest time by the entire village. Some of the permanent or mirasdar balutedars received small plots of inam land to cultivate. The permanent balutedars' rights (or miras) could be subdivided and sold or transferred.

The 1870 gazetteer notes (p. 206) that in Amravati district (of which Murtizapur was then a part) the twelve balutedars (menials and artisans) were:

Wadhi	carpenter
Khati	blacksmith
Garpagari	hail-averter
Mhar	village servant[a]
Chambhar	currier
Kumbhar	potter
Mahali	barber
Warthi	washerman
Gura	temple-cleaner
Joshi	astrologer
Bhat	bard
Moolla	Muslim divine[a]

The gazetteer also speaks of alutedars, who did not appear to have any customary rights or *hakks* at that time (cf. Kulkarni, 1966).

Sonar	goldsmith[a]
Jangam	*Lingayat guru*
Mang	musician[a]
Simpi	tailor
Teli	oil presser[a]
Koli	water carrier
Gosain	—
Kurki	piper and snake-charmer
Bari	*pan* seller
Gondali	drum beater

Each *pargana* or subdistrict, had its hereditary chiefs, the deshmukhs, and hereditary accountants, the deshpandes. This rural aristocracy was expected

---

[a] The occupations of village servant, Muslim divine, goldsmith, musician, and oil presser were not in the original and have been added.

to enforce the peace locally and to assist the state in times of war. In return, they were given inam lands and allowed to collect certain customary dues from the villages in their charge. Earlier, in addition to these dues, these officials had received a share of the land revenue collected by them on behalf of the state. But in Berar, both Malik Ambar and the Marathas after him attempted to do away with intermediaries and collect revenue directly from the village headmen, thus reducing the power of the pargana aristocracy. Contrasting the deshmukhs near Sholapur, a town in a district neighboring Berar, who had managed to become landed proprietors of the villages in their parganas with the deshmukhs of Berar, the 1870 gazetteer notes, "But in Berar the Nizam and the Marathas were struggling for the revenue; they were too powerful to let any subjects stand between them and the full demand; while wherever the Marathas got complete mastery those keen financiers dispensed altogether with the services, and therefore with the claims, of untrustworthy and influential collectors not directly subordinate to themselves" (p. 100). As a result, even the most powerful deshmukhs wielding authority over several parganas and receiving customary dues from several hundred villages were unable to retain any land beyond their inam holdings. Kanzara, with its large deshmukh community, is a deshmukh village, that is, a village that was held largely in inam by deshmukhs.

The position of the menial castes, the mahars and mangs as they were called in the seventeenth and eighteenth centuries, is not clear. On the one hand, they were clearly excluded from large-scale landholding. For example, noting that the village "system in its integrity is a thing of the past," the 1870 gazetteer (p. 205) adds that the system "did not contemplate village Mahars vying with Kunbis in the cultivation of the soil, still less their being landholders in other villages." But on the other hand, there is no reference to their having any source of livelihood but their customary dues. Nor is it clear what proportion of the population belonged to these castes or whether these castes provided the bulk of the agricultural labor required on the fields of the mirasdars and uparis. Were the latter peasants relying on family labor for cultivation? It should be noted that for North India under the Moghuls, Habib (1982, p. 249) concludes that these "menial" castes, forming between a fifth and a fourth of the population, must have served as a labor reserve. In any case, by the late nineteenth century, the "menial" castes were by and large nothing but agricultural laborers. As the 1881 census report notes (Berar, 1881, p. 145), the mahars accounted for about an eighth of the population. Less than 5 percent of them were employed as village servants. The report estimates that these servants' grain dues would have sufficed to support at most twice their number. Of the rest, most were agricultural laborers. Similarly, the mangs were 2 percent of the population. Only a sixth gave their traditional occupation of village musician as their primary source of income. A quarter of the males and a third of the females were estimated to be

Table 4.4. *Caste and landownership*
(1930–1931)

Caste	Households	Land (acres)
Deshmukh	34	584.8
Patil	8	206.8
Gosavi	4	110.8
Jiremali	21	381.3
Barber	3	20.7
Mahar	1	4.5
Others	7	66.2

agricultural laborers. Overall, the mahars provided 32.5 percent of the male daily labor force and 44.8 percent of the female daily labor force, while the *kunbis* accounted for 22.1 percent and 29.7 percent and the malis 22 percent and 37 percent (Berar, 1881, p. 188).[5]

The only balutedars still holding hakks today are the barbers, carpenter, and potter, who retain ties with some landowning families in this and nearby villages and are paid in kind by them. These balutedars also work for others for payment in cash or kind. Table 4.4 shows how much of Kanzara's land was owned by each caste in 1930. While Tables 4.3 and 4.4 cannot be directly compared because some of Kanzara's land was (and is) owned by outsiders and Kanzara residents own (and owned) land elsewhere, Table 4.4 does suggest that the jiremali were already in the ascendant in the 1930s. It is clear, however, that in the intervening years (1931–1985) the lowest castes, the mahars and mangs, who had owned little land in the past, and the Muslims have made sizable gains. Table 4.3 also shows the caste composition of the five household groups. The three most numerous castes (the deshmukhs, jiremalis, and navbudhs) are found in every land-operating stratum. Even among the noncultivating deshmukh households in groups I and II, wage labor is reported as the primary source of income for four out of nine households. Unlike in the past, wage labor is not the lot of the lowest castes alone.

Agriculture

In areas of rain-fed agriculture, soil type and the pattern and variability of rainfall greatly influence cropping patterns and agricultural practices. For example, the deep black soils of some areas in SAT India absorb so much

5. This census defined *kunbi* to include kunbis proper and deshmukhs and certain other agricultural castes.

water that the fields are impassable during the monsoon, and agricultural operations have to be put off until the monsoon has passed. Elsewhere, deeper soils may permit the farmer to raise a second crop using moisture retained in the soil. Most of Kanzara's soils are medium-deep vertisoils; only 10 percent or less are deep enough to permit double-cropping, and 15 percent are shallow soils. Little land is left fallow and little uncultivated land is available. Before 1971, the census did not provide land use data for each village, so little can be said about the availability of fallow and uncultivated land in the past. Between 1971 and 1981, cultivated area increased by 2.3 percent to 90 percent of total area, and area used for nonagricultural purposes more than doubled, leaving little room for further expansion. For the district as a whole, the 1961 census notes that in 1959–1960 net sown area was 80.15 percent, and current and other fallows were 5.45 percent of total area. As the expansion of cultivation between 1860 and 1869 demonstrated, there was much uncultivated land before the cotton boom. However, by 1869, if the gazetteer is to be believed, 84.9 percent of the cultivable area was under cultivation.[6]

The Akola region is better situated than many other regions of SAT India in that it receives adequate rainfall in most years. The cumulative distribution of annual rainfall (1891–1970) at Akola (the district seat fifty kilometers from Kanzara), superposed on annual rainfall at Kanzara for the eleven years from 1975 to 1985, reveals that Kanzara has relatively assured rainfall and the rains were adequate in seven out of the eleven years (Walker and Ryan, 1990).[7] Average rainfall at Akola during 1891–1970 was 790 millimeters.

Two key features of agriculture in this region are the predominance of cotton and the practice of intercropping. In intercropping, several crops are grown together, with a certain number of rows of one crop followed by a number of rows of the next crop, and so on, in a definite ratio. Cotton has been grown in the region for several centuries. Cotton and cotton mixtures with sorghum and pulses such as mung and pigeon pea account for about half the cropped area for the kharif crop, which is sown at the onset of the southwest monsoon. Sorghum and sorghum-pulse mixtures occupy another 22 to 33 percent of the kharif area, with the remainder planted in groundnut and groundnut-pulse-sorghum mixtures. Except for local sorghum, which is planted in the first week of July, the other kharif crops are planted in the third week of June. Weeding, hoeing, and the application of pesticides are taken

6. The gazetteer (pp. 264–265) notes that cultivated area rose from 61.6 percent of culturable area in 1868 to 84.9 percent in 1869. It is not clear how reliable this increase in cultivation is because only one other taluka in Berar (Mekhar) shows a large increase in cultivated area (85 percent), while the others show small increases and, in some cases, decreases.
7. Rainfall data for Murtizapur would be more suitable but were unavailable after 1950. The cumulative distribution shown is obtained by smoothing the empirical cumulative distribution function.

up in July and August. The mung harvest is in September, followed by hybrid sorghum in October, cotton in November and early December, and local sorghum in December. The *rabi* season starts in October soon after the mung and hybrid sorghum harvests, when wheat and vegetables are planted on irrigated land and chick-pea and safflower on plots that have deep, water-retentive soils. These crops are harvested in February. Over the period of the ICRISAT study, the rabi area was between 2.2 percent and 7.7 percent of the kharif area. Depending on the availability of water, some irrigated land, ranging from nil in 1975 to 5 percent of the kharif area in 1983, was planted to vegetables and groundnut in the summer.

Intercropping has several advantages. It lowers the risk of complete crop failure because it is less likely that all components of a crop mixture will fail. In addition, where the soil does not retain enough moisture for two crops to be taken one after the other, intercropping a mixture of short- and long-duration crops allows the farmer to use the moisture in the soil more efficiently. The combination of short- and long-duration crops also provides a more evenly spaced cash flow and spreads out labor demand. But yields on intercropped plots are lower because they receive less fertilizer than do sole crops, perhaps because the different components of a crop mixture respond differently to applications of fertilizer.

Estimates of the area sown to each crop may be made by allocating the area of each plot to each crop in the ratio of the rows occupied by that crop.[8] These estimates are presented in Table 4.5. The kharif area occupied by cotton was between 39 and 50 percent, while that sown to sorghum ranged between 21 and 32 percent, that sown to pulses from 17 to 26 percent, and oilseeds, 3 to 12 percent. While there was no major reallocation between cotton, sorghum, and pulses, hybrid sorghum fast overtook the local variety, and mung came to be as important a pulse as pigeon pea, formerly the main pulse grown here. The switch to hybrid sorghum was occasioned by the release of a new hybrid that had higher-quality grain and fetched a higher price than the earlier hybrids. The shift to mung took the form of a shift from a mixture of cotton, pigeon pea, local sorghum, and another pulse to the cotton-mung-pigeon-pea intercrop. As Walker and Ryan point out (1990, p. 37), the first combination has the disadvantage that the three major components are all long-duration crops maturing in November and December, whereas the second combines mung, which is harvested in September, with two long-duration crops.

8. Ideally the observed row ratios should be used, but these were not entered in the data set. Average ratios for two-crop, three-crop, four-crop, and five-crop mixtures provided by ICRISAT were used. However, the row ratios are known to be sensitive to relative prices, and the price of pulses went up relative to that of other crops over the period of the ICRISAT study (Walker and Ryan, 1990, p. 26). For 1984, the actual row ratios were available and were used.

Table 4.5. *Kharif cropping patterns (1975–1984)*

Crop	Fraction of total area (%)										
	1975	1976	1977	1978	1979	1980	1981	1982	1983	1984	1984[a]
Cotton	42.01	36.97	42.52	48.73	38.44	43.6	39.39	39.29	40.42	48.31	49.30
Hybrid cotton	2.17	2.07	2.34	1.71	1.92	2.81	1.80	2.89	1.43	0.50	0.50
Local sorghum	17.89	19.53	16.91	13.11	22.33	12.86	17.60	11.62	11.39	4.51	3.45
Hybrid sorghum	7.07	9.49	11.10	7.01	7.16	10.42	11.33	12.65	16.69	16.62	15.51
Other cereals	2.88	2.52	3.01	2.27	3.03	2.08	1.50	1.67	0.99	1.03	1.17
Pigeon-pea (tur)	13.31	10.62	10.39	13.40	15.33	14.32	11.88	11.01	9.60	13.79	13.79
Mung	1.45	3.08	3.88	4.70	4.18	5.64	9.09	11.48	11.01	9.60	2.08
Urad	3.64	3.17	5.08	3.75	3.05	1.67	1.38	4.20	3.24	1.07	2.08
Other pulses	0	0.17	0.25	0.19	0.15	0.13	0.09	0.26	0.43	0.11	0.13
Groundnut	8.95	11.34	3.65	4.67	3.11	5.12	3.63	3.00	3.11	4.69	4.67
Other oilseeds	0.14	0.56	0.19	0.17	0.74	0.08	0.07	0.10	0.15	1.11	0.70
Other crops	0.48	0.47	0.76	0.29	0.55	1.27	1.79	2.36	1.29	1.10	1.11
Total area (ha)	169.4	177.5	176.1	153.8	165.6	159.2	150.6	167.1	156.6	162.1	

[a]In this column areas were allocated to crops according to observed row ratios whereas in the other columns the standard row ratio were supplied by ICRISAT.
Source: Computed from ICRISAT VLS data.

Table 4.6. *Growth rates of yields in Akola district (1956–1984)*

Crop	Growth rate	t-statistic (%)	R^2
Wheat	3.34	5.15	0.505
Sorghum	1.94	2.64	0.205
Chick-pea	0.11	0.16	0.0001
Pigeon-pea	−0.68	−0.81	0.024
Groundnut	−0.75	−0.48	0.009
Cotton[a]	−0.12	−0.26	0.002

[a] Cotton yields cover the period 1942–1984.

Yield increases in agriculture

Unlike the wheat-growing regions of north India, where the adoption of high-yielding varieties brought large increases in yield and output and massive changes in the production process and cropping patterns, the adoption of sorghum hybrids in this region of SAT India has not led to sharp changes in cropping patterns and land distribution or to widespread mechanization. Moreover, hybrid varieties of pulses and oilseeds have made little headway, and hybrid cotton, which requires high levels of fertilizer application and careful attention, is grown only by the biggest farmers on a few irrigated plots. That little change in cropping patterns has taken place is confirmed by the data for 1893–1897 and 1926–1930 (SR, 1931). On the average, for Murtizapur taluka as a whole, cotton accounted for 48 and 54 percent of kharif acreage during these periods, sorghum for 45 and 34 percent, and pigeon-pea for 5 percent in both periods. In the 1980s, the major change was that less land was devoted to sorghum and more to pigeon-pea and other pulses.

The contrast between sorghum and wheat, improved varieties of which have spread rapidly through the district, and other crops is striking. Table 4.6 presents estimates of growth rates over the period 1956 to 1984 for the yields of major crops in Akola district.[9] While the growth rate for yield is 3.3 percent for wheat and 1.9 percent for sorghum, the growth rates for pigeon-pea, cotton, groundnut, and chick-pea are not significantly different from zero. These growth rates are similar to growth rates for nationwide crop

9. The estimates were obtained by fitting a linear time trend to the logarithm of yield. For most crops, reliable yield data from sample surveys became available only in the 1950s. However, for cotton, yield estimates from 1942 to 1946 are available because a pilot study (Madhya Pradesh, 1954) was conducted in Akola. All other yield data are from *Agricultural Situation in India (ASI)*, various issues.

Table 4.7. *Labor requirements for common crops*

	Time (hours/acre)			Yield (kg/acre)
	Male	Female	Bullock	
Cotton-pigeon-pea				
1951	77.58	126.2	41.68	108.16
	(5.68)	(10.44)	(2.45)	
1983	75.40	121.43	43.90	137.11
	(17.7)	(10.54)	(3.90)	(19.2)
1984	56.06	131.6	36.26	142.5
	(4.51)	(8.01)	(2.73)	(12.2)
Sorghum				
1951	90	53.8	41.9	406.8
	(6.52)	(7.17)	(2.90)	
1975	138.1	64	50.6	256
	(12.04)	(13.6)	(5.2)	(45.7)

Note: Figures in parentheses represent standard errors.
Source: ICAR (1954) for 1951, for the other years computed from ICRI-SAT VLS data.

yields, except for cotton, for which the all-India yield growth rate is positive.

Cultivation practices have changed little or not at all since the 1860s. Then, as now, draft animals supplied most of the power, and the implements *wakhar*, *tifan* (a seed drill), and *daura* (a kind of harrow) are still used today. The major changes are the gradual displacement of the wooden plow by the iron plow in the 1930s (SR, 1931, para. 9), the introduction of pumps for lifting water, driven by oil engines and, later, electric motors in the 1950s and 1960s (Dhawan, 1986), and the advent of threshing machines in 1976. Though they were first introduced to this taluka by big landowners before 1931, as the settlement report (SR, 1931) notes, tractors are still uncommon. In 1971, thirteen out of thirty talukas (including Murtizapur) in the four-district region around Akola had between one and three tractors per 100 square kilometers (Jodha, Asokan, and Ryan, 1977, app. 1). The apparent lack of change in agricultural techniques is borne out by an examination of changes in labor requirements per acre since 1951. Table 4.7 shows bullock and human labor use per acre for the common cotton-pigeon-pea intercrop in 1951–1952, 1983, and 1984 and for local sorghum in 1951–1952 and 1975.[10] The 1951–1952 figures are two-year averages for Murtizapur taluka and are from a cost

10. The 1975 data are used for sorghum because in later years most sorghum was threshed by machine.

of cultivation survey (ICAR, 1954). As can be seen, for the major cotton-pigeon-pea intercrop, there has been little change in labor requirements.

Other sources of increases in yield are the increasing use of fertilizers and pesticides and an increase in irrigation from wells. As Walker and Ryan observe (1990, p. 32), "Irrigation and fertilizer [use] go hand in hand." In 1984, irrigated land in Kanzara received 2.6 times as much fertilizer and 9.8 times as much pesticide as did dry land. Fertilizer use on the rain-fed kharif crop was 23.6 kilograms per hectare in 1975 and remained at about that level until 1979, after which it increased steadily to reach 93 kilograms per hectare in 1984. Fertilizer use on dry land is higher than in other parts of SAT India because the Akola region has higher and more assured rainfall. However, few farmers apply fertilizer to each plot every year, and those who use fertilizer less frequently are also those who apply it less intensively (Walker and Ryan, 1990, p. 34). But at least in 1984, average fertilizer use (Table 4.8) was the same for small and medium farmers (groups III and IV) as for big farmers (group V).

Overall, irrigated land increased from 4.45 to 9.81 percent of the total. Most of this increase was confined to the large farmers (group V). According to the 1985 census, small farmers had 4.10 percent, medium farmers 16.3 percent, and large farmers 78.4 percent of the irrigated land. But the increase in irrigation did not lead to a commensurate increase in rabi, or, except in 1983, summer crop areas. Instead, the increased irrigation was used largely to supplement the rain-fed kharif crop. It did not bring about any significant change in cropping patterns except for hybrid cotton. The other kharif crops grown on irrigated land are the same as those on unirrigated land.

The data

The data used to estimate the SAM were collected by ICRISAT as part of its village studies program.[11] Two ICRISAT publications, *Manual of Instructions for Economic Investigators* (November 1978) and *ICRISAT Village Level Studies Data Management System* (October 1985) explain how the sample households were selected and how the data were collected and coded. Included in these publications are lists of codes and sample questionnaires and coding sheets used in the study. ICRISAT's investigators lived in the study villages and collected data in eight to twelve rounds over each survey year. Generally speaking, the rounds were equally spaced, except during the slack season, when they were further apart. Annual data were collected on particulars of members of sample households, farm assets, commodity stocks, and financial assets. Other data on labor, machinery and draft animal utilization,

11. Walker and Ryan (1990) provide a detailed account of the major findings of this program.

Table 4.8. *Characteristics of agriculture (1984)*

	Dry				Wet	
	Small and medium		Large			
	Rs	(%)	Rs	(%)	Rs	(%)
Value and composition of agricultural output						
Coarse cereals	38,339	11.5	155,265	17	48,785	9.5
Rice and wheat	0	0	119	0	68,904	13.5
Pulses	93,549	28.0	170,285	18.6	66,470	13.0
Vegetables and oilseeds	15,079	4.5	106,205	11.6	104,809	20.5
Cotton	167,388	50.1	414,990	45.4	195,876	38.3
Fodder	19,815	5.9	67,108	7.3	26,654	5.2
		hours/100		hours/100		hours/100
Labor use	hours/acre	Rs output	hours/acre	Rs output	hours/acre	Rs output
Male	98.0	10.12	99.0	11.54	200.5	12.98
Female	179.6	19.22	119.1	13.67	201.2	12.97
		per 100		per 100		per 100
Input use (in Rs)	per acre	Rs output	per acre	Rs output	per acre	Rs output
Pesticide	2.04		5.2	0.78	55.6	3.03
Fertilizer	73.6	8.2	60.6	9.04	209	11.4
Bullock power		8.18		10.73		6.75
Seeds (village)		2.95		2.51		2.98
Seeds (imported)		1.2		2.01		5.13
Electricity and fuel	0	0	0	0		1.76
Farmyard manure		1.71		1.75		0.90
Agricultural services		0.77		0.76		1.04
Miscellaneous inputs		0.85		0.49		0.66

Source: Computed from ICRISAT data.

all economic transactions, and farm operations were collected at each round. For major transactions and those involving crops of interest to ICRISAT, the identity of the partner (such as regulated market or trader) and the distance were also (but not always) recorded.

The other data used for constructing the SAM were information on input use, factor payments, and revenues for all nonagricultural activities; sources of income and composition of expenditure for the village government and temple; all salaries received; all transactions with a cooperative credit society;

the ration shop's requisition of cereals and oil; and estimates by the shopkeepers of their volume of sales, cost price, and sale price by commodity. The data for this SAM were collected in May–June 1986, a year after the end of the 1984 crop year. Data were based on recall, except for data on the credit society and the ration shop.

Estimating the SAM

Estimates of most quantities in the SAM were found by taking the group means for groups I and II combined and for groups III, IV, and V from the data and then dividing by the sample fraction for these groups. The combined estimates for groups I and II were separated when necessary, using the supplementary data described earlier on group I's income, expenditure, and consumption. The only exceptions to this procedure were for the village government and temple, nonagricultural activities, salaries, and transactions with the credit society. For these the supplementary data and the data on the nonagricultural activities of the artisans in the ICRISAT sample provided direct estimates of the quantities in question.[12]

Although many items in the SAM are found directly from the data, others can only be found as residuals, as will be seen making use of the fact that in a SAM a row account and the corresponding column account have the same sum.

The village SAM

In this section the structure of the village economy is examined using the SAM. The focus is on the structure of production activities, savings, consumption and investment, the generation and distribution of income and external trade, and on linkages in the village economy. A schematic SAM is presented in Table 4.9, and an aggregated version of the estimated SAM is shown in Table 4.10. The aggregated SAM has accounts for nine activities, six commodities, nine factors, five household classes, the village temple, the village government, capital, maintenance, stock changes, and the rest of India. This SAM has fewer activities than the typical national SAM because of the predominance of agriculture and the absence of any manufacturing except handicraft production. However, greater attention is paid to labor flows, transfers, and income generation and distribution.

The first row (activities) of the schematic SAM has only one nonzero entry, for the supply of commodities by village activities. The first entry in the commodity (second) row is for purchases of intermediate inputs by activities.

---

12. A detailed account of issues relating to the data, such as correcting the valuation of output and labor use, and of the estimation of each block in the SAM is provided in Subramanian, 1988, appendix.

Table 4.9. *Schematic of the social accounting matrix*

	Activities	Commodities	Factors	Institutions	Capital	Maintenance	Stocks	Rest of India
Activities		Commodity supplies						
Commodities	Intermediate demands	Composite commodities		Consumption expenditures	Investment demand	Maintenance expenditures	Stock changes	Exports
Factors	Wages, interest, salaries, rents			Interest paid on consumption	Payments to labor for investment	Payments to labor for maintenance		Factors earnings from outside
Institutions	Profits to households, taxes to government		Factor payments to households	Transfers between households				Transfers from outside
Capital stocks				Savings changes in private stocks				
Maintenance	Maintenance expenses			Maintenance of consumer durables				
Rest of India	Taxes to rest of India	Imports	Factor payments outside	Transfers to rest of India	Capital outflows			

Table 4.10a. *Social accounting matrix for Kanzara: Activity accounts (rupees)*

	Dry agriculture		Wet agriculture	Livestock	Agricultural services	Village production
	Small	Large				
Dry agriculture (small)	—	—	—	—	—	—
Dry agriculture (large)	—	—	—	—	—	—
Wet agriculture	—	—	—	—	—	—
Livestock	—	—	—	—	—	—
Agricultural services	—	—	—	—	—	—
Village production	—	—	—	—	—	—
Retail trade	—	—	—	—	—	—
Government services	—	—	—	—	—	—
All activities	—	—	—	—	—	—
Social expenditures	—	—	—	—	—	—
Cereals	15	344	4,684	—	—	—
Pulses	3,566	5,913	1,250	7,926	—	—
Milk	—	—	—	—	—	—
Other foods	2,889	9,541	8,240	—	—	—
Sugar	—	—	—	—	—	195
Nonfoods	3,377	7,772	10,068	—	1,665	2,731
Consumer durables	—	—	—	—	—	—
Agricultural inputs	70,767	233,637	147,815	177,034	157	6,040
Livestock	—	—	—	—	—	—
Producer durables	—	—	—	—	—	—
All commodities	80,614	257,197	172,056	184,959	1,822	8,966
Family male	20,745	42,330	23,609	—	—	—
Family female	21,820	12,798	2,047	—	—	—
Hired male	9,627	30,390	19,849	—	2,070	1,094
Hired female	13,817	56,480	34,540	—	—	—
Farm servants	—	18,011	14,397	26,316	—	—
Salaried workers	—	—	—	—	—	—
Rent	21,212	61,805	1,857	—	—	—
Private credit	7,450	520	—	—	—	—
Public credit	11,417	21,186	16,315	15,188	600	200
All factors	106,088	243,519	112,613	41,503	2,670	1,294
Landless salaried	—	—	—	—	—	—
Landless unsalaried	8,615	—	111	4,159	—	15,830
Small farmers	31,421	—	10,602	7,463	19,970	1,300
Medium farmers	103,323	—	572	10,375	—	8,376
Large farmers	—	403,879	212,506	156,572	15,349	24,074
All households	144,359	403,879	222,426	178,570	35,319	49,580
Temple	—	—	—	—	—	—
Village government	28	563	412	—	—	—
Capital	—	—	—	—	—	—
Maintenance	1,647	4,121	2,458	—	980	1,000
Stock changes	—	—	—	—	—	—
Rest of India	1,434	4,693	1,531	—	—	1,000
Total	334,169	913,971	511,497	405,032	40,791	61,840

Retail trade	Government services	All Activities	Commodities	Factors	Households	Others	Total
—	—	—	334,169	—	—	—	334,169
—	—	—	913,972	—	—	—	913,972
—	—	—	511,497	—	—	—	511,497
—	—	—	405,032	—	—	—	405,032
—	—	—	40,791	—	—	—	40,791
—	—	—	61,840	—	—	—	61,840
—	—	—	476,066	—	—	—	476,066
—	—	—	47,400	—	—	—	47,400
—	—	—	2,790,768	—	—	—	2,790,768
—	—	—	—	—	105,212	—	105,212
43,870	—	48,913	31,725	—	431,911	66,695	579,244
20,815	—	39,469	8,128	—	248,535	228,867	525,000
—	—	—	—	—	93,477	117,346	210,823
112,477	—	133,146	8,148	—	208,146	240,597	590,025
42,217	—	42,412	2,362	—	79,119	30,050	153,943
185,222	15,000	225,824	54,849	—	390,829	881,872	1,553,374
17,120	—	17,120	—	—	54,256	16,131	87,508
—	—	635,451	—	—	9,242	21,323	666,016
—	—	—	—	—	—	102,036	102,036
—	—	—	—	—	—	145,790	145,790
421,721	15,000	1,142,335	105,121	—	1,620,726	1,850,697	4,718,970
—	—	86,685	—	—	—	—	86,685
—	—	36,664	—	—	—	—	36,664
2,080	—	63,110	—	—	—	196,005	261,115
—	—	104,837	—	—	—	27,864	132,701
—	—	58,724	—	—	—	62,537	121,260
—	32,400	32,400	—	—	—	226,159	258,559
—	—	84,874	—	—	—	—	84,874
—	—	7,970	—	—	11,299	—	19,269
400	—	65,305	—	—	—	—	65,305
2,480	32,400	542,568	—	—	11,299	512,565	1,066,432
—	—	—	—	78,743	872	1,327	80,943
3,860	—	32,353	—	213,226	29,231	13,459	288,268
—	—	71,757	—	137,820	6,733	2,651	218,963
21,158	—	142,661	—	275,840	13,023	—	431,524
26,847	—	839,227	—	260,091	36,418	62,939	1,198,676
51,865	—	1,085,999	—	965,721	86,277	80,375	2,218,373
—	—	—	—	6,475	—	—	6,475
—	—	1,003	—	126	1,733	5,372	8,234
—	—	—	—	—	350,088	6,552	356,640
—	—	10,206	—	—	7,842	—	18,048
—	—	—	90,718	—	44,331	—	135,049
—	—	8,658	173,273	94,110	96,076	135,860	2,066,976
476,066	47,400	2,790,768	4,718,970	1,066,432	2,218,373	2,591,421	0

Table 4.10b. *Social accounting matrix for Kanzara: Institutions accounts (Rupees)*

	All			Landless households		Farming households		
	Activities	Commodities	Factors	Salaried	Unsalaried	Small	Medium	Large
Dry agriculture (small)	—	334,168	—	—	—	—	—	—
Dry agriculture (large)	—	913,972	—	—	—	—	—	—
Wet agricultural	—	511,497	—	—	—	—	—	—
Livestock	—	405,032	—	—	—	—	—	—
Agricultural services	—	40,791	—	—	—	—	—	—
Village production	—	61,840	—	—	—	—	—	—
Retail trade	—	476,066	—	—	—	—	—	—
Government services	—	47,400	—	—	—	—	—	—
All activities	—	2,790,768	—	—	—	—	—	—
Social expenditures	—	—	—	5,504	29,162	6,866	30,843	32,837
Cereals	48,913	31,725	—	12,546	90,815	62,916	123,323	142,311
Pulses	39,469	8,128	—	9,645	38,888	31,808	52,874	115,320
Milk	—	—	—	3,605	7,945	8,553	20,752	52,621
Other foods	133,146	8,148	—	5,722	30,325	22,369	66,212	83,517
Sugar	42,412	2,362	—	2,104	13,458	8,930	23,920	30,707
Nonfoods	225,824	54,849	—	11,831	61,876	38,318	106,117	172,688
Consumer durables	17,120	—	—	2,188	11,604	11,800	10,833	17,832
Agricultural inputs	635,451	—	—	472	212	122	1,542	6,893
Livestock	—	—	—	—	—	—	—	—
Producer durables	—	—	—	—	—	—	—	—
All commodities	1,142,335	105,212	—	53,617	284,285	191,683	436,414	654,727
Family male	86,685	—	—	—	—	—	—	—
Family female	36,664	12,798	—	—	—	—	—	—
Hired male	65,110	—	—	—	—	—	—	—
Hired female	104,837	—	—	—	—	—	—	—
Farm servants	58,724	—	—	—	—	—	—	—
Salaried workers	32,400	—	—	—	—	—	—	—
Rent	84,874	—	—	—	—	—	—	—
Private credit	7,970	—	—	526	2,789	2,031	530	5,423
Public credit	65,305	—	—	—	—	—	—	—
All factors	542,568	—	—	526	2,789	2,031	530	5,423
Landless salaried	—	—	78,743	41	162	176	115	379
Landless unsalaried	32,353	—	213,226	305	9,895	6,507	5,794	6,730
Small farmers	71,757	—	137,820	140	1,477	1,544	1,745	1,828
Medium farmers	142,661	—	275,840	116	4,003	3,403	1,905	3,597
Large farmers	839,227	—	260,091	135	1,516	1,282	1,516	31,969
All households	1,085,999	—	965,721	737	17,052	12,912	11,074	44,503
Temple	—	—	6,475	—	—	—	—	—
Village government	1,003	—	126	49	257	652	175	601
Capital	—	—	—	34,333	22,335	−6,633	4,327	295,726
Maintenance	10,206	—	—	12	65	581	2,531	4,653
Stock changes	—	90,718	—	−8,762	−40,795	9,818	−38,137	122,208
Rest of India	8,658	1,732,273	94,110	431	2,281	7,919	14,610	70,835
Total	2,790,768	4,718,970	1,066,432	80,943	288,268	218,963	431,524	1,198,676

All households	Temple	Village government	Capital	Maintenance	Stock changes	Rest of India	Total
—	—	—	—	—	—	—	334,169
—	—	—	—	—	—	—	913,972
—	—	—	—	—	—	—	511,497
—	—	—	—	—	—	—	405,032
—	—	—	—	—	—	—	40,791
—	—	—	—	—	—	—	61,840
—	—	—	—	—	—	—	476,066
—	—	—	—	—	—	—	47,400
—	—	—	—	—	—	—	2,790,768
105,212	—	—	—	—	—	—	105,212
431,911	—	—	—	—	8,549	58,146	579,244
248,535	—	—	—	—	75,642	153,225	525,000
93,477	—	—	—	—	—	117,346	210,823
208,145	—	—	—	—	34,121	206,374	590,025
79,119	—	—	—	—	—	30,050	153,943
390,829	4,955	445	—	640	4,434	871,398	1,553,374
54,256	—	—	—	—	—	16,131	87,508
9,242	—	—	—	4,975	12,211	4,137	666,016
—	—	—	102,036	—	—	—	102,036
—	—	—	100,965	10,282	—	34,543	145,790
1,620,726	4,955	445	203,001	15,897	135,049	1,491,350	4,718,970
—	—	—	—	—	—	—	86,685
—	—	—	—	—	—	—	36,664
—	720	2,037	17,779	2,150	—	173,319	261,115
—	—	—	—	—	—	27,864	132,701
—	—	—	—	—	—	62,537	121,260
—	—	—	—	—	—	226,159	258,559
—	—	—	—	—	—	—	84,874
11,299	—	—	—	—	—	—	19,269
—	—	—	—	—	—	—	65,305
11,299	720	2,037	17,779	2,150	—	489,878	1,066,432
872	—	—	—	—	—	—	80,943
29,231	—	—	—	—	—	13,459	288,268
6,733	—	—	—	—	—	2,651	218,963
13,023	—	—	—	—	—	—	431,524
36,418	—	—	—	—	—	62,939	1,198,676
86,277	—	—	—	—	—	80,375	2,218,373
—	—	—	—	—	—	—	6,475
1,733	—	—	—	—	—	5,372	8,234
350,088	800	5,752	—	—	—	—	356,640
7,842	—	—	—	—	—	—	18,048
44,331	—	—	—	—	—	—	135,049
96,076	—	—	135,860	—	—	—	2,066,976
2,218,373	6,475	8,234	356,640	18,048	135,049	2,066,976	

Table 4.10c. *Social accounting matrix for Kanzara: Commodity accounts (rupees)*

	All activities	Social expenditures	Cereals	Pulses	Milk	Other food	Sugar	Nonfood
Dry agriculture (small)	—	—	38,339	93,549	—	15,079	—	167,388
Dry agriculture (large)	—	—	155,384	170,285	—	106,205	—	414,990
Wet agriculture	—	—	117,689	66,470	—	104,809	—	195,876
Livestock	—	—	—	—	210,823	—	—	—
Agricultural services	—	—	—	—	—	—	—	—
Village production	—	—	—	—	—	—	—	59,550
Retail trade	—	—	60,532	23,312	—	155,246	93,437	122,094
Government services	—	—	—	—	—	—	—	47,400
All activities	—	—	371,944	35,365	210,823	381,340	93,437	1,007,298
Social expenditures	—	—	—	—	—	—	—	—
Cereals	48,913	31,725	—	—	—	—	—	—
Pulses	39,469	8,128	—	—	—	—	—	—
Milk	—	—	—	—	—	—	—	—
Other food	133,146	8,148	—	—	—	—	—	—
Sugar	42,412	2,362	—	—	—	—	—	—
Nonfood	225,824	54,849	—	—	—	—	—	—
Consumer durables	17,120	—	—	—	—	—	—	—
Agricultural inputs	635,451	—	—	—	—	—	—	—
Livestock	—	—	—	—	—	—	—	—
Producer durables	—	—	—	—	—	—	—	—
All commodities	1,114,335	105,212	—	—	—	—	—	—
Family male	86,685	—	—	—	—	—	—	—
Family female	36,664	—	—	—	—	—	—	—
Hired male	65,110	—	—	—	—	—	—	—
Hired female	104,837	—	—	—	—	—	—	—
Farm servants	58,724	—	—	—	—	—	—	—
Salaried workers	32,400	—	—	—	—	—	—	—
Rent	84,874	—	—	—	—	—	—	—
Private credit	7,970	—	—	—	—	—	—	—
Public credit	65,305	—	—	—	—	—	—	—
All factors	342,568	—	—	—	—	—	—	—
Landless salaried	—	—	—	—	—	—	—	—
Landless unsalaried	32,353	—	—	—	—	—	—	—
Small farmers	71,757	—	—	—	—	—	—	—
Medium farmers	142,661	—	—	—	—	—	—	—
Large farmers	839,227	—	—	—	—	—	—	—
All households	1,085,999	—	—	—	—	—	—	—
Temple	—	—	—	—	—	—	—	—
Village government	1,003	—	—	—	—	—	—	—
Capital	—	—	—	—	—	—	—	—
Maintenance	10,206	—	—	—	—	—	—	—
Stock changes	—	—	2,375	—	—	—	—	—
Rest of India	8,658	—	204,925	171,384	—	208,686	60,506	546,076
Total	2,790,768	105,212	579,244	525,000	210,823	590,025	153,943	1,553,374

Consumer durables	Agricultural inputs	Livestock	Producer durables	All Commodities	Factors	Households	Others	Total
—	19,814	—	—	334,169	—	—	—	334,169
—	67,108	—	—	913,972	—	—	—	913,971
—	26,654	—	—	511,497	—	—	—	511,497
—	194,210	—	—	405,032	—	—	—	405,032
—	40,791	—	—	40,791	—	—	—	40,791
—	2,290	—	—	61,840	—	—	—	61,840
20,240	—	—	1,204	476,066	—	—	—	476,066
—	—	—	—	47,400	—	—	—	47,400
20,240	350,867	—	1,204	2,790,768	—	—	—	2,790,768
—	—	—	—	—	—	105,212	—	105,212
—	—	—	—	31,725	—	431,911	66,695	579,244
—	—	—	—	8,128	—	248,535	228,867	525,000
—	—	—	—	—	—	93,477	117,346	210,823
—	—	—	—	8,148	—	208,145	240,586	590,025
—	—	—	—	2,362	—	79,119	30,050	153,943
—	—	—	—	54,849	—	390,829	881,872	1,553,374
—	—	—	—	—	—	54,256	16,131	87,508
—	—	—	—	—	—	9,242	21,323	666,016
—	—	—	—	—	—	—	102,036	102,036
—	—	—	—	—	—	—	145,790	145,790
—	—	—	—	105,212	—	1,620,726	1,850,697	4,718,970
—	—	—	—	—	—	—	—	86,685
—	—	—	—	—	—	—	—	36,664
—	—	—	—	—	—	—	196,005	261,115
—	—	—	—	—	—	—	27,864	132,701
—	—	—	—	—	—	—	62,537	121,260
—	—	—	—	—	—	—	226,159	258,559
—	—	—	—	—	—	—	—	84,874
—	—	—	—	—	—	11,299	—	19,269
—	—	—	—	—	—	—	—	65,305
—	—	—	—	—	—	11,299	512,565	1,066,432
—	—	—	—	—	78,743	872	1,327	80,943
—	—	—	—	—	213,226	29,231	13,459	288,268
—	—	—	—	—	137,820	6,733	2,651	218,963
—	—	—	—	—	275,840	13,023	—	431,524
—	—	—	—	—	260,091	36,418	62,939	1,198,676
—	—	—	—	—	965,721	86,277	80,375	2,218,373
—	—	—	—	—	6,475	—	—	6,475
—	—	—	—	—	126	1,733	5,372	8,234
—	—	—	—	—	—	350,088	6,552	356,640
—	—	—	—	—	—	7,842	—	18,048
—	53,800	—	34,543	90,718	—	44,331	—	135,049
67,268	261,349	102,036	110,043	1,732,273	94,110	96,076	135,860	2,066,976
87,508	666,016	102,036	145,790	4,718,970	1,066,432	2,218,373	2,591,421	0

Table 4.10d. *Social accounting matrix for Kanzara: Factor accounts*

	All		Family		Hired		Farm servants
	Activities	Commodities	Male	Female	Male	Female	
Dry agriculture (small)	—	334,169	—	—	—	—	—
Dry agriculture (large)	—	913,972	—	—	—	—	—
Wet agriculture	—	511,497	—	—	—	—	—
Livestock	—	405,032	—	—	—	—	—
Agricultural services	—	40,791	—	—	—	—	—
Village production	—	61,840	—	—	—	—	—
Retail trade	—	476,066	—	—	—	—	—
Government services	—	47,400	—	—	—	—	—
All activities	—	2,790,768	—	—	—	—	—
Social expenditures	—	—	—	—	—	—	—
Cereals	48,913	31,725	—	—	—	—	—
Pulses	39,469	8,128	—	—	—	—	—
Milk	—	—	—	—	—	—	—
Other food	133,146	8,148	—	—	—	—	—
Sugar	42,412	2,362	—	—	—	—	—
Nonfood	225,824	54,849	—	—	—	—	—
Consumer durables	17,120	—	—	—	—	—	—
Agricultural inputs	635,451	—	—	—	—	—	—
Livestock	—	—	—	—	—	—	—
Producer durables	—	—	—	—	—	—	—
All commodities	1,142,335	105,212	—	—	—	—	—
Family male	86,685	—	—	—	—	—	—
Family female	36,664	—	—	—	—	—	—
Hired male	65,110	—	—	—	—	—	—
Hired female	104,837	—	—	—	—	—	—
Farm servants	58,724	—	—	—	—	—	—
Salaried workers	32,400	—	—	—	—	—	—
Rent	84,874	—	—	—	—	—	—
Private credit	7,970	—	—	—	—	—	—
Public credit	65,305	—	—	—	—	—	—
All factors	542,568	—	—	—	—	—	—
Landless salaried	—	—	—	—	3,064	1,681	—
Landless unsalaried	32,353	—	1,588	1,019	104,036	60,957	32,810
Small farmers	71,757	—	5,006	5,816	54,950	39,455	22,500
Medium farmers	142,661	—	15,273	15,083	79,989	26,380	48,530
Large farmers	839,227	—	64,818	14,747	19,076	4,228	17,420
All households	1,085,999	—	86,685	36,664	261,115	132,701	121,260
Temple	—	—	—	—	—	—	—
Village government	1,003	—	—	—	—	—	—
Capital	—	—	—	—	—	—	—
Maintenance	10,206	—	—	—	—	—	—
Stock changes	—	90,718	—	—	—	—	—
Rest of India	8,658	1,732,273	—	—	—	—	—
Total	2,790,768	4,718,970	86,685	36,664	261,115	132,701	121,260

Salaried workers	Rent	Private credit	Public credit	All		Others	Total
				Factors	Households		
—	—	—	—	—	—	—	334,169
—	—	—	—	—	—	—	913,971
—	—	—	—	—	—	—	511,497
—	—	—	—	—	—	—	405,032
—	—	—	—	—	—	—	40,791
—	—	—	—	—	—	—	61,840
—	—	—	—	—	—	—	476,066
—	—	—	—	—	—	—	47,400
—	—	—	—	—	—	—	2,790,768
—	—	—	—	—	105,212	—	105,212
—	—	—	—	—	431,911	66,695	579,244
—	—	—	—	—	248,535	228,867	525,000
—	—	—	—	—	93,477	117,346	210,823
—	—	—	—	—	208,145	240,586	590,025
—	—	—	—	—	79,119	30,050	153,943
—	—	—	—	—	390,829	881,872	1,553,374
—	—	—	—	—	54,256	16,131	87,508
—	—	—	—	—	9,242	21,323	666,016
—	—	—	—	—	—	102,036	102,036
—	—	—	—	—	—	145,790	145,790
—	—	—	—	—	1,620,726	1,850,697	4,718,970
—	—	—	—	—	—	—	86,685
—	—	—	—	—	—	—	36,664
—	—	—	—	—	—	196,005	261,115
—	—	—	—	—	—	27,864	132,701
—	—	—	—	—	—	62,537	121,260
—	—	—	—	—	—	226,159	258,559
—	—	—	—	—	—	—	84,874
—	—	—	—	—	11,299	—	19,269
—	—	—	—	—	—	—	65,305
—	—	—	—	—	11,299	512,565	1,066,432
71,269	2,230	500	—	78,743	872	1,327	80,943
—	10,316	2,500	—	213,226	29,231	13,459	288,268
—	8,594	1,500	—	137,820	6,733	2,651	218,963
76,005	13,080	1,500	—	275,840	13,023	—	431,524
111,285	24,517	4,000	—	260,091	36,418	62,939	1,198,676
258,559	58,737	10,000	—	965,721	86,277	80,375	2,218,373
—	6,475	—	—	6,475	—	—	6,475
—	—	—	126	126	1,733	5,372	8,234
—	—	—	—	—	350,088	6,552	356,640
—	—	—	—	—	7,842	—	18,048
—	—	—	—	—	44,331	—	135,049
—	19,661	9,269	65,179	94,110	96,076	135,860	2,066,976
258,559	84,874	19,269	65,305	1,066,432	2,218,373	2,591,421	

The second entry in this row gives the commodity composition of composite commodities.[13] The fourth entry shows the institutions' consumption expenditures; the fifth, investment demand; the sixth, purchases of commodities for maintenance activities; the seventh, changes in stocks; and the eighth, exports to the rest of India. The third row is for payments to factors. The only accounts making these payments are the production activities (which pay wages, rent, and salaries), the capital and maintenance accounts (which employ labor for creating capital assets and for maintenance and repair), and the rest of the world (which pays labor employed outside the village). In the first entry in the institutions row, households receive residual profits and the village government taxes from the activities.[14] Factor payments from the factor accounts to households and payment of rent to the temple appear as the third entry in this row. The fourth entry is interhousehold group transfers (there are no transfers involving the other village institutions), and the last, transfers from the rest of India to the village (including transfers from the state government to households and the village government).

The fifth row is for the capital account and contains entries for savings by households, the village government, and the temple. Since there is a separate row for stocks (the sixth), household savings do not include changes in stocks. The stocks row contains two entries, one for supply of commodities from stocks (i.e., the drawing down of stocks), and the other for changes in stocks held by households. The seventh row is for maintenance expenditures and has entries for spending by activities on maintenance of production assets and spending by households on maintenance of consumer durables. The last row is for the rest of India. Activities pay taxes such as land revenue and market access to the rest of India. The commodity account buys imports. The third entry contains factor payments to the outside world, primarily interest payments to banks and private moneylenders and rent on land rented from outsiders. The fourth entry contains transfers by households to outsiders. The fifth entry is for net capital outflow, that is, investment by villagers in real estate in Murtizapur, in bank deposits and insurance policies, less capital inflows, including bank credit.

There are some other divergences from the standard SAM structure. First, construction and financial services are not treated as activities. Construction work is carried out by the investing households by hiring labor and purchas-

---

13. The ICRISAT consumption data distinguish between ordinary consumption expenses and spending for social and ceremonial occasions, such as weddings, funerals, and religious feasts. These social expenses are treated as a separate, composite commodity.
14. The usual practice is to combine all profits in a single factor account and then distribute total profit to the institutions. The disadvantage of such an approach is that all groups will share in any change in profit in an activity, regardless of whether that group actually receives any profit from that activity. This can be avoided by having activity-specific profit accounts or by allowing profits to flow to households directly, as is done here.

ing materials, and therefore this activity has no profits and can be dropped by allowing the capital account to hire labor and buy materials. Financial services in the village hire no labor and require no material inputs, so interest payments can flow direct to the lending households. Second, three sets of prices are distinguished in the unaggregated SAM. Commodities are supplied by village activities at wholesale price, the average price at which farmers sell their crop within the village and in Murtizapur. The village shops sell items at retail price and purchase at wholesale price. The ration shop sells commodities at a subsidized price. Consequently, each commodity is treated as three separate commodities, one at wholesale price, another at retail price, and a third at subsidized price. The aggregated SAM presented here (Table 4.10) does not make this distinction and combines wholesale, retail, and subsidized commodity flows.

The structure of production

Agriculture. A feature of the aggregated SAM is that agriculture is not disaggregated by crop but into rain-fed and irrigated agriculture. The reasons for this choice are set out here. Their contribution to value-added is 55.2 percent and 20.6 percent, respectively. The other activities and their shares in value-added are livestock, 13.4 percent; agricultural services, 2.36 percent; handicraft production and village services, 3.21 percent; trade, 3.30 percent; and government services, 1.97 percent.

One reason for separating irrigated and unirrigated agriculture is that input intensities, labor use, composition of output, and distribution of land differ markedly across the two. Another is that intercropping predominates and few crops are grown singly. Therefore, joint production is common and input use is hard to allocate separately by crop. Because input intensities and labor use differ across farm size classes, dry agriculture is further divided into small farms (including small and medium farms) and large farms. Small and medium farms are not separated, and wet agriculture is not disaggregated because the number of plots is too small to warrant such a division.

As Table 4.8 shows, the major difference in cropping patterns is that wheat and many vegetables are grown only under irrigation.[15] Within dry agriculture, the small farms grow more pulses, less oilseeds and vegetables, and less coarse cereals than the large farms. Cotton accounts for 44 percent of the value of output. Turning to input use, bullock power, fertilizer, and seed are the most important, accounting for 20.4 and 24.3 percent of the value of output in small-farm and large-farm dry agriculture and 26 percent in wet agriculture. The cash outlay on inputs ranges from 10.6 and 12.3 percent of the value of output in dry agriculture on small farms and large

15. Rice and wheat are aggregated for reasons discussed later, but rice production is negligible.

farms, respectively, to 22 percent in wet agriculture.[16] In dry agriculture, fertilizer use per acre on small farms was somewhat larger than that on large farms. Pesticide and fertilizer use in wet agriculture is several times that used in dry agriculture.

Five types of labor are distinguished: family male, family female, hired male, hired female, and "regular farm servants" (male workers hired for a period of several months, often in exchange for a loan provided by the employer).[17] Female wage labor accounts for 40.6 percent, and women provide 55.4 percent of labor used in agriculture. The average wage for women is about 60 percent of that for men, while regular farm servants receive 74 percent of the male wage. The share of total labor provided by family labor varies across household classes and is substantially lower for large farms and in wet agriculture (which is dominated by large farms). For small and medium farms, around 35 percent of total labor costs are for hired labor, while for large farms and irrigated agriculture, about 70 percent of total labor costs are for hired labor.

Labor absorption per acre also differs substantially. Male labor use per acre in dry agriculture is the same for small and large farms and twice as high in wet agriculture. Female labor use per acre in dry agriculture is 50 percent higher for small farms than for large farms and 66 percent higher in wet agriculture. The significance of this labor difference between small and large farms is hard to assess because of the tremendous variety (43 combinations on 165 plots) of intercropping mixtures used and the small number of plots belonging to small and medium farmers.

Land is rented both by small landowners who lack the wherewithal to farm to large farmers and by large landowners to smaller landowners. Most land is rented on sharecropping contracts, except the land owned by the temple, which is given out on fixed rent. Rents in-kind were valued at wholesale price. Little irrigated land is rented. Rents as a fraction of value of output are similar for small- and large-farm dry agriculture. Interest payments are estimated from the ICRISAT data (which distinguish between consumption and production loans) and information on credit from the cooperative society and a bank in Murtizapur. Most loans are for purchases of inputs; these are divided between wet and dry agriculture in proportion to these activities' use

16. Seeds from outside the village, pesticide, fertilizer, electricity, and miscellaneous inputs are assumed to be paid for in cash.
17. Wage rates for family labor were imputed by ICRISAT's investigators using operation-specific wage rates then current for hired labor. Because family labor and wage labor are not used in the same proportions for all operations, the average imputed wage rates differ from the average hired wage rates. The wage rate for each regular farm servant is imputed after finding out how much labor he or she supplies for agriculture, livestock, and other activities.

of material inputs. Most of the interest payments to private moneylenders are from small and medium farmers.

Other activities. Livestock is the most significant noncrop activity. Milk accounts for 52.1 percent of the livestock sector's output, draft animal power for 39.3 percent, and farmyard manure for 8.6 percent. Some 55 percent of the milk is sold outside the village. Many of the large farmers employ regular farm servants for field labor and to care for their livestock. On the basis of time allocation data, 45 percent of the farm servants' wages were attributed to the livestock sector. No data were available on family labor use. Locally grown fodder (62 percent), imported concentrates (20.6 percent), and grazing and other village services (10.8 percent) are the major inputs to the livestock sector.

The other activities are of minor importance. Agricultural services include the hiring out of agricultural machinery (50.1 percent), grazing services (37.7 percent), and carpenters' services (12.2 percent). Village production encompasses contraband alcohol (24.2 percent), flour milling (24.3 percent), tailors' services (23.3 percent), barbers' services (14.8 percent), and several minor items such as roof tiles and clay pots and baskets. Most inputs for agricultural services and village production are from outside the village, except for agricultural residues and cow dung used by the potter and basket makers. Some 26 percent of the alcohol and 30 percent of tailors', barbers', and millers' services are exported.

The trade sector consists of the shops, a tailor who also sells cloth, and an itinerant seller of pots and pans. The trade sector obtains its supplies from Murtizapur and from the village. Part of the sales are on credit and shopkeepers often charge a higher price on these sales, depending on the status of the buyer. However, the data were not detailed enough or reliable enough to permit disentangling purchases from these two sources or to estimate interest income from sales on credit. As a result, the trade sector simply buys at wholesale price and sells at retail price. The markup rates range from 7.4 percent for cooking oil to 19.2 percent for the commodity group tea, tobacco, soap, and other nonfoods. Data on family labor use were not available. The only hired labor used is for bringing supplies from Murtizapur. The government services sector consists of the primary health center. It imports 15,000 rupees (Rs) of supplies from outside, and its two employees' salaries amount to Rs 32,400. By convention, its output is consumed by the state government – that is, its output is exported.

Factor incomes and household income distribution. Independent estimates of factor payments made by village activities and of factor payments received by households can be obtained from the ICRISAT data.

However, the data do not identify the source of factor payments to households, so factor payments received from the village and factor payments received from outside cannot be separated. Consequently, only net factor payments from the outside world can be identified by taking the difference between payments to a particular factor and payments received from that factor. Salaries and interest payments are an exception. The sources and amounts of all salaries are known. Total salary income is large (Rs 258,559 or 11.6 percent of total household income), and of this amount, Rs 32,400 is earned by the health center's employees in the village. The rest is received by government workers in the village who work elsewhere. In the case of interest payments, all payments to private moneylenders are assumed to be to households in the village, and all payments to the formal sector flow to the outside world.[18] Net factor earnings for labor are positive and large – that is, earnings from employment outside the village are a large part of total earnings for male and female labor and for regular farm servants. For male labor, 66 percent of total earnings is from outside; for regular farm servants, 52 percent; and for female labor, 21 percent. The reason for these large labor outflows is that Kanzara has a higher population density than the neighboring villages. Based on the per acre labor absorption figures for Kanzara in 1984 and the 1981 population and area data for villages within 1.5 kilometers of Kanzara, total employment, including family labor of Kanzara's work force, should be 354,000 hours for men and 737,000 hours for women. Labor use in Kanzara is 206,000 hours for men and 255,000 hours for women. The difference should be employment outside: 148,000 hours for men and 482,000 hours for women. On converting the net wage payments from outside to hours of labor at the appropriate average wage, outside employment for men (including farm servants) is 239,000 hours, but only 44,000 hours for women. The two estimates of labor outflow are of similar magnitude for men, but the expected outflow for women is almost eleven times that observed, which may be because women do not or cannot work far from the village.

Unlike factor payments, for transfers the location of the other party was usually recorded so that intravillage transfers could be separated from transfers between households and the outside world. However, while total intravillage transfers to or from a household group can be estimated directly, they cannot be disaggregated into a matrix of intergroup transfers without making further assumptions, because one does not know the household group to which the other party in a transfer belongs. However, most intravillage transfers are between caste fellows. For each caste, these are allocated to the different household groups in proportion to the number of households of that

---

18. No estimates of interest payments received by village households on bank deposits were available.

caste in the household groups. By adding up over castes, an estimate of the transfer matrix is obtained.[19]

Rents, profits, and salaries are unequally distributed, as can be seen from the aggregated SAM. The landless and small farmers receive only 3.0 and 4.6 percent of total profits. Their combined share of livestock profits is only 6.5 percent, suggesting that investment in dairy production, which in theory is open to small farmers and the landless, is in reality restricted to the large farmers, whose share in livestock profits is 87 percent. Seventy-four percent of profits in dry agriculture and 95 percent of profits in wet agriculture accrue to large farmers, who also have a large share in other activities. (The flour mills, threshers, and fodder cutter, and three out of five shops are owned by them.) Large farmers also receive 39 percent of salaries, 42 percent of rents, and 75 percent of imputed payments to male family labor. Female labor force participation is lower in group V, so groups IV and V have nearly equal shares in imputed wages to female family labor.

The composition of household income is shown in Table 4.11. Households not operating land are in groups I and II. Salaried employment is the main source of income for households in group I. Group II obtains its livelihood principally from wage labor. Groups III, IV, and V are small, medium, and large farm households. Wage labor is the single most important source of income for all except groups I and V. Moving from the landless to large farmers, the share of wages declines and that of profits increases. Medium farmers obtain about a third of their income from profits and another third from wages, while large farmers derive 70 percent of their income from profits. Average per capita income for the salaried landless is Rs 1,686, which is higher than that for medium farmers (Rs 1,332), but this masks a great deal of variation because among this salaried group are the employees of the health center, whose per capita income is several times the average. Per capita income increases with size of landholding, from Rs 801 for the landless unsalaried to Rs 2,931 for the large farmers.

Savings, consumption, and investment. Consumption could not be directly estimated from the ICRISAT data for two reasons. First, consumption of items other than cereals, pulses, durables, and social expenses was not recorded after 1981. Second, consumption of cereals and pulses can only be found as a residual from the data on harvests, beginning and closing stocks, sales, and the like, and the consumption series so obtained shows extremely large year-to-year variations. Hence, the following procedure was adopted. Total expenditure for 1980 and 1981 was first estimated by using data on consumption of items other than cereals and pulses for those years and Engel curves for cereals and pulses obtained from National Sample Survey

19. For details, see Subramanian, 1988, p. 45.

Table 4.11. *Household characteristics and composition of income*

	Landless households		Farming households		
	I Salaried	II Unsalaried	III Small	IV Medium	V Large
Distribution of land					
Number of households	8	79	53	50	52
Number of members	46	397	244	293	291
Land owned (acres)	6.88	66.6	57.3	139.7	416.5
Land operated (acres)	0	0	53.9	163.1	506.7
Average operational holding					
(acres)	0	0	1.02	3.26	9.74
Share of irrigated land (%)	0	0	3.93	15.65	80.42
Composition of household					
income (%)					
Profits					
Dry agriculture	0	2.99	14.81	23.94	33.69
Wet agriculture	0	−0.04	4.84	−0.13	17.73
Livestock	0	1.44	3.41	2.4	13.06
Agricultural services	0	0	9.12	0	1.28
Village production	0	5.49	0.59	1.94	2.01
Retail trade	0	1.34	0	4.9	2.24
Total	0	11.22	32.77	33.06	70.01
Wages					
Hired male	3.79	36.09	25.1	18.54	1.59
Hired female	2.08	21.15	18.02	6.11	0.35
Farm servant	0	11.38	10.28	11.25	1.45
Total	5.86	68.62	53.39	35.9	3.4
Imputed wages					
Family male	0	0.55	2.29	3.54	5.41
Family female	0	0.35	2.66	3.5	1.23
Salary	88.05	0	0	17.61	9.28
Rent	2.76	3.58	3.92	3.03	2.05
Interest	0.62	0.87	0.69	0.35	0.33
Transfers	2.72	14.82	4.29	3.02	8.29

Source: Computed from the social accounting matrix.

consumption data for rural Maharashtra for 1972 and 1973.[20] From these estimates of total expenditure and estimates of income from the ICRISAT data, savings rates for each group were worked out. These savings rates were then used with the income estimates for 1984 to work out expenditure in 1984. From these expenditure figures and the Engel curves, estimates of

20. NSS data for the early 1980s would have been more suitable but were not readily available.

Table 4.12. *Savings and consumption*

	Landless households		Farming households		
	I Salaried	II Unsalaried	III Small	IV Medium	V Large
Savings rate (%)					
Net	42.4	7.7	−3.0	1.0	24.7
Including stock accumulation	31.6	−6.4	1.5	−7.8	34.9
Consumption shares (%)					
Social expenditures	10.27	10.26	3.58	7.07	5.02
Coarse cereals	1,190	25.46	26.53	21.0	10.93
Rice and wheat	11.50	648	6.30	7.26	10.81
Pulses	17.99	13.68	16.59	12.12	17.61
Milk	6.72	2.79	4.46	4.76	8.04
Other food	10.67	10.67	11.67	15.17	12.76
Sugar	3.92	4.73	4.66	5.48	4.69
Nonfood	22.06	21.77	19.99	24.32	26.38
Consumer durables	4.08	4.08	6.16	2.48	2.72
Agricultural inputs	0.88	0.07	0.06	0.35	1.05
Consumption per capita (Rs)	1,117	790	805	1,347	1,601
Consumption shares by *source (%)*					
Dry agriculture	15.9	21.1	23.0	19.5	17.3
Wet agriculture	9.3	9.1	8.2	8.8	9.1
Livestock	6.8	2.9	4.5	4.8	8.0
Village production	2.5	2.7	2.1	2.9	2.7
Retail trade	21.3	22.5	22.2	21.9	18.9
Stocks	0.2	0.1	0.1	0.1	0.2
Imports	44.0	41.7	40.0	42.0	43.7

Source: Computed from the social accounting matrix.

expenditure on pulses and cereals were obtained. For the other commodities, deflated budget shares from 1980 and 1981 were used. For cereals and pulses estimates of stock changes follow from the estimates of consumption and the harvest and sales data. For the other agricultural products, stock changes were found after making allowances for consumption (e.g., of chilies and oilseeds) and seed use. Savings net of accumulation of physical assets was then found as a residual for each group. Net and gross savings rates are shown in Table 4.12. Since these are relatively crude estimates, little can be said about the savings rates of groups II–IV except that they are low. The high savings rate of group I is accounted for by the high savings of the employees of the village health center. The savings rate and rate of stock accumulation are high for the large farmers, which may not be unrealistic.

Table 4.12 shows the pattern of consumption by commodity group. These budget shares should be viewed with caution because they are not based on actual consumption data. The share of food ranges between 62 and 70 percent. As per capita consumption rises, rice and wheat are substituted for coarse cereals and milk consumption increases. The share of subsidized commodities in total consumption is small at 4 percent, but is large for individual commodities, such as cooking oil (26 percent) and sugar (40 percent).[21]

By "collapsing" the SAM, consumption can be allocated to the village's production activities and the rest-of-India account, that is, to local production and to imports. Table 4.12 shows that about a quarter of consumption is from village agriculture, about a fifth is from the shops, while some 40 percent is from village imports. The share of village production (i.e., baskets, tiles, pots, and tailors', barbers', and millers' services) is small. Although large farmers might be expected to consume more from their own production, this will not be evident here because the data used to construct the SAM did not reveal whether a purchase was from the village or from outside.

Investment activities are carried out by households and the village government, but the government's share is only 1.6 percent. Households and village government both invest in wells and in buildings. Households also invest in implements, livestock, machinery, and land. Livestock purchases are from outside, and no household specializes in animal breeding. Investment in livestock accounts for 46.4 percent of total investment of Rs 220,780. Some investment expenditures are not identified; these are assumed to be for construction materials. Implements and machinery account for 25.4 percent of investment, construction and other materials for 20.3 percent, and payments to labor, 8.05 percent. Total savings is Rs 356,640. The difference between savings and investment, Rs 135,860, is the net capital outflow from the village, which is more than a third of total savings. The net capital outflow represents financial investments (estimated at Rs 76,702) and purchases of property outside the village less bank and other credit to the village and purchases of village land by outsiders. In the absence of estimates of credit and purchases of property, no independent check of this estimate of net capital outflow is possible.

External trade. The village exports crops, milk, retail commodities, small amounts of locally produced goods and services, and, by convention, the output of the government services sector. The only commodities not imported are fodder, locally produced goods and services, and, by definition, retail commodities sold by village shops. Imports of all other commodities are found as residuals because, as noted earlier, information on sources of

21. These figures are obtained from the unaggregated SAM.

Table 4.13a. *Collapsed social accounting matrix for Kanzara: Activity accounts (rupees)*

	Dry agriculture		Wet agriculture	Livestock	Agricultural services	Village production	Retail trade	Government services	All				
	Small	Large							Activities	Factors	Households	Others	Total
Dry agriculture (small)	1,533	3,145	889	19,640	—	145	7,534	—	32,887	—	79,847	221,436	334,169
Dry agriculture (large)	4,053	9,400	4,017	64,200	—	490	24,630	—	106,790	—	231,326	575,855	913,972
Wet agriculture	2,360	6,070	5,152	25,480	—	195	20,104	—	59,360	—	144,783	307,354	511,497
Livestock	33,175	114,048	39,092	—	—	24	—	—	186,339	—	93,477	125,216	405,032
Agricultural services	2,513	6,796	5,209	19,667	—	—	854	—	34,185	—	—	6,606	40,791
Village production	609	962	720	—	—	—	—	—	3,144	—	43,557	15,140	61,840
Retail trade	—	—	—	—	—	—	—	—	—	—	336,942	139,124	476,066
Government services	—	—	—	—	—	—	—	—	—	—	47,400	—	47,400
All activities	44,243	140,422	55,078	128,987	—	854	53,122	—	422,705	—	929,932	1,438,130	2,790,767
Family male	20,745	42,330	23,609	—	—	—	—	—	86,685	—	—	—	86,685
Family female	21,820	12,798	2,047	—	—	—	—	—	36,664	—	—	—	36,664
Hired male	9,627	30,390	19,849	—	2,070	1,094	2,080	—	65,110	—	—	196,005	261,115
Hired female	13,817	56,480	34,540	—	—	—	—	—	104,837	—	—	27,864	132,701
Farm servants	—	18,011	14,397	26,316	—	—	—	—	58,724	—	—	62,537	121,260
Salaried workers	—	—	—	—	—	—	—	32,400	32,400	—	—	226,159	258,559
Rent	21,212	61,805	1,857	—	—	—	—	—	84,874	—	—	—	84,874
Private credit	7,450	520	—	—	—	—	—	—	7,970	—	11,299	—	19,269
Public credit	11,417	21,186	16,315	15,188	600	200	400	—	65,305	—	—	—	65,305
All factors	106,088	243,519	112,613	41,503	2,670	1,294	2,480	32,400	542,568	—	11,299	512,565	1,066,432
Landless salaried	—	—	—	—	—	—	—	—	—	78,743	872	1,327	80,943
Landless unsalaried	8,615	—	−111	4,159	—	15,830	3,860	—	32,353	213,226	29,231	13,459	288,268
Small farmers	32,421	—	10,602	7,463	—	1,300	21,158	—	71,757	137,820	6,733	2,651	218,963
Medium farmers	103,323	—	−572	10,375	19,970	8,376	—	—	142,661	275,840	13,023	—	431,524
Large farmers	—	403,879	212,506	156,572	15,349	24,074	26,847	—	839,227	260,091	36,418	62,939	1,198,675
All households	144,359	403,879	222,426	178,570	35,319	49,580	51,865	—	1,085,999	965,721	86,277	80,375	2,218,373
Temple	28	—	412	—	—	—	—	—	1,003	6,475	1,733	5,372	6,475
Village government	—	563	—	—	—	—	—	—	—	126	7,842	6,552	8,234
Capital	1,647	4,121	2,458	—	980	1,000	—	—	10,206	—	350,088	—	356,640
Maintenance	6,676	—	14,267	11,710	1,822	93	257	15,000	53,145	—	47,101	—	18,048
Stock changes	31,128	20,142	14,242	44,263	1,822	9,019	—	—	—	94,110	784,100	34,803	135,049
Rest of India	—	101,326	104,242	—	—	9,019	368,342	—	675,142	—	—	513,624	2,066,976
Total	334,169	913,972	511,497	405,032	40,792	61,840	476,066	47,400	2,790,767	1,066,432	2,218,373	2,591,422	

Table 4.13b. *Collapsed social accounting matrix for Kanzara: Institution accounts (rupees)*

	All		Landless		Farming		
	Activities	Factors	Salaried	Unsalaried	Small	Medium	Large
Dry agriculture (small)	32,887	—	2,388	14,416	10,978	2,065	31,460
Dry agriculture (large)	106,790	—	6,129	45,670	33,122	64,636	81,770
Wet agriculture	59,360	—	4,964	25,756	15,735	38,444	59,885
Livestock	186,339	—	3,605	7,945	8,553	20,752	52,621
Agricultural services	34,185	—	—	—	—	—	—
Village production	3,144	—	1,357	7,654	4,026	12,634	17,886
Retail trade	—	—	11,438	63,930	42,504	95,390	123,679
Government services	—	—	—	—	—	—	—
All activities	422,705	—	29,881	165,370	114,918	252,461	367,301
Family male	86,685	—	—	—	—	—	—
Family female	36,664	—	—	—	—	—	—
Hired male	65,110	—	—	—	—	—	—
Hired female	104,837	—	—	—	—	—	—
Farm servants	58,724	—	—	—	—	—	—
Salaried workers	32,400	—	—	—	—	—	—
Rent	84,874	—	—	—	—	—	—
Private credit	7,970	—	526	2,789	2,031	530	5,423
Public credit	65,305	—	—	—	—	—	—
All factors	542,568	—	526	2,789	2,031	530	5,423
Landless salaried	—	78,743	41	162	176	115	3,769
Landless unsalaried	32,353	213,226	305	9,895	6,507	5,794	6,730
Small farmers	71,757	137,820	140	1,477	1,544	1,745	1,828
Medium farmers	142,661	275,840	116	4,003	3,403	1,905	3,597
Large farmers	839,227	260,091	135	1,516	1,282	1,516	31,969
All households	1,085,999	965,721	737	17,052	12,912	11,074	44,503
Temple	—	6,475	—	—	—	—	—
Village government	1,003	126	49	257	652	175	601
Capital	—	—	34,333	22,335	−6,633	4,327	295,726
Maintenance	10,206	—	12	65	581	2,531	4,653
Stock changes	53,145	—	−8,631	−40,496	9,954	−37,546	123,820
Rest of India	675,142	94,110	24,035	120,897	84,548	197,972	356,649
Total	2,790,767	1,066,432	80,943	288,268	218,963	431,524	1,198,675

purchases was not recorded in the consumption data. As a result, estimates of imports should be interpreted with caution.

The village is both importer and exporter of the major food crops, partly because of the aggregation involved and partly because some products are both imported and exported (e.g., wheat and pigeon-pea). Overall, the village is a net importer of cereals and pulses. The proportion of consumption of these staples that is met by imports is 52 percent. Although this result must be viewed with caution because the import and consumption estimates are not reliable, it may not be grossly incorrect for three reasons. First, those with a large marketable surplus may prefer to sell in the regulated market soon after the harvest to maintain their cash flow. Second, about 22 percent

All households	Temple	Village government	Capital	Maintenance	Stock changes	Rest of India	Total
79,847	—	—	—	—	17,816	203,620	334,169
231,326	—	—	—	—	44,572	531,283	913,972
144,783	—	—	—	—	24,786	282,568	511,497
93,477	—	—	—	—	5,883	119,333	405,032
—	—	—	—	4,869	—	1,737	40,791
43,557	1,000	—	—	640	—	13,500	61,840
336,942	—	—	979	225	—	137,920	476,066
—	—	—	—	—	—	47,400	47,400
929,932	1,000	—	979	5,734	93,057	1,337,360	2,790,767
—	—	—	—	—	—	—	86,685
—	—	—	—	—	—	—	36,664
—	720	2,037	17,779	2,150	—	173,319	261,115
—	—	—	—	—	—	27,864	132,701
—	—	—	—	—	—	62,537	121,260
—	—	—	—	—	—	226,159	258,559
—	—	—	—	—	—	—	84,874
11,299	—	—	—	—	—	—	19,269
—	—	—	—	—	—	—	65,305
11,299	720	2,037	17,779	2,150	—	489,878	1,066,432
872	—	—	—	—	—	1,327	80,943
29,231	—	—	—	—	—	13,459	288,268
6,733	—	—	—	—	—	2,651	218,963
13,023	—	—	—	—	—	—	431,524
36,418	—	—	—	—	—	62,939	1,198,675
86,277	—	—	—	—	—	80,375	2,218,373
—	—	—	—	—	—	—	6,475
1,733	—	—	—	—	—	5,372	8,234
350,088	800	5,752	—	—	—	—	356,640
7,842	—	—	—	—	—	—	18,048
47,101	—	—	—	—	—	34,803	135,049
784,100	3,955	445	337,881	10,163	41,991	119,188	2,066,976
2,218,373	6,475	8,234	356,640	18,048	135,049	2,066,976	

of household income is earned outside the village, and those working outside may well import cereals bought or received as wages outside. Third, imports of food grains may be high because of the high degree of specialization in cotton production, which accounts for 44 percent of agricultural output.

As the SAM's rest-of-India account shows, the village economy is extremely open. Total imports are Rs 1.73 million, or 57 percent of domestic absorption. Cereals and pulses have a share of 21.7 percent in imports; other foods, 15.5 percent; nonfoods, 31.5 percent; agricultural inputs, 15.1 percent; and durables, 16.1 percent. Total exports are Rs 1.49 million. The major exports are cotton (with a share of 52 percent), vegetables and oilseeds (11 percent), pulses (10 percent), and milk (7.9 percent). The trade gap is Rs

Table 4.13c. *Collapsed social accounting matrix for Kanzara: Factor accounts (rupees)*

| | | Family | | Hired | | | | | | | All | | | |
	All activities	Male	Female	Male	Female	Farm servants	Salaried workers	Rent	Private credit	Public credit	Factors	Households	Others	Total
Dry agriculture (small)	32,887	—	—	—	—	—	—	—	—	—	—	79,847	221,436	334,169
Wet agriculture (large)	106,790	—	—	—	—	—	—	—	—	—	—	231,326	575,855	913,972
Wet agriculture	59,360	—	—	—	—	—	—	—	—	—	—	144,783	307,354	511,497
Livestock	186,339	—	—	—	—	—	—	—	—	—	—	93,477	125,216	405,032
Agricultural services	34,185	—	—	—	—	—	—	—	—	—	—	—	6,606	40,791
Village production	3,144	—	—	—	—	—	—	—	—	—	—	43,557	15,140	61,840
Retail trade	—	—	—	—	—	—	—	—	—	—	—	336,942	139,124	476,066
Government services	—	—	—	—	—	—	—	—	—	—	—	—	47,400	47,400
All activities	422,705	—	—	—	—	—	—	—	—	—	—	929,932	1,438,130	2,790,767
Family male	86,685	—	—	—	—	—	—	—	—	—	—	—	—	86,685
Family female	36,664	—	—	—	—	—	—	—	—	—	—	—	—	36,664
Hired male	65,110	—	—	—	—	—	—	—	—	—	—	—	196,005	261,115
Hired female	104,837	—	—	—	—	—	—	—	—	—	—	—	27,864	132,701
Farm servants	58,724	—	—	—	—	—	—	—	—	—	—	—	62,537	121,260
Salaried workers	32,400	—	—	—	—	—	—	—	—	—	—	—	226,159	258,559
Rent	84,874	—	—	—	—	—	—	—	—	—	—	—	—	84,874
Private credit	7,970	—	—	—	—	—	—	—	—	—	—	11,299	—	19,269
Public credit	65,305	—	—	—	—	—	—	—	—	—	—	—	—	65,305
All factors	542,568	—	—	—	—	—	—	—	—	—	—	11,299	512,565	1,066,432
Landless salaried	—	—	—	3,064	1,681	—	71,269	2,230	500	—	78,743	872	1,327	80,943
Landless unsalaried	32,353	1,588	1,019	104,036	60,957	32,810	—	10,316	2,500	—	213,226	29,231	13,459	288,268
Small farmers	71,757	5,006	5,816	54,950	39,455	22,500	—	8,594	1,500	—	137,820	6,733	2,651	218,963
Medium farmers	142,661	15,273	15,083	79,989	26,380	48,530	76,005	13,080	1,500	—	275,840	13,023	—	431,524
Large farmers	839,227	64,818	14,747	19,076	4,228	17,420	111,285	24,517	4,000	—	260,091	36,418	62,939	1,198,675
All households	1,085,999	86,685	36,664	261,115	132,701	121,260	258,559	58,737	10,000	—	965,721	86,277	80,375	2,218,373
Temple	—	—	—	—	—	—	—	6,475	—	—	6,475	—	—	6,475
Village government	1,003	—	—	—	—	—	—	—	—	126	126	1,733	5,372	8,234
Capital	—	—	—	—	—	—	—	—	—	—	—	350,088	6,552	356,640
Maintenance	10,206	—	—	—	—	—	—	—	—	—	—	7,842	—	18,048
Stock changes	53,145	—	—	—	—	—	—	—	—	—	—	47,101	34,803	135,049
Rest of India	675,142	—	—	—	—	—	—	19,661	9,269	65,179	94,110	784,100	513,624	2,066,976
Total	2,790,767	86,685	36,664	261,115	132,701	121,260	258,559	84,874	19,269	65,305	1,066,432	2,218,373	2,591,422	0

240,923, which is met by net factor earnings (Rs 395,770) and net transfers (− Rs 18,986) from the outside world, leaving a net capital outflow of Rs 135,860, as discussed already.

Production linkages

Activities use commodities produced by other activities as intermediate inputs. An increase in a particular activity's level of output will produce an increase in demand for intermediate inputs and thence an increase in the output level of other activities. These production linkages become apparent when the commodity accounts in the SAM are deleted and each commodity's intermediate use and final demand is allocated among domestic activities, stock changes, and imports. This is best done using Pyatt's (1985) ingenious technique for "collapsing" SAMs. The collapsed SAM has no commodity accounts. The rest-of-India and stock changes rows now have a different interpretation. The rest-of-India row now contains both transfers and tax payments from village institutions and activities *and* these accounts' consumption of imports. These imports can be found by taking the difference between the rest-of-India row in the collapsed and uncollapsed SAMs.

Examination of the activity blocks of the collapsed SAM (Table 4.13) shows the most significant links are those between agriculture and the livestock sector and between the livestock sector and agricultural services. The only other significant linkage is from the trade sector to agriculture. The absence of strong linkages between agriculture and nonagriculture is the result of the predominance of agriculture in the village's economy.

Conclusion

In brief, the SAM provides a consistent framework for viewing aggregate flows within the village economy and between the village and the rest of India. The SAM shows Kanzara to be a highly commercialized village, exporting 64 percent of its agricultural output and importing 52 percent of the staple cereals and pulses. Kanzara is also a labor-exporting village, with over half its wage income derived from outside the village. Agriculture provides over 75 percent of value-added, followed by the livestock sector at 13.4 percent. Wages and salaries from outside amount to 22.7 percent, and factor payments to the outside world are 4.37 percent of total factor income. Labor income is the single largest component of total income for all except the salaried landless and the large farmers. These two groups have high savings rates, while the others' savings rates are much smaller. Capital outflows are large, about 28 percent of total savings. Production linkages are weak except between agriculture and livestock, and from trade to agriculture.

The predominance of agriculture in this village and region suggests that agricultural development remains indispensable to growth. Since value-added per acre and labor absorption per acre are almost twice as high in irrigated as in dry-land agriculture, investment in irrigation can make an important contribution to growth. But the extension of irrigation is limited by the scarcity of surface and groundwater resources in the region. The importance of wage labor as the chief source of income for the landless and small and medium farmers suggests that employment programs could effectively stabilize the incomes of the poor in this region of unstable agriculture.

5

Migration and the changing structure of a Mexican village economy

Migration is tightly woven into the economic, cultural, and political fabric of communities on both sides of the Mexico–U.S. border. Nowhere is this more evident than in the economies from which migrants come. Official International Monetary Fund (IMF) estimates place total international migrant remittances to Mexico at \$2.3 billion in 1989, an amount equal to 10 percent of Mexico's total merchandise exports, making migrants that country's major source of foreign exchange after oil and tourism (Russell and Teitelbaum, 1992).[1] The activity of migration and the income migrants remit to their households of origin are a structural feature of village economies throughout Mexico. Because of this, a change in almost any aspect of economic policy in Mexico has implications for Mexico-to-U.S. migration. This fact has not been lost on policymakers in Mexico and in the United States, who fear that market reforms initiated in the 1980s and continuing in the 1990s will create new pressures for increased migration.

As migration links villages with the global economy, Mexico's rural economy is directly influenced by the international economic and political environment. Economic conditions in the United States, exchange rate devaluations, and changes in U.S. immigration policies can alter injections of migrant remittances into Mexico. Changes in remittances initially affect the households that receive them. The expenditure and production patterns of these households, however, quickly transmit impacts to other households. Second- and higher-order remittance effects generate villagewide "remittance multipliers," which may be large relative to the initial injection of remittances (Adelman, Taylor, and Vogel, 1988).

1. These estimates grossly understate total remittances from Mexico-to-U.S. migrants, which include a large amount of clandestine and in-kind remittances.

Despite the economic importance of international migration for rural Mexico, few economists have attempted to understand the influence of migration and remittances on the village economy. A wealth of ethnographic data is available from anthropological studies of Mexican villages, but these data are not quantitative enough for formal economic analysis. Villages have largely been perceived as lying outside the economist's domain.

Remittances and the village economy

The SAM-based villagewide modeling framework developed by Adelman, Taylor, and Vogel (1988) focuses on the complex role played by migrant remittances in village economies of central Mexico. This chapter extends that analysis by using the village SAM framework to explore the changing structure of one migrant village economy over time, using new matched-longitudinal village data. The study covers most of the 1980s (1982–1988), a decade during which Mexico-to-U.S. migration from the village increased while internal migration was discouraged by economic distress in Mexico. Migrant remittances from the United States had profound direct and indirect effects on the village economy during this period (Taylor, 1992).

The Mexican rural economy is organized around farm households clustered together in villages. Income from migrants abroad frequently represents an important component of these households' income portfolios. Assessing the impacts of migrant remittances on the rural economy requires understanding: (1) the magnitude of remittances; (2) the economic behavior of household-farms that send migrants abroad; and (3) the linkages between these and other household-farms within the village. In the past studies of migration and development have focused on (1) and (2), ignoring the potentially important villagewide effects of migration implied by (3).

The impact of migrant remittances on village economies in Mexico has been a subject of controversy in the economics literature. A pessimistic view has emerged from remittance-use surveys, concluding that migrant remittances are spent primarily for consumption rather than investment (for a critical review of these studies, see Massey, Arango, Hugo, Kouaci, Pellegrino, and Taylor, 1994). Such surveys, which focus on a single income source (remittances), offer limited insight into how that income source affects a household-farm's full income and economic choices. The effect of remittances on expenditures is unlikely to be reflected in the way remittances themselves are utilized. Migrant remittances loosen household-farm budget constraints, potentially resulting in changes in household-farm expenditures (and investments) across a range of goods and services.

Ascertaining the impact of remittances on investment requires identifying what constitutes "investment goods." Machinery, land, new technologies, animals as capital inputs for livestock or crop production, family education (human capital), and improved housing, which can contribute to family health and productivity, are all examples of household-farm investments. Remarkably few of these investment categories are included in past studies of remittance use in Mexico. Yet, together they typically absorb a large share of household-farm expenditures.

Furthermore, consumption and investment linkages among village households generate important second and higher-round remittance effects rarely considered in remittance-use studies. Households that "consume" their remittances may be an important source of demand for goods and services supplied by other households in the village and a stimulus for production and investments by those households. The production and expenditure patterns of households that benefit indirectly from remittances help shape the overall impact of remittances on village incomes, employment, and investment.

Even when production is intensive in family inputs, consumption and factor-demand linkages may be strong. Village consumption goods include staples, meat and other animal products, and perhaps some nonagricultural goods. They also include leisure, which migrant households may "purchase" by substituting hired labor for family labor on the farm. Investments may assume many forms, with varying short- and long-run linkage effects on the village economy. Housing investments (sometimes treated as consumption) may generate demand linkages with suppliers of building materials outside the village, but will also call upon village households that supply labor for construction activities. Machinery investments, which studies of Mexican villages generally find to be small, normally flow outside the village, because few villages possess any kind of machinery-producing sector. The village livestock sector, however, may be an important source of both consumption (meat, dairy products) and capital goods (draft animals, breeding stock). Expenditures on secondary and postsecondary education for family members (human capital) tend to flow out of the village; most Mexican villages have, at best, a primary school. However, schooling may be a stimulus for future remittances by educated family migrants (Taylor, 1986).

The remainder of this chapter concerns the study area; an overview of village income sources and structural changes in the economy in 1982 and 1988; the Mexico village SAM framework; and an example of a 1988 SAM for the village modeled in Adelman, Taylor, and Vogel's earlier study (the two village SAMs are compared to explore structural changes that occurred in the village economy between 1982 and 1988).

The study area

The village of Napízaro is located at the edge of the Tarascan highlands on the western shore of Lake Pátzcuaro, in the central Mexican state of Michoacán. It has a semitropical climate. At 2,050 meters, Lake Pátzcuaro is one of the highest spring-fed lakes in the world. It is surrounded by a skirt of relatively flat, intensively farmed land (*tierras de temporal*), which rises first gently and then steeply up to a series of ridges and peaks that define the outer border of the Pátzcuaro basin. At its lower elevations, the hillside land (*tierra de humedad*) has been cleared and intensively farmed. Much of this land has been taken out of crop production in recent years, however, because of what farmers describe as declining productivity (there is striking evidence of erosion on the lower *humedad* lands) and to accommodate an expanding livestock sector. The higher elevations are covered by a patchwork of pastures and forests, which have benefited in the past decade from government-sponsored reforestation projects to combat erosion.

Migrant roots

Napízaro is itself a product of migration. Early colonial maps of the Lake Pátzcuaro region do not show evidence of a settlement in what is now the village. Contemporary Napízaro is the descendant of the Napízaro Hacienda, an artifact of Spanish colonial rule in Mexico. The hacienda house (*la casa grande*), granary, and stables were destroyed after the revolution. The adobe *templo* (chapel) was demolished in 1982 to make room for a new brick and concrete church financed by the community of Napízaro migrants in southern California. The foundations of the old hacienda buildings are still visible to the knowing eye.

Village legend speaks of five *caballeros* (horsemen) who migrated to Napízaro from El Bajío in the north to oversee the hacienda's livestock operation. Although Purépecha-speaking peoples are found throughout the region, Napízareños do not consider themselves to be *indígenas* (Indian), but instead descendants of the *caballeros*. Genealogical research by Fletcher (cited in Fletcher and Taylor, 1992) reveals five important male ancestors of the present population who lived and worked on the hacienda, and a number of others who appear to have migrated to Napízaro from outside the lake region during and after the hacienda period. However, this research also uncovered Purépecha (Tarascan)-speaking ancestors from indigenous *comunidades* (communities) around the lake.

Village elders reminisce about the difficult years during and just after the hacienda period, when many Napízareños lived in stone-and-wood dwellings, wore burlap clothing, and often used acorn meal to extend their *nixtamal* (maize dough) for making tortillas. The village was, for the most part, self-sufficient. Fish from the nearby lake provided an important complement to the traditional Mexican corn and beans diet. Wood for construction and cooking was obtained from the hillsides surrounding the Pátzcuaro basin. The lake supplied some inputs for nonagricultural production, such as reeds for baskets, broomsticks, and *petates* (mats). Some of these were carried by foot or canoe to be sold at weekly markets around the lake, including one twenty kilometers away in Pátzcuaro, in exchange for pottery, cloth, and other items.

The dismantling of the hacienda and redistribution of hacienda lands under Mexico's *ejido* law in the 1930s and 1940s created a class of small family farms with rights to 8.5 hectares of land each. The *ejiditarios*, beneficiaries of the land reform, originally comprised all adult males in the village. Under ejido law, rights to ejido land are secure as long as the ejiditario's family works the land, and they can be passed down to a successor, usually one of the ejiditario's sons. The ejiditarios of Napízaro, like caballeros of the hacienda before them, were classic *milpa* (intercropped corn, beans, and occasionally squash) producers working on marginal, mostly hilly, rain-fed lands and using traditional, low-input agricultural techniques. Economic returns to crop production were low; farm profits could be increased primarily by making more extensive use of the farmer's land with family labor.

The first two generations of ejiditarios fathered large families: eight to twelve children were not uncommon. This demographic growth reflects decreasing mortality rates, supported in part, no doubt, by the improved nutritional status of the new small-farm sector and by the need for family labor to farm ejido land. However, in time it put pressure on the local resource base and created a class of landless sons and daughters of ejiditarios with few economic options in the village.

The arrival of labor recruiters to Napízaro from the United States under the series of bilateral agreements known as the bracero program represents a watershed in the economic, social, and cultural history of the village. This program, initiated in 1917 and expanded in the 1940s to relieve labor shortages during the Second World War, actively recruited adult males to work in agriculture and on infrastructure projects (e.g., railroad construction) in the United States. It covered all facets of labor recruitment. Starting in 1946, Napízaro were issued work permits, put on trains and channeled to specific jobs in the United States. The program targeted villages in Central Mexico, in some of the poorest regions of the country, including the state of Michoacán. It offered large numbers of villagers contact with a foreign land and forged links between Mexican villages and labor markets in the American Southwest, especially California, providing the institutional means for a massive influx of migrant workers from rural Mexico. In 1982 nearly one-half (47 percent) of all male household heads in Napízaro had worked in the United States under the bracero program. Of these, nearly three-quarters (71 percent) had also worked illegally at some time in the United States, and 93 percent had at least one son or daughter living and working in the United States by 1983.

The braceros typically made several trips over a ten- or fifteen-year period, remaining abroad for only a few months at a time. Some were young and unmarried; married workers left their families behind. Their goals were often specific, for example, saving to buy a team of oxen, to build a new adobe house, or to add a cement floor to an existing house. U.S. migration was seen as instrumental to improving families' lives within the traditional corn and beans economy of the village (Fletcher, 1996). After the bracero program ended in 1964, men from Napízaro continued to come to the United States illegally, often working seasonally in agriculture or in low-paying service and industrial jobs, usually for short periods of time.

This short-term, shuttle migration pattern changed in the 1970s and 1980s, as sons and daughters of ex-braceros began to migrate, often at a young age. Migrants stayed longer, eventually moving out of seasonal agricultural jobs into more stable and higher-paying manufacturing work. Communities of Napízaro migrants formed in North Hollywood, San Fernando, and Pacoima, California. Young men brought their families to the United States or else married migrants they met abroad. Their original goal may have been to return to the village, but they also began to have an increasing stake in the United States. Some bought houses. Others saw a benefit in a U.S. education for their children. Amnesty provisions in the 1986 Immigration Reform and Control Act (IRCA) gave many of these families a larger stake in the United States: legal residence, and eventually citizenship. As stated earlier, 93 percent of Napízaro's residents had a child working in the United States in 1983. Under IRCA, individuals who had resided continuously in the United States between 1982 and 1986 as unauthorized immigrants could become legal U.S. residents.

Alternatives to migration

In Napízaro, the only local employment alternatives to household-farm production in our sample are a small government-sponsored reforestation project, a furniture factory in Erongarícuaro that currently employs two people from Napízaro, and some local seasonal wage work in house construction and agriculture.

Household-farms are the main employers of village labor. Although the majority of work is performed by family labor, hired workers are used by some households for seeding, weeding, and harvesting. Hired labor, along with the use of purchased inputs in crop production, partly represents an effort to substitute for family labor lost to migration (Fletcher and Taylor, 1992).

Until the 1970s, crop production in the village used few modern inputs. Draft animals are the major capital input, but tractors are used increasingly to plow and occasionally to plant seed. Fertilizers, pesticides, and herbicides were introduced to village farmers through government programs in the 1970s and early 1980s, that promoted high-input and monocrop agricultural practices and subsidized fertilizer inputs.

Increasingly, the traditional mix of corn and beans in the milpa has given way to a monocrop of maize, as farmers use an herbicide incompatible with beans and squash as a labor substitute. These lands typically are cultivated on a two-year rotation, planted in pasture crops or else left fallow every other year.

Although maize and beans production is the major employer of family labor and the social and cultural foundation of the village, productivity is low (about one metric ton of maize per hectare), and net profits (total revenue minus purchased inputs) from maize and beans production make up a relatively small share of total village income. Most of the output from this production is consumed by the household; relatively few farmers are net surplus producers of maize or beans.

At the time of the surveys that are the basis for this reasearch, Napízaro was connected to Erongarícuaro, the county seat and nearest town two kilometers away, by a poorly maintained dirt road (*brecha*), which became impassable for most vehicles during the rainy season. Because of low productivity and high transactions costs, few farmers sell maize on the national market, despite a high government-guaranteed price for corn. (The nearest government [CONASUPO] purchase point at which the guaranteed price can be obtained is in Pátzcuaro, twenty kilometers away.) Surplus production is either sold locally, at a price below the government-guaranteed price, or fed to livestock. Five village stores stock soft drinks, beer, and such household necessities as cooking oil, eggs, flour, soaps, and paper products. Livestock products are either locally produced or bought in town, depending on the item: Milk and poultry are supplied locally, whereas beef, for which local demand is too limited to support a village butcher except at fiesta time, is bought in town. There is no produce market in the village, but a weekly market in Erongarícuaro (the *tiangis*) provides fresh produce as well as a variety of small manufactured goods from outside the region, including clothing, electronic goods, and other small manufactures from the United States.

In Napízaro the land base is divided into three land-tenure categories. The majority of lands are ejido, or reform-sector, lands expropriated from the Napízaro hacienda and redistributed in the 1930s. The standard ejido holding consists of 4 hectares of temporal land and 4.5 of humedad. As of 1989, these lands could not be bought, sold, or rented; under Mexico's ejido law, they were required to be farmed by the holder of the ejido right (the ejidatario) or his (her) family. There is a limited amount of private farmland (*propiedad*), consisting of lands that were retained by members of the old hacienda family but later sold to villagers. Since the inception of the ejido, a new land source and tenure category has emerged as Lake Pátzcuaro has receded, uncovering a band of land around the lake (*tierras de orilla*) varying in width from 100 to 200 meters in and around the village. The new lakeside lands are controlled

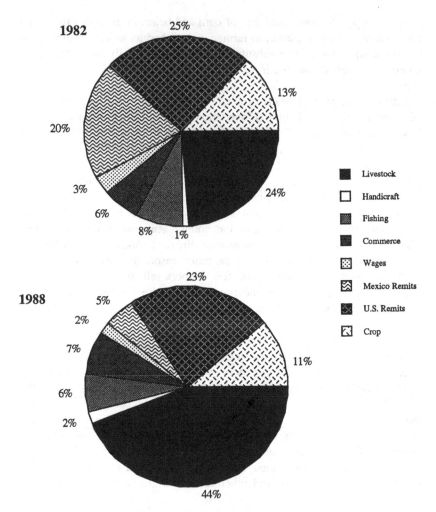

Figure 5.1. Composition of village income, 1982 and 1988.

by the federal government but leased to farmers annually for a small fee. In practice, these *federal* lands are treated as an extension of bordering ejido plots. Ejidatarios with plots contiguous to the new lakeside lands claim preferential rights to lease them from the government. This has been a source of conflict in the village. Ejido holders now represent only one-half of Napízaro households. Local population growth has generated pressures by the landless to obtain access to the lakeside lands, which some view as an alternative to migration.

Table 5.1. *Incidence of migration: 1982 and 1988*

	1982	1988
Average number of migrants per household		
Total	2.6	3.1
Rural–urban	1.2	1.4
United States	1.1	2.0
Share of households with migrants (%)		
Total	70.0	90.0
Rural–urban	40.0	43.3
United States	63.3	83.3

Structural change in the village economy: 1982–1988

Figure 5.1 summarizes the components of village income in 1982 and 1988, the years covered by the two surveys. In 1982, crop production accounted for no more than 13 percent of total village income. Remittances from internal and international migrants accounted for nearly one-half (45 percent) of income, the share of livestock income was 24 percent, and wage labor accounted for 3 percent. Other noncrop activities, including handicrafts, commerce, and renewable resource extraction (fishing, firewood gathering), accounted for the remaining 15 percent.

Migration and the structure of the Napízaro economy changed during the 1980s. Table 5.1, together with Figure 5.1, reveals the increasing importance of U.S. migration relative to internal migration in Napízaro households. The average number of migrants (internal and U.S.) per village household was 2.6 in 1982 and rose to 3.1 by 1988 (Table 5.1). The average number of migrants in urban Mexico, however, rose only slightly during this period of economic crisis and adjustment, from 1.2 to 1.4. By contrast, the average number of U.S. migrants per household nearly doubled, from 1.1 to 2. By 1988, more than 80 percent of all households had at least one family member in the United States, and more than one in three villagers were living and working in California.

During this same period, the direct share of village income from total (internal plus international) migrant remittances declined sharply, from 45 to 28 percent (Figure 5.1). The share of U.S. migrant remittances declined only slightly, from 25 to 23 percent; however, internal migrant remittances plunged from 20 to 5 percent, reflecting a contraction in economic opportunities for village migrants in Mexico. Although Mexico-to-U.S. migrant remittances fell in relative terms, they increased by nearly one-fifth in absolute dollar terms. Nonmigration income, however, increased more quickly than U.S. remittances.

Still, much of this increased income from nonremittance sources can actually be explained by migration. For example, remittances from migration appear to have loosened financial and possibly risk constraints on production in the village, enabling households with migrants to accumulate livestock (which accounted for the largest increase in village income). The sale of animals and animal products amounted to 24 percent of village income in 1982 and 44 percent in 1988. By taking into account the indirect effects of remittances on village incomes, an estimated 35 percent of 1988 village income could be attributed to U.S. migrant remittances, and 9 percent could be attributed to remittances from internal migrants (Taylor, 1992). This concrete example of the indirect effects of remittances demonstrates how Mexico-to-U.S. migration is becoming an increasingly integral part of the economic fabric of the village.

The village SAM framework and data

The Napízaro SAMs in Adelman, Taylor, and Vogel (1988) and in this chapter were elaborated to highlight the role of remittances in the village economy. The structure of the SAM reflects the economic structure of the household-farms that compose the village. Village production accounts (as summarized by an input–output matrix) are relatively simple and do not fully describe the resource allocations that occur within households. The SAM, by contrast, is able to capture the complex factor-income flows and household-farm expenditure patterns, both of which are critical in shaping the village economy over time.

The Napízaro SAM follows the outline presented in Table 2.1 (Chapter 2). The input–output (I-O) matrix for the village consists of five sectors: farming (principally maize), livestock, renewable resources (fishing and wood gathering), construction, and retail activities. The last sector is less a production sector than a catchall category for manufactured and processed goods "imported" into the village from the rest of Mexico. The village economy has a large import component. Labor exports play a key role in financing these imports.

Production activities result in income payments to capital, labor, and land. Payments to capital, or capital value-added, include explicit payments for capital services ranging from ox-and-plow to tractor services. They also include imputed returns to capital when no explicit payment takes place (e.g., use of own oxen for plowing). Both types of payments are contained in the capital factor account. Separate entries are included in the SAM for hired and nonhired (family) labor services (or labor value-added) in order to highlight interhousehold labor linkages and to reflect the imperfect substitutability of family and hired labor in village production. Land rents include explicit and implicit payments for land. These were estimated econometrically (Taylor and Wyatt, 1993). The factor accounts summarize the factor distribution of village income.

Value-added and migrant remittances are channeled into three village household institutions and government. The household institutions are defined by size of landholdings. They include landless (less than one hectare), smallholder (two to eight hectares), and largeholder (more than eight hectares) households. (Because of a lack of markets for ejido lands, the membership of these household groups was stable throughout the 1982–1986 period, with the exception of a few households that abandoned the village; see the next section.

The institution accounts provide a breakdown of payments for services supplied by village households to employers both inside and outside the village. Factor accounts channel value-added from village production activities into the three household groups. Remittances from internal labor migrants are represented as an income flow into households from the rest of Mexico. International migrant remittances are represented as a flow from the rest of the world, with the prevailing exchange rate utilized to translate the latter into local currency. International exchange rate fluctuations have a direct and immediate impact on the value of migrant remittances, with possible repercussions throughout the village economy. The three household rows summarize the household distribution of village value-added and remittances.

The household accounts channel income into consumption demand for village products, imports, and savings. The village SAM contains two capital accounts. The first of these collects household and government savings and purchases physical capital investment goods. The second, in keeping with the SAM's labor focus, is a human capital account. The purpose of this account is to capture household expenditures on schooling. This activity is intertemporally linked with internal migration: The more villagers attain formal schooling, the more likely they are to become internal migrants as opposed to working in the village or migrating illegally to the United States (Taylor, 1986).

Data

Data to construct the village SAMs are from household surveys carried out in 1983 (for the 1982 calendar year) and 1989 (for the 1988 calendar year) in the Pátzcuaro region of the state of Michoacán, Mexico, approximately 2,000 kilometers south of the Mexico–California border. The 1983 sample for Napízaro consists of 222 adults thirteen years of age or older representing the total adult population of thirty households, or 10 percent of the village household population. All but four of the households were successfully reinterviewed by Fletcher and Taylor (see Fletcher and Taylor, 1992) in 1989. (In the four unsuccessful cases, all household members had moved to the

United States prior to the second survey year.) Detailed data were collected on each individual's labor allocations and contributions to household income in the calendar year preceding the survey. Data were also gathered on income from household-farm production (farming, fishing, livestock, commerce, etc.) and rental income, expenditures on consumer goods produced inside and outside the village, savings, and investments.

The household economy is defined in relation to randomly selected housing units, which were the basis of our sample design. All income and expenditures centered in the housing unit are considered part of the household economy. Income remittances to the village are part of these household economies, as are "reverse remittances" (support of absent migrants by villagers), which were rare. Income earned and spent by migrants while away from the village (i.e., income that does not enter the village economy) is not included. In-kind remittances are not counted in household-farm income or in expenditures.

Household members in the village provided information on sociodemographic characteristics and income remittances from migrants who were absent at the time of the survey. In 1982 most U.S. migrants were working illegally in the United States. There was reason to expect a priori that some villagers might not be forthcoming with information about these missing family members in a standard survey situation.

Our survey design addressed this problem first by drawing a random sample of housing units for inclusion in the survey and becoming personally acquainted with the families associated with these units before conducting the formal interview, in a process more akin to anthropological fieldwork than to economic household surveys. Often, villagers we had already interviewed introduced us to our subsequent interviewees. They made a valuable contribution to our study by assuring fellow villagers and by explaining the survey and interview procedures from a villager's perspective.

Responses to the survey were recorded in matrix form on data sheets that did not explicitly identify households. These and other efforts to ensure the anonymity of family members in Mexico and in the United States were carefully explained to all interviewees. Although participation in the survey was entirely voluntary, no one in our sample refused to participate or to answer specific questions, including questions about family migrants in the United States.

As word of our study spread through the village, families began to anticipate our arrival. This facilitated many of our interviews. The trust we had won from village families was particularly evident as our survey was nearing completion, when nearly one-third of the village sample gave us letters and other small items to hand-carry to family members in California. A number of families that had not been part of our random sample approached us and wanted to know why we had left them out of our interviews. We attempted to explain the basics of the scientific sampling procedure, and then usually arranged a time for an informal visit to their house. Our extensive interactions with villagers outside of formal interview situations deepened our understanding of village economic life and provided important contextual information for our quantitative research.

Comparison of village SAMs

A 1982 SAM for the village appears in Adelman, Taylor, and Vogel (1988). The remainder of this chapter presents the 1988 SAM and explores the structural changes in the village economy during the 1980s, reflected in the two SAMs. To facilitate the comparison of these two SAMs, we will focus on SAM coefficient matrices. Differences in SAM coefficients between the two years may be attributable to any of three events: (1) changes in real-income linkages; (2) changes in the village household sample (the four households that were lost from the village sample through migration); or (3) changes in relative prices. Events (1) and (2) represent real changes in village economic structure. In the case of (1), SAM coefficients are altered by changes in the structure of production or household demand patterns; in the case of (2), the emigration of households from the village eliminates some households' influence on the SAM coefficients. There was a net loss of households because the six-year period did not witness the formation of new households in the village. If production or demand patterns in migrant households had differed from those of nonmigrant households in 1982, the disappearance of emigrant households from the sample in 1988 may have strengthened or weakened village income linkages.

Changes in relative prices (event 3) produce nominal changes in SAM production and consumption linkages and in factor demands. However, changes in relative factor prices translate into real changes in household incomes when factor incomes are unequally distributed across households, as was clearly the case in 1982 (Adelman, Taylor, and Vogel, 1988). For example, an increase in the price of capital, land, or family labor relative to the price of hired labor redistributes village value-added away from wage-labor households. This, ceteris paribus, reduces the influence of wage-labor households' demand patterns on village consumption linkages.

Price deflators in 1988 (relative to 1982) for the major commodities in the SAM appear in Table 5.2. The largest price increase in the village is for physical capital, a labor substitute (more than twice the increase in corn prices), followed by renewable resources, land, labor, and nonagricultural goods (including village nontradables). This pattern of price changes is consistent with a village that is losing labor to migration, demanding labor substitutes in production, switching to land-intensive livestock production, and placing increasing pressure on the local resource base. Prices for live-

Table 5.2. *Village price deflators for 1988 (relative to 1982)*

	Deflator	Relative to staple price deflator
Activities		
Staples (BG)	0.0174	1.00
Livestock (LV)	0.0162	0.93
Renewable resources (RR)	0.0237	1.36
Nonagricultural (NAG)	0.0214	1.23
Commerce (COM)	0.0196	1.13
Factors		
Labor	0.0214	1.23
Capital	0.0429	2.47
Land	0.0230	1.32
Mexico-to-U.S. migration (exchange rate)	0.0166	0.95

stock products, by contrast, rise less rapidly than the price of corn during this period, as does the exchange rate. Both livestock prices and the exchange rate are determined in markets outside the village.

The 1988 SAM

The estimated 1988 SAM and accompanying SAM coefficient matrix (both in 1988 prices) are shown in Tables 5.3 and 5.4. The SAM offers a snapshot view of the structure of production, the distribution of factor and household income, expenditures, and trade in the village at the end of the 1980s.

The 1988 SAM, like its 1982 counterpart, reveals that the Mexican village economy is relatively simple on the production side but integrated in complex ways with regional commodity markets and with both regional and international factor markets. Nevertheless, there is evidence of structural changes in the village during the 1980s.

Village production is dominated by an export-oriented livestock sector (LV), producing both capital and consumer goods, together with a basic grains (principally corn and beans) sector (BG) producing food for subsistence and feed for livestock. These two sectors combined account for more than four-fifths of total village value-added in 1988. In addition, two relatively minor sectors are engaged in renewable-resource-based production (RR: mostly fishing and firewood gathering, along with some harvesting of reeds for basket making in neighboring villages) and small industry (NAG: mostly handicrafts and construction, with some needlework in a piecework

Table 5.3. *1988 Napizaro village SAM*

	Production sectors					Factors		Capital & land		Households			Exogenous accounts					
	BG	LV	RR	NAG	COM	Fam	Hir	Cap	Land	Subs	Med	Large	G	Sav	HKSav	ROM	ROW	Total
Production sectors																		
BG	926	28,734			12,104					3,803	10,193	9,595				5,135		58,386
LV										3,475	18,196	17,849		41,699		148,914		230,133
RR					8,070					1,890	6,155	8,029				5,637		21,711
NAG			62								9,299	594				9,073		19,028
COM	6,827			7,113						7,632	119,390	84,679						225,641
Factors																		
Family labor	14,873	17,970	12,450	1,178						1,366	31,309	31,900						64,575
Hired labor	2,916		3,745	1,485						663	2,047	5,436						8,146
Capital	8,467	44,507	17,978	3,190						4,235	31,878	29,918						66,031
Land	17,413	108,588	3,719							7,413	62,666	59,641						129,720
Households																		
Subsistence						1,366	663	4,235	7,413							1,915	2,878	18,470
Mediumholder						31,309	2,047	31,878	62,666							17	36,950	164,867
Largeholder						31,900	5,436	29,918	59,641							14,520	25,983	167,398
Exogenous accounts																		
Government										7	180	169						356
Savings										1,663	196	39,840	356					42,055
Human capital savings											1,258	6,643						7,901
Imports	6,964	30,334			205,467									356	7,901			251,022
Total	58,386	230,133	21,711	19,028	225,641	64,575	8,146	66,031	129,720	18,470	164,867	167,398	356	42,055	7,901	185,211	65,811	251,022

Table 5.4. SAM coefficient matrix

	Production sectors					Factors		Capital & land		Households			Exogenous accounts				
	BG	LV	RR	NAG	COM	Fam	Hir	Cap	Land	Subs	Med	Large	G	Sav	HKSav	ROM	ROW
Production sectors																	
BG	0.02	0.12								0.21	0.06	0.06		1.00		0.03	0.04
LV										0.14	0.11	0.11				0.80	0.56
RR					0.05					0.10	0.04	.045				0.03	0.39
NAG				0.00	0.04					0	0.05	0.08				0.05	
COM	0.12			0.37						0.41	0.72	0.51					
Factors																	
Family labor	0.25	0.08	0.57	0.38													
Hired labor	0.05		0.17	0.08													
Capital	0.14	0.19	0.08	0.17													
Land	0.30	0.47	0.17														
Households																	
Subsistence						0.02	0.08	0.06	0.06								
Mediumholder						0.48	0.25	0.48	0.48								
Largeholder						0.49	0.67	0.45	0.46								
Exogenous accounts																	
Government										0.09	0.00	0.03	1				
Savings											0.00	0.24					
Human capital savings											0.00	0.04		0.01	1		
Imports	0.12	0.13			0.91						0.01						
Total	1	1	1	1	1	1	1	1	1	1	1	1	1	1	1	1	1

Table 5.5. *Real (inflation-adjusted) input–output shares,*
1988 (1982)

	BG	LV	RR	NAG	COM
BG	1.12	8.48			0.00
	(4.10)	(1.30)			(4.30)
LV					0.00
					(3.60)
RR					0.00
					(1.30)
NAG				0.29	
				(16.50)	
COM	9.36		0.00	30.12	
	(8.60)		(0.10)	(50.30)	

arrangement with a factory in Pátzcuaro). The retail sector (COM) generates little village value-added and primarily serves as an import account.

Some real changes are evident in the input–output coefficients between 1982 and 1988. Basic grains production becomes slightly more intensive in commercial inputs, as reflected by a real increase in the commerce-sector input share in village basic grains production from 8 percent in 1982 to 9.5 percent in 1988 (Table 5.5). Significantly, the increase in purchased-input intensity occurs despite a phaseout of state subsidies for fertilizer and other inputs. As livestock production expands in the 1980s, this sector's demand for locally produced feed grains increases (from 1 to 8.6 percent of the value of village livestock output, in 1982 prices). The remaining sectors, however, become less dependent on village intermediate inputs.

The composition of value-added from the five village production activities reveals the family factor intensity of village production (Table 5.3). Family labor and land combined account for 43 to 69 percent of value-added in the five production sectors. By contrast, hired labor accounts for a maximum of 15 percent of value-added (in renewable resource extraction) and only 5.4 percent of value-added in basic grains production. No hired labor is used in livestock production, the highest value-added sector in the village.

Table 5.6 reports striking changes in the functional distribution of real (factor-price-adjusted) income, as the Napízaro village economy becomes less labor-intensive.[2] The share of family-labor value-added in the total gross value of village output declines from 25 to 18 percent, while the hired-labor share falls slightly (from 2.6 to 2.3 percent). Meanwhile, the real capital share

2. Land value-added was not separated out in the 1982 SAM. The numbers presented here were obtained by recalculating 1988 value-added without a separate land account, using the same procedure as for 1982.

Table 5.6. *Factor value-added and*
import shares in gross village output,
1982 and 1988 (%)

	1982	1988
Value-added shares		
Family labor	24.84	17.99
Hired labor	2.62	2.27
Capital	20.92	36.79
Import shares	40.21	36.84

nearly doubles, from 21 to 37 percent, as Napízaro farmers substitute capital for increasingly costly hired and family labor. The share of imported intermediate inputs is relatively unchanged over the decade.

Households rely on local factor income for four-fifths of their total income (Table 5.3). Family, land, and capital value-added are concentrated almost entirely in smallholder and largeholder households; landless households receive only 2 to 6 percent of these factor incomes. They also receive a small share of wage income in the village (8 percent).

These shares stand in contrast to 1982, when landless households captured more than 10 percent of family-labor value-added, just under 10 percent of capital value-added, and most of the village's wage income. As livestock replaces traditional crop activities and as village production becomes more capital-intensive, income opportunities in the form of sharecropping and wage work appear to be shrinking for landless households. This poorest household group also lacks access to high-paying international migration work, as evidenced by its small share in U.S. migrant remittances (4 percent; see Table 5.4).

Landless households found themselves in a double squeeze in the 1980s, losing income from both village and internal migration without gaining access to migrant labor markets in the United States. In fact, internal migrant remittances accounted for nearly one-third of landless-household income in 1982 (Adelman, Taylor, and Vogel, 1988, p. 15) but only 7 percent in 1988 .

Migrant remittances, like factor incomes, are unequally distributed (Table 5.7). Only 6 percent of 1988 migrant remittances accrued to landless households, with the rest roughly equally divided between smallholder and largeholder households. The changing origin of migrant remittances reflects the combined influence of economic crisis in Mexico and an expansion and strengthening of U.S. migration networks in the 1980s. In 1982, total remittances were nearly equally divided between internal and Mexico-to-U.S. migration. By 1989, Mexico-to-U.S. migration generated nearly three times

Table 5.7. *Distribution of migrant remittances, by origin and household group*

Household group	1982			1988		
	Internal migration	Mexico–U.S. migration	Total	Internal migration	Mexico–U.S. migration	Total
Landless	41.9	32.9	36.9	11.6	4.4	6.2
Smallholder	34.2	38.6	36.6	0.1	56.1	41.7
Largeholder	23.9	28.6	26.5	88.3	39.5	52.1
Total	1.0	1.0	1.0	1.0	1.0	1.0

more income for the village than internal migration (adjusted for real exchange rate changes).

The most striking change in village income sources during the 1980s is a shift away from traditional (maize and beans) production to livestock. In 1982, livestock production was not significantly greater than maize and beans production (Figure 5.1), and livestock export earnings were dwarfed by migrant remittances. By 1988, livestock was far and away the largest village production activity (despite a fourfold increase in the output of the corn and beans sector), and livestock was the largest source of village "exports." Interviews with villagers reveal that the accumulation of livestock was widely viewed as an alternative form of savings during a decade of high inflation, economic uncertainty, and negative real interest rates, and that migrants were the principal source for this potential savings by village households. As one villager remarked, "The animals are our bank now." The expansion of livestock was supported by an abundance of hillside (humedad) lands. It was further encouraged by declining profitability of maize production on those lands, due to rising input costs and probably also to ecological decline.

Consumption and investment linkages

Although production (I-O) linkages in this village are weak, the Adelman, Taylor, and Vogel (1988) study found that consumption and investment linkages were important in shaping the impacts of income changes on the village economy. But the village produces mostly primary goods for which income elasticities of demand are inferior to those of "imported" manufactured goods. For this reason, village consumption linkages may diminish over time as real incomes increase.

Table 5.8 presents household consumption and savings propensities from the 1982 and 1988 SAMs (both in 1982 prices). Village consumption goods (sectors 1 through 4) accounted for one-fifth (for smallholder households) to

Table 5.8. *Household consumption and savings shares 1982 and 1988 (%)*

	1982				1988			
Consumption	Landless	Small	Large	Total	Landless	Small	Large	Total
BG	21.71	9.21	26.36	20.08	18.96	5.55	5.18	6.07
LV	5.39	5.79	4.22	4.96	16.17	9.24	9.00	9.48
RR	6.69	7.09	5.37	6.19	12.85	4.57	5.91	5.64
NAG	0.00	0.00	0.00	0.00	0.00	6.24	0.40	3.14
Total village production (sectors 1–4)	33.79	22.09	35.95	31.23	47.98	25.60	20.39	24.33
COM	51.18	54.16	43.21	48.33	42.97	73.40	51.64	61.47
Savings								
Physical capital	13.06	14.47	12.13	13.05	9.00	0.12	23.80	11.85
Human capital	1.96	9.27	8.71	7.39	0.00	0.76	3.97	2.25

one-third (for largeholder and landless households) of total expenditures in 1982, while imports (most of the retail sector's output) accounted for 43 to 54 percent. Nearly 60 percent of household savings were channeled into investment demand for livestock, which has a low village "import" component. (The remainder was absorbed by construction, which relied heavily on imported materials in 1982.) These shares suggest a potentially important role for consumption and investment linkages in promoting the second- and higher-round growth effects of village income changes.

Village consumption linkages from largeholder households weaken in 1988, while those for landless households increase substantially. The consumption propensity for village goods (sectors 1 through 4) decreases to just over 0.20 in the largeholder group but rises to nearly one-half in the landless group. It increases by a few percentage points in the smallholder group. Consumption propensities for staples decline in all three groups, while the propensities to consume animal products increase. These shifting consumption patterns increase the potential importance of the livestock sector in generating income linkages in the village. The importance of imported consumer goods increases for all but landless households.

The most important expenditure linkage with village production for the largeholder households in 1988 is through physical capital investment. This investment absorbs nearly one-fourth of the largeholder group's total income in 1988 (Table 5.8), and nearly all of this investment is in the form of livestock demand (Table 5.4). Thus, while landless households generate the strongest village income linkages on the consumption side, largeholder households produce the largest linkages on the investment side.

Human capital (schooling), a leakage from the village, absorbed important shares of village incomes in 1982 (2 to 9 percent), when the combined returns to schooling and internal migration were high (Taylor, 1987). Schooling investments almost disappear in 1988, however, in the wake of Mexico's economic crisis and the accompanying contraction of international migration opportunities.

Conclusions

This chapter presents an overview of changing economic linkages in a migrant-sending village over time. The Mexican village of Napízaro is characterized by strong networks of family ties with migrants in California, which make labor exports the most important source of village income from the rest of the world, next to livestock. In addition to being closely integrated with outside labor markets, the village is incorporated into regional and national consumer markets, which provide households with a variety of consumer goods. The SAM reveals strong consumption and investment linkages within the village, especially for food and livestock. As is typical for villages that are relatively well integrated with regional markets, production activities in this village are simple and specialized, centered on the household-farm.

A comparison of the 1988 SAM with the earlier (1982) SAM for the same village reveals evidence of growth in new village production activities and production technologies during a decade of economic crisis and restructuring in Mexico. It also shows a virtual collapse of internal migration but a persistence of migrant remittances from the United States. The 1988 SAM is the starting point for constructing the Mexican villagewide CGE model presented in Chapter 8.

6

Economic linkages in a small regional economy: The case of Kutus region, Kenya

BLAINE D. LEWIS AND ERIK THORBECKE

This chapter offers an empirical study of the economic linkages that exist in one small region in Kenya.[1] The region in question is defined by a market center and its hinterland. The chosen center is Kutus town, located in Kirinyaga district of Central Province in Kenya. Data collected to reveal production, consumption, income, and employment linkages in the Kutus area are used to estimate a social accounting matrix (SAM) for the region.

The chapter begins with some background information on the Kutus region; then the Kutus SAM is developed and presented; and finally the SAM is used to provide a further empirical picture of the local economy.

Kutus town and its hinterland

Kutus town is located in Kirinyaga District, Central Province.[2] The district is located between latitude 1° 1' south and 0° 0.8' south and between longitude 37° and 38° east. It spans approximately 1,437 square kilometers, about 21 percent of which is occupied by Mount Kenya Forest. The district encompasses about 10.9 percent of the area of Central Province and 0.3 percent of the area of the entire nation. The district is bordered by Nyeri and Murang'a districts of Central Province and Embu and Machakos districts of Eastern Province.

Blane D. Lewis is an Economist at the Harvard Institute for International Development, Jakarta, Indonesia, and Erik Thorbecke is H. E. Babcock Professor of Economics and Food Economics at Cornell University.
1. Portions of this chapter are adapted, in part, from Lewis and Thorbecke, 1992.
2. Much of the following descriptive information is contained in Republic of Kenya, 1984.

Kutus lies virtually in the center of the district at the junction of the district's three divisions: Mwea, Ndia, and Gichugu. Kutus has been officially "twinned" with Kerugoya to form the Kerugoya-Kutus town council. Kerugoya is located ten kilometers northwest of Kutus and is the site of the district administrative offices. This twinning was necessitated by local officials' desire to upgrade Kerugoya's urban council to a town council, and in no real economic sense are the two towns one. Other important centers in the district include Sagana, Baricho, Wanguru, and Kianyaga.

The Ministry of Planning has estimated hinterland boundaries for many small urban centers in Kenya. These estimates are based on field research in and around those towns and also on more formal methods used in some geographical research.[3] Kutus is one of those centers for which hinterland boundaries have been estimated. [4] The hinterland can be thought of, although somewhat imprecisely, as a circle having a radius of between seven and eight kilometers with Kutus as its center.

Within the boundaries of the region lie the so-called shopping centers. These places are small centers of residence, usually possessing at least a minimal amount of economic activity. They range in size from several households to just under 100 households. There are twenty such centers in the Kutus region as defined.

Physical features

The land is characterized as a midlands transition area with land elevations ranging from 4,800 feet in the north to 3,900 feet in the south. The land is rated at medium to high potential for agricultural production. Kutus region land has been designated as especially suitable for the growing of coffee and maize.

Mean annual rainfall in the region is over 1,000 millimeters in the north and drops to under 800 in the south. There are two rainy seasons: October through November and April through July.

There are numerous rivers and streams in the district which run down from Mount Kenya through the Kutus region. The Thiba and Ragati Rivers are of the most importance to the Kutus area. The Thiba runs directly through the town, and the Ragati serves as a source for the Ndia water project, which provides potable water to much of the district.

---

3. See Gaile, 1987.
4. In defining the precise economic boundaries used in the study described here, the research team took the original ministry estimates and made adjustments based on household shopping location information garnered through field-testing the research instruments.

Infrastructure

Kutus town is well served by major overland transportation systems. It is, in fact, at the hub of a network of bitumen-surfaced trunk roads linking it with important towns in the district and with major cities outside. In addition to Kerugoya, Sagana (20 kilometers to the southwest), Embu (17 kilometers to the east), and Nairobi (150 kilometers to the south) are the most important such connections. Kutus is linked to the hinterland by an adequate system of farm-to-market roads, although they are unpaved and during the rains can become virtually impassable. Numerous small feeder roads also exist in the area linking farming areas to coffee factories.

The major rail connection in the district is at Sagana. Partly because of this, Sagana is the location of major grain storage facilities. Private interdistrict grain trade is prohibited in Kenya; consequently, grain storage facilities and access to them are of great importance. Sagana also serves as a depot for farming inputs brought into the region by the coffee cooperatives.

Kutus town receives electricity via its own step-down transformer, and potable water is supplied by virtue of the Ndia water project. Kutus town has a functional telephone service, used almost exclusively by businesses. There is one call box in town for public use. Electricity has not yet come to the rural areas. Local rivers and streams serve as the water source for farm households.

The Kutus region possesses a well-developed social infrastructure. There are twenty-three primary schools and seven secondary schools located within the area. In addition, there is a major government livestock research station just south of town. There is a maternity center in Kutus town and four health clinics. A major public hospital, which offers its services free of charge, is in Kerugoya.

Population

The population of Kutus region comprises town households, farm households, and rural nonfarm households of which there are 1,294, 4,617, and 671, respectively. Rural nonfarm households live in the scattered "shopping centers" mentioned earlier.

Average size of a household is 3.69, 8.37, and 5.33 for town, farm, and rural nonfarm households, respectively. Total population in town is 4,775, on farms, 38,644, and rural nonfarms, 3,576. Total regional population is therefore 46,995; this estimate is in keeping with government expectations about catchment populations for centers the size of Kutus. The government anticipates such towns to be serving populations of not less than 40,000 people. The above population information is summarized in Table 6.1.

Given an estimate of 175 square kilometers for the area of Kutus region

Table 6.1. *Town, farm, and rural nonfarm population estimates: Kutus region, Kenya, 1987*

	Town	Farm	RNF	Region
Number of households	1,294	4,617	617	6,528
Average household size	3.69	8.37	5.33	7.20
Total population	4,775	38,644	3,576	46,995
Percent total	10.16	82.23	7.61	100.00

Table 6.2. *Selected demographic statistics: Kutus, hinterland, and region, 1987*

	Kutus	Hinterland	Region
Heads of households born in district (%)	50	97	87
Heads of households in region less than 10 yrs. (%)	63	13	24
Average age of head (yrs.)	36	52	48
Heads with no schooling (%)	14	25	23
Population that is female (%)	52	53	53
Population less than 15 yrs (%)	55	52	53

and the above regional population estimate, density in the region is estimated at 269 persons per square kilometer. Densities in the district as a whole have been estimated at 110, 146, and 202 persons per square kilometer for 1962, 1969, and 1979 respectively.

The 1979 population of Kutus town was estimated at 2,224 by the government census. Given the above 1988 estimate of 4,775, this means that the town has been growing at a rate of 8.9 percent per annum. The Ministry of Planning estimates that many small rural centers such as Kutus have been growing at around 9 to 10 percent per year over recent years. World Bank figures indicate that urban population in Kenya as a whole is growing at a rate of 6.3 percent annually.

There are no previous estimates of regional farm and rural nonfarm populations, so their rates of growth are not possible to estimate. Population in the district as a whole has been estimated to be growing at a rate of 3.65 percent in recent years.[5] National population growth has been estimated at 4.0 percent per annum.[6]

These and other demographic statistics concerning the town and hinterland population can be found in Table 6.2. Of particular note is that the town

5. Republic of Kenya, 1984.   6. Republic of Kenya, 1988.

Table 6.3. *Average coffee and foodcrops acreage for small and large farmers in Kutus region, Kenya, 1987*

	Small farmers	(%)	Large farmers	(%)	All farmers	(%)
Average coffee acreage	0.64	(17.11)	1.43	(14.61)	1.12	(15.05)
Average foodcrop acreage	3.10	(82.89)	8.36	(85.39)	6.32	(84.95)
Total	3.74	(100.00)	9.79	(100.00)	7.44	(100.00)

population appears to be more recently settled, younger, and somewhat better educated than the rural population.

Economic activity

Not surprisingly, the region's economic activity is dominated by agriculture. There are an estimated 5,162 farms in the area, including those of town households and rural nonfarm households. Farm production in the area is almost exclusively rain-fed, and the level of agricultural output in any given period is highly correlated with the amount of rainfall. In addition to the level of rainfall, output may be constrained by seasonal labor shortages.[7]

Farm sizes are small in the region. The average acreage under crop production is 7.44. Thirty-nine percent of holdings are 5 acres or under, and 84 percent are 10 acres or fewer. Although about 16 percent of farm families rent land in the region, the rented portion serves to augment land which is owned. There is no sharecropping in the area.

Coffee is the dominant cash crop in the Kutus region. Eighty-seven percent of farm households in the area grow coffee, and the average amount of land under coffee production is 1.12 acres. Sales of coffee account for slightly over 50 percent of gross farm income.

Maize and beans are the important food crops. One hundred percent of farmers in the region grow at least some maize and beans. The two are most often intercropped, and average acreage is 3.19. Other food crops of importance include tomatoes, bananas, potatoes, and sorghum. The average amount of land under all other food crops combined is 3.13 acres. Food crops in total account for just over 30 percent of gross farm revenues.

There is apparently little crop specialization vis-à-vis farm size in the Kutus region. Table 6.3 shows average acreage under coffee and food crops production for small and large farmers in the area. Here, small refers to those

7. See Avrom Bendavid-Val et al., 1988 for the details.

farmers whose total landholdings are five acres or fewer. Five acres is the cutoff point that local officials use to distinguish between small and large farmers.

As can be seen from the table, small farmers have slightly more than the average acreage of land under coffee production, as a percentage of total landholdings, and slightly less than the average amount under food crops. The converse is true for large farmers. The main point, however, is that cropping patterns are very similar among small and large farmers in the region.

The raising of livestock is also an important economic activity. Eighty-six percent of farmers in the region garner some income from livestock. Sales of livestock and dairy and other livestock products account for a little less than 20 percent of farm income. Many local officials believe that livestock production has nearly reached its limit due to the increasing scarcity of grazing land.

Nonagricultural production in the region is closely tied to agriculture. Coffee processing is the major economic activity in the nonagricultural sector. Coffee processing in the region falls exclusively within the purview of the Kirinyaga District Cooperative Union (KDCU). The KDCU is made up of a number of coffee "societies" established in the district, of which there are five in the Kutus region. Each coffee society manages several coffee factories. There were seventeen coffee factories, scattered throughout the rural areas, in operation in the region during the study period. Coffee factories are the direct link to the farmer, and it is here where the initial coffee processing takes place.

Most farmers live within a very short distance of the factory to which they belong, the average being 3.2 kilometers. Coffee spoils quickly once picked and so expeditious transport to factories is a necessity. In Kenya, if a farmer has more than ten acres under coffee, then private processing of the product may be allowed. There were no such cases in Kutus region during the time of the study.

Other important nonagricultural activities in the region include manufacturing and construction, wholesale and retail trade, transportation, and services of all kinds. Production in these sectors is carried out largely in Kutus town, although a limited amount of such activity takes place in the shopping centers. A list of the types and numbers of activities by sector in Kutus town is provided in Table 6.4.

Businesses are mostly owner-operated and small. For fixed businesses in Kutus, the average number of paid full-time employees is 1.1 and the average number of paid part-time employees is 0.4. Average capital start-up costs is KSh 16,709 Kenyan shillings (KSh). The breakdown of average numbers of employees, both full- and part-time, and start-up costs for manufacturing, retail, and service sector operations is given in Table 6.5.

Table 6.4. *Manufacture, trade, and service production activities in Kutus town*

	Number
Manufacturing activities	
Tailoring and shoemaking	20
Blacksmithing	8
Woodworking and construction	7
Tobacco processing	5
Sawmilling	3
Leather goods making	2
Slaughterhouse activities	1
Honey processing	1
Printing	1
Brakebonding	1
Electrical equipment manufacturing	1
Total manufacturing	50
Trade activities	
General goods retail	72
Hardwares retail	38
Grain wholesale and retail	33
Hotels, bars, and restaurants	31
Tobacco, miraa, and sugarcane retail	30
Shoes and clothes retail	26
Motor spares and tires retail	10
Butcheries	9
Charcoal and wood retail	9
Soda and wine wholesale and retail	4
Books and school supplies retail	4
Furniture retail	3
Newspapers retail	3
Handicrafts retail	3
Petro retail	2
Total trade	277
Service activities	
Motor and bicycle repair	18
Shoeshining	13
Health care	5
Photography	3
Laundry	3
Repair other	3
Barbering and hair styling	3
Car washing	1
Auctioneering	1
Total service	50

Table 6.5. *Capital start-up costs, full- and part-time employees in fixed manufacturing, trade and service businesses in Kutus town, 1987*

	Capital start-up (KSh)	Full-time employees (Avg. no.)	Part-time employees (Avg. no.)
Manufacturing	33,729	1.2	1.1
Wholesale and retail trade	15,083	1.2	0.3
Services	8,698	0.8	0.4
All businesses	16,709	1.1	0.4

Trade and transportation are the dominant activities in town. Of the 377 established businesses in Kutus town, 277, or 73 percent, are wholesale or retail operations. In addition, Kutus is a very active market center and possesses one of the largest open-air markets in the province. On an active market day there may be well over 1,000 individual food and nonfood traders hawking their goods in the market. Not surprisingly, given its market center character, Kutus is also somewhat of a transportation hub for the greater region. During the course of a market day there are often as many as 300 buses and *matatus* (vehicles for hire) in town, the services of which are available for purchase.

Manufacturing and service activity is small compared with the distribution sector activity. There are fifty establishments each of manufacturing and service businesses in Kutus town. Although limited in terms of numbers of establishments, manufacturing and service sectors have relatively strong backward and forward linkages with other sectors in the regional economy. The processing of rural product, the manufacture and repair of farm inputs, and the repair of transportation equipment are especially important activities in this regard.

Employment and incomes

Household employment and income in the region are marked by a diversity of sources. Consider farm households, for example. Besides farming, major sources of income include farm-based nonfarm activities, town business self-employment, and wage earnings, mostly from town-based activities. Eleven percent of farm households are engaged in farm-based, nonfarm activities, 22 percent in town business self-employment, and 41 percent in wage employment. Looked at another way, of all farm households in the area, 58.56 percent earn income from at least one other source besides farming, and 13.51 percent have earnings from at least two additional sources.

Table 6.6. *Farm, town, and rural nonfarm household income generation by type of activity, Kutus region, Kenya, 1987*

	% of farm households	% of town households	% of RNF households
Farm production	100	25	33
Farm-based nonfarm production	11	0	0
Town-based self-employment	22	67	44
Wage employment	41	38	44

All households in town are engaged in either business self-employment or wage employment or both. Besides those two activities, farm production is the only other major source of employment and income. Sixty-seven percent of town households are engaged in business self-employment, 38 percent in wage employment, and 33 percent in farm production. Almost 31 percent of town households have at least one extra source of income, besides their primary one, and almost 8 percent have two such sources.

Rural nonfarm households in the region are somewhat less diversified in terms of income sources. Thirty-three percent of such households are engaged in farming, 44 percent in town-based self-employment, and 44 percent in wage employment. Only 22 percent of rural nonfarm households have more than one source of income. Data on household income sources is given in Table 6.6.

A SAM for Kutus

Data collected in the research effort have been used to estimate a social accounting matrix (SAM) for the region. An enumeration of the various production, value-added, institutional, capital, and rest-of-the-world accounts in the Kutus SAM is shown in Table 6.7. Further information on the specification and estimation of Kutus SAM accounts follows, beginning with a brief description of the research effort that produced the data to estimate the SAM.

The bulk of the Kutus study[8] consists of surveys at the household, farm, and firms. Separate surveys were undertaken of farm households and produc-

8. The study was commissioned by the Ministry of Planning and National Development, Government of Kenya. The research itself was conducted by Settlement and Resource Systems Analysis (SARSA), a research and field support project of the United States Agency for International Development (USAID), Bureau for Science and Technology, Office of Rural and Institutional Development. Additional support was contributed by USAID/Nairobi and the Regional Housing and Urban Development Organization (RHUDO)/Nairobi. Inside the Ministry, the RMRD project of the Harvard Institute for International Development (HIID) provided technical and administrative assistance.

Table 6.7. *Sectors defined in Kutus SAM*

Production activities	Factors of production	Institutions	Combined capital	Rest of world
Coffee	Land	Households	Capital	Activities
Foodcrops	Capital services	Rural nonfarm	Harambee	Labor
Livestock	Hired labor	Small farm	Human	Others
Farm-based nonfarm	Family labor	Large farm		
Coffee processing		Low ed town		
Manufacturing		High ed town		
Retail		KDCU		
Transport		Government		
Services				
Govt services				
Housing				
Finance				

tion activities, rural nonfarm households, rural nonfarm businesses, town households, town businesses, and town open-air market activities. In particular, 111 farms and farm households, 17 rural nonfarm households, 11 rural nonfarm businesses, 52 town households, 78 town businesses, and 63 open-air market trading activities were surveyed.

The survey team consisted of six local Kenyan enumerators and two principal researchers, including a Kenyan and one of the present authors. The survey questionnaires were designed and tested by the researchers and administered on-site by the enumerators. Fieldwork was conducted between September 1987 and February 1988. Data collected pertain to the previous 12 months' activities. The analysis and reporting period of the project extended from March to August 1988.

On the household side, detailed information was collected on demographic variables, consumption expenditures, and incomes. Concerning demographics, basic data on gender, age, ethnicity, education, and mobility were enumerated. Household expenditure data on a full range of budget items were gathered, including food, clothes and footwear, consumer expendables, housing, transport, consumer durables, education, health, personal services, and social obligations. Income data on both primary and secondary sources were compiled.

For production activities, both farm and firm, exhaustive purchases and sales data were collected. Quantities and prices concerning the use of land, labor, capital, and intermediate goods were recorded. Output data included cash sales and own-use of goods produced. Virtually all production, consumption, and income data were location-specific. That is, along with prices and quantities, place of purchase, sale, and employment were also recorded.

Production activities

Production activities in the SAM include farm, rural nonfarm, town, and other activities. Further disaggregation is based on type of commodity produced. Farm sectors include coffee, food crops, livestock, and farm-based nonfarm production. Coffee, as already noted, is the most important cash crop in the area and is grown exclusively for cash sale. Food crops production consists mostly of maize and beans, although tomatoes, bananas, potatoes, sorghum, peas, and other fruits and vegetables are also included. Food crops are grown both for sale and for own consumption. The livestock sector comprises all animals kept on the farm and includes cattle, goats, chicken, pigs, rabbits, and donkeys. Manure is the major product from livestock and most is used for fertilizer on the farm. A modicum of meat, milk, cheese, eggs, and hides is also derived from the animals, both for own-use and for sale or barter. No data were available on the reproduction of livestock through breeding. Farm-based nonfarm activities consist of beer brewing, basket making, masonry, carpentry, blacksmithing, painting, tailoring, posho milling, retailing, and other similar activities. In SAM estimation, both real and imputed production are incorporated in the figures. Unsold output is evaluated at market prices, as are all transactions in the SAM.

Coffee processing is the only rural nonfarm production activity highlighted in the SAM. Coffee processing consists of the sorting, pulping, drying, bagging, and transporting of coffee cherry grown by area farmers. Processing is done by the coffee cooperatives, which also retail farm inputs, especially fertilizers, pesticides, and other chemicals to farmers. Both processing and retailing activities are included in the coffee processing account. Revenue and expenditure information on the coffee factories was derived from balance sheets and income and expenditure accounts from four coffee societies operating in the area.

Also in the rural areas, located in the shopping centers, a limited amount of manufacture, retail, and service activity is carried out by local households. Unfortunately, scanty locational information concerning sales and purchases of this rural nonfarm production was available, and as a result all such production is subsumed under the appropriate town activity accounts.

Town sectors include manufacture, retail, transportation, and services. Specific activities in the manufacturing sector have already been enumerated. Retail activities, in addition to those listed, include all open-air market activities. The transportation sector includes both matatu transportation, that is, vehicle hire, and *mokokotani* services, or internal-to-market goods transportation. The service sector includes those activities inventoried earlier and, in addition, personal services, that is, houseboys and housegirls. As before, production for own-consumption is evaluated at market prices and included in the total figures where data were available.

Government, housing, and financial services round out the production activities. Government services are made up of livestock immunization, water and electricity provision, slaughterhouse services, health services, and most important, educational services. Production figures for these activities, with the exception of the slaughterhouse, are estimated from household, farm, and firm expenditure data. Slaughterhouse production is based directly on a production survey of that activity. Most schools, although not all, in the area are government run, and revenues are derived from household tuition expenditures. In the Kutus SAM, we assume all household tuition expenditures end up as revenues to government services. Housing services is a dummy account that serves to collect housing rental payments, both real and imputed, made by households and to distribute housing rental income to various household groups. The financial services account collects repayments on loans for personal consumption. It is assumed that all such loans are garnered outside the region, since there are no formal banking services offered in the region and no data were available on informal money lending activities.

Factors

Four groups of factors are delineated in the SAM: land, capital services, hired labor, and family labor. Factor payments to land consist of both real and imputed payments for the use of farmland. Real payments for farmland rental were collected as part of the survey. Imputed payments for land were calculated at the average real rental price, KSh 356 per acre per year, determined from the survey.

Capital services value-added includes both real and imputed payments for the rental of tools and equipment and building stock. Information with which to estimate the imputed rental of building stock was only available for coffee factories and town businesses and not for farming operations. Again, figures for real rental payments were collected directly from the survey. The current value of the different types of capital stock was also collected in the survey, with the aforementioned exception of building stock for farming operations. Imputed capital service payments were calculated on the current value of capital stock using rates of .37 for tools and equipment, .25 for temporary building stock, and .04 for permanent buildings. These are the figures that are used by the coffee factories to depreciate their capital stock, and so for the sake of consistency they are also used in the imputed capital services estimations.

Hired labor consists of wage payments to full- and part-time hired workers who are not family members. These wages include both money wages and some imputed wages (transportation and lunch money, for example, which are often given to workers, are also included where appropriate). Family labor includes real and imputed wage payments to family members who work in family-owned farms and businesses. These are almost exclusively imputed payments; only very rarely does the owner-operator pay real wages to himself or herself or to family members. The imputed amount was determined as the residual of gross income from production, minus all operating and capital costs. Calculations reveal that the resultant family member wage rate is comparable to the real wage rate.

Institutions

Institutions in the SAM include households, companies, and government. Households are of five types: rural nonfarm, small farm, large farm, low-education town, and high-education town. Rural nonfarm households are those households that reside in the shopping centers. Small farm households are composed of those farm families who live and work on farms of five acres and less. Large farm households have farms of over five acres. Acreage includes farmland that is under crop production as well as that which is left fallow for the grazing of animals. Low-education town households are those households whose head has had formal education not higher than the lower primary level. High-education households are those families in which the head has had at least some upper-primary-level education.

The disaggregation of farm and town households is based on the ownership of major assets. The most important asset farm families own is land, while it is felt that the asset of most importance to town families is human capital.

It should be noted that no attempt was made to estimate transfers among individual types of households within the region. Total remittances made and received by households were collected as part of the survey. Unfortunately, information regarding the location of origin of remittance receipts and location of destination of remittance expenditures proved unreliable. Therefore, in the SAM all remittances received and sent are assumed to be acquired from and delivered to households outside the region. This is not too serious since remittances of this type account for only about 2 percent of total household income and expenditure in the region.

The companies' institution is the Kirinyaga District Cooperative Union, the head of the coffee cooperative system in the district. The KDCU collects real profits from the processing of coffee and the retailing of farm inputs carried out by its coffee factories, as well as imputed factor income from the ownership of coffee factory capital stock. The KDCU makes no current expenditures in the region apart from those that its member factories make in carrying out their coffee processing and retailing operations. Profits are assumed to be reinvested in the region.

Government includes both local and national government. The government account serves to collect taxes from the production activities only; there are no personal income taxes in the area. No information was available on direct transfers from government to households or subsidies of production activities by government.

Capital

There are three capital accounts in the Kutus SAM. In addition to the usual capital account that serves to collect household and other institutional savings and to purchase physical investment goods, there exist separate accounts for *harambee*[9] capital and human capital. Household savings data proved difficult to obtain in the surveys, and therefore savings by households in the region are estimated as the residual of total income minus total expenditures. Harambee savings consists of pecuniary contributions by households to official harambee functions held by the government to raise funds for various projects, especially education-related construction. Human capital savings consists of savings by households to educate their children. These savings go to expenditures on school fees, building fund, books, and uniforms.

These three capital savings accounts determine the amount available for investment in each respective category. Relative amounts of physical capital investment inside and outside the region are estimated from capital stock data collected in the survey, which notes sector and location of purchase. Most investment goods purchased inside the region are from the retail sector which has brought them in from outside, although some capital goods are produced and sold directly by the local manufacturing sector. Harambee investment is all assumed to go toward local construction projects, and all investment purchases are assumed to be from the local manufacturing sector. Human capital investment purchases are from local sellers of education-related items if the child goes to school inside the region and to firms outside the region if the child is sent away for schooling.

Rest of the world

The rest-of-the-world account is disaggregated into separate accounts for activities, hired labor, and other. These accounts serve to collect imports and exports of commodities, hired labor, and other factor income. All imported commodities are those goods and services that are purchased directly outside the region by households, farms, and firms. Labor imports are those wage payments to laborers who live outside the region and commute in to work. Other factor imports consist of factor payments and profits that accrue to owners of area businesses who reside outside the region and of remittance expenditures made by Kutus region residents. Exports of commodities pro-

9. *Harambee* is the Kiswahili word for "to pull together."

duced by area production activities are both goods sent directly outside the region and purchases of area goods by those who reside outside. Labor exports consist of outside wage earnings by residents. Other factor exports are residents' factor earnings from outside businesses and remittances received by area households.

In this set of accounts, "rest of the world" refers to everywhere outside the Kutus region. It would have been preferable to disaggregate the rest-of-the-world account into separate accounts for the rest of Kenya and rest of the world, as in the Adelman-Taylor-Vogel (1988) SAM described elsewhere in this book. In this way one would have been able to separate trade flows between Kutus region and the rest of Kenya from those between Kutus region and the rest of the world outside Kenya. In addition, trade flows between the rest of Kenya and the rest of the world could have been incorporated into the SAM. Unfortunately data collected on the origin and final destination of goods, labor, and other factors imported into and exported out of the region could not be distinguished between the rest of Kenya and the rest of the world outside Kenya.

Balancing the SAM

Since most of the entries in the SAM are estimated from survey data, it is expected that initially some discrepancies in the row and column sums would exist. Such imbalances may be a function of sampling errors, incorrect responses from those surveyed, enumerator errors, or coding and computer input errors. In general, initial row and column imbalances in the estimation of the Kutus SAM were quite small, within the 3 to 7 percent range.

Reconciliation of imbalances was based entirely on the judgment of the authors. Miernyk makes a strong argument for using such subjective reconciliations when the personnel involved are intimately familiar with the region under study and the research process, as is the case here.[10] When reconciliations of row and column sums needed to be made in the Kutus SAM, in general relatively more weight was put on expenditure data, and income data were adjusted when necessary.

The estimated Kutus SAM

The full Kutus SAM reflects twenty-nine different sectors. The estimated SAM is presented in Table 6.8. The SAM is used to give a further description of the Kutus area. More specifically, some descriptive information on Kutus concerning production, factors of production, institutions, capital, and rest of the world is presented.

10. Miernyk, 1979, pp. 36–38.

Production

Table 6.9 shows sectoral output and value-added. Total sectoral output in the region is KSh 640,446,000. Retail has the greatest share of total output with 39 percent, followed by coffee processing with 15 percent, and coffee with 12 percent. Total value-added in the region is KSh 253,211,000. Coffee's share of value-added is greatest at 25 percent. Retail's share of value-added, 24 percent, is considerably less than its relative share of total output. Following retail is food crops production with 15 percent of total regional value-added. The final column of the table gives value-added as a percentage of output. As can be seen, value-added is almost 40 percent of total output, at the aggregate level.

Table 6.10 shows sectoral output by intermediate and final demand. At the aggregate level, just over 28 percent of sales are to producers in the region while approximately one-third of all sales go to households in the region. It is common among developing countries, of course, to find that consumption sales exceed sales to producers. Just over 6 percent of sales go to investment, including physical capital, harambee capital, and human capital investment. Finally, approximately one-third of all output is exported out of the region.

Factors

Table 6.11 shows the distribution of sectoral value-added across factors. Value-added shares of land, capital services, hired labor, and family labor are 5.45 percent, 28.53 percent, 12.37 percent, and 53.65 percent, respectively. Production in the area is highly labor-intensive. At the aggregate level, just over 66 percent of total value-added goes to labor factors.

Institutions

Households receive just under 97 percent of all regional value-added, the remainder being divided between the government and KDCU. In addition to regional factor income, Kutus households receive income from outside sources. Table 6.12 gives household income by source as well as figures for per household income and per capita income. Average 1987 income per household in the region is KSh 42,449, which is KSh 5,979 per capita or approximately $350. High-education households are best off in terms of per capita incomes with KSh 11,044, followed by rural nonfarm households with KSh 6,432, large farm households with KSh 6,055, small farm households with KSh 4,593, and finally low-education town households with KSh 4,506.

Table 6.13 shows how household income is spent. Overall, households

Table 6.8. Kutus region SAM, 1987 (000 KSh)

	Cof 1	Fcrp 2	Lvstk 3	Fbnf 4	C Proc 5	Man 6	Retail 7	Trans 8	Srvc 9	Hsing 10	Govt S 11	Finan 12	Land 13	Cap S 14	H Lab 15
Activities															
Coffee	0	0	0	0	80,022	0	0	0	0	0	0	0	0	0	0
Food crops	0	1,044	0	0	0	0	15,148	0	0	0	0	0	0	0	0
Livestock	3,314	1,607	0	0	0	0	4,267	0	0	0	0	0	0	0	0
FBNF	0	0	0	0	0	0	53	0	0	0	0	0	0	0	0
Coffee processing	3,953	1,822	0	0	0	0	0	0	0	0	0	0	0	0	0
Manufacture	0	0	0	3,196	0	304	0	0	0	0	30	0	0	0	0
Retail	4,353	3,230	1,642	278	0	3,197	17,606	17,903	1,526	0	30	0	0	0	0
Transportation	320	343	0	216	0	586	6,585	0	183	0	0	0	0	0	0
Services	906	463	0	0	0	132	3,436	735	180	0	0	0	0	0	0
Housing services	0	0	0	0	0	0	0	0	0	0	0	0	0	0	0
Government services	0	0	429	117	0	52	298	0	288	0	24	0	0	0	0
Financial services	0	0	0	0	0	0	0	0	0	0	0	0	0	0	0
Factors															
Land	1,903	10,730	1,173	0	0	0	0	0	0	0	0	0	0	0	0
Capital services	12,485	6,317	15,326	1,412	4,470	1,858	12,578	5,590	1,288	10,916	7	0	0	0	0
Hired labor	1,687	1,049	0	933	979	798	3,550	1,296	1,437	0	19,588	0	0	0	0
Family labor	46,885	18,951	5,099	5,493	0	2,715	45,468	6,193	5,039	0	0	0	0	0	0
Institutions															
Rural Nonfarm Hhs	0	0	0	0	0	0	0	0	0	0	0	0	173	3,442	5,816
Small farm hhs	0	0	0	0	0	0	0	0	0	0	0	0	2,614	14,005	3,743
Large farm hhs	0	0	0	0	0	0	0	0	0	0	0	0	10,333	40,778	18,232
Low ed town hhs	0	0	0	0	0	0	0	0	0	0	0	0	113	1,591	1,038
High ed town hhs	0	0	0	0	0	0	0	0	0	0	0	0	573	7,311	2,488
Companies	0	0	0	0	0	0	0	0	0	0	0	0	0	5,112	0
Harambee capital account	0	0	0	0	0	0	0	0	0	0	0	0	0	0	0
Human capital account	0	0	0	0	0	0	0	0	0	0	0	0	0	0	0
Government	0	0	0	91	1,107	151	914	1,123	70	0	13	0	0	7	0
Capital account	0	0	0	0	0	0	0	0	0	0	0	0	0	0	0
Rest of World															
Rest of Kenya activities	1,898	1,155	1,110	304	10,475	3,470	124,025	4,857	1,877	0	0	0	0	0	0
Rest of Kenya labor	2,319	1,484	0	0	1,233	188	807	2,573	1,234	0	0	0	0	0	0
Rest of Kenya other	0	0	0	0	0	0	15,105	15,025	181	5,512	0	9,115	0	0	0
Totals	80,022	48,195	24,779	12,040	98,287	13,450	249,839	55,294	13,304	16,428	19,692	9,115	13,806	72,246	31,316

	F Lab 16	Rnf 17	Fhh1 18	Fhh2 19	Thh1 20	Thh2 21	Comp 22	Hmbee 23	Humanc 24	Govt 25	Cap 26	RoK Act 27	RoK HL 28	RoK Ot 29	Totals 30
Coffee	0	0	0	0	0	0	00	0	0	0	0	0	0	0	80,022
Food crops	0	1,749	8,238	18,860	406	292	0	0	0	0	0	2,458	0	0	48,195
Livestock	0	147	3,424	9,723	0	92	0	0	0	0	0	2,205	0	0	24,779
FBNF	0	0	2,854	6,794	0	0	0	0	00	0	1,858	482	0	0	12,040
Coffee processing	0	0	0	0	0	0	0	0	0	0	0	92,511	0	0	98,287
Manufacture	0	844	1,002	3,411	203	674	0	4,120	2,811	0	0	52	0	0	13,450
Retail	0	9,260	19,516	64,795	5,683	15,014	0	0	3,267	0	17,920	61,701	0	0	249,839
Transportation	0	1,351	2,780	4,163	359	1,541	0	0	0	0	0	36,806	0	0	55,294
Services	0	400	1,022	2,146	67	1,259	0	0	0	0	0	2,318	0	0	13,304
Housing services	0	3,170	3,250	6,596	1,246	2,166	0	0	0	0	0	0	0	0	16,428
Government services	0	58	0	0	0	64	0	0	8,950	0	0	9,435	0	0	19,692
Financial services	0	0	2,376	6,157	0	583	0	0	0	0	0	0	0	0	9,115
Land	0	0	0	0	0	0	0	0	0	0	0	0	0	0	13,806
Capital services	0	0	0	0	0	0	0	0	0	0	0	0	0	0	72,246
Hired labor	0	0	0	0	0	0	0	0	0	0	0	0	0	0	31,316
Family labor	0	0	0	0	0	0	0	0	0	0	0	0	0	0	135,843
Rural Nonfarm Hhs	10,760	0	0	0	0	0	0	0	0	0	0	0	0	0	23,005
Small farm hhs	24,412	0	0	0	0	0	0	0	0	0	0	0	2,684	130	54,479
Large farm hhs	78,584	0	0	0	0	0	0	0	0	0	0	0	7,979	1,726	162,155
Low ed town hhs	5,105	0	0	0	0	0	0	0	0	0	0	0	12,797	1,431	8,977
High ed town hhs	16,982	0	0	0	0	0	0	0	0	0	0	0	0	1,130	30,782
Companies	0	0	0	0	0	0	0	0	0	0	0	0	289	3,139	5,112
Harambee capital account	0	13	506	3,436	13	151	0	0	0	0	0	0	0	0	4,120
Human capital account	0	2,014	4,047	11,419	155	622	0	0	0	0	0	0	0	0	18,257
Government	0	0	0	0	0	0	0	0	0	3,464	0	0	0	0	3,464
Capital account	0	3,015	4,046	18,725	416	5,372	5,112	0	0	0	0	0	0	0	40,149
Rest of Kenya activities	0	825	1,301	4,480	306	2,224	0	0	3,229	0	20,371	0	0	0	181,905
Rest of Kenya labor	0	0	0	0	0	0	0	0	0	0	0	0	0	0	9,851
Rest of Kenya other	0	158	118	1,451	123	731	0	0	0	0	0	0	0	0	47,518
Totals	135,843	23,005	54,479	162,155	8,977	30,782	5,112	4,120	18,257	3,464	40,149	207,969	23,749	7,556	1,483,429

Table 6.9. *Sectoral output and value-added, Kutus region, Kenya, 1987 (000 KSh)*

Sector	Total Output	%	Regional Value-added	%	Value-added/total output (%)
Coffee	80,023	12.49	62,960	24.86	78.68
Foodcrops	48,195	7.53	37,047	14.63	76.87
Livestock	24,779	3.87	21,598	8.53	87.16
Farm-based nonfarm	12,040	1.88	7,837	3.10	65.09
Coffee processing	98,287	15.35	5,449	2.15	5.54
Manufacturing	13,450	2.10	5,371	2.12	39.93
Retail	249,839	39.01	61,596	24.33	24.65
Transport	55,294	8.63	13,078	5.16	23.65
Services	13,304	2.08	7,763	3.07	58.35
Housing	16,428	2.57	10,916	4.31	66.45
Finance	9,115	1.42	0	0.00	0.00
Government service	19,692	3.07	19,596	7.74	99.51
Totals	640,446	100.00	253,211	100.00	39.54

Table 6.10. *Sectoral output by destination, Kutus region, Kenya, 1987 (000 KSh)*

Sector	Intermediate sales	Household sales	Investment sales	Export sales	Total sales
Coffee	80,022	0	0	0	80,022
Foodcrops	16,192	29,545	0	2,458	48,195
Livestock	9,188	13,385	0	2,205	24,778
Farm-based nonfarm	53	9,648	1,858	482	12,041
Coffee processing	5,775	0	0	92,511	98,286
Manufacturing	334	6,133	6,931	52	13,450
Retail	52,683	114,268	21,186	61,701	249,838
Transport	8,295	10,195	0	36,806	55,296
Services	6,092	4,894	0	2,318	13,304
Government services	1,184	122	8,950	9,435	19,691
Housing	0	16,428	0	0	16,428
Finance	0	9,115	0	0	9,115
Totals	179,818	213,733	38,925	207,968	640,444
%	28.08	33.37	6.08	32.47	100.00

Table 6.11. *Disaggregation of sectoral value-added, Kutus region, Kenya, 1987 (000 KSh)*

Sectors	Capital	Land	Labor Hired services	Family	Total
Coffee	1,903	12,485	1,687	46,885	62,960
Foodcrops	10,730	6,317	1,049	18,951	37,047
Livestock	1,173	15,326	0	5,099	21,598
Farm-based nonfarm	0	1,412	933	5,493	7,838
Coffee processing	0	4,470	979	0	5,449
Manufacturing	0	1,858	798	2,715	5,371
Retail	0	12,578	3,550	45,468	61,596
Transport	0	5,590	1,296	6,193	13,079
Services	0	1,288	1,437	5,039	7,764
Government services	0	7	19,588	0	19,595
Housing	0	10,916	0	0	10,916
Finance	0	0	0	0	0
Totals	13,806	72,247	31,317	135,843	253,213
%	5.45	28.53	12.37	53.65	100.00

use about 81 percent of their income on expenditure. Regional households, therefore, save approximately 19 percent, including about 7 percent for human capital savings and 1 percent for harambee savings. Table 6.14 presents the average and marginal expenditure propensities for Kutus region households.[11] These parameter estimates are useful in transforming the SAM from a simple set of accounts into a more realistic model of the regional economy.

Capital

Total gross investment in the region is KSh 62,526,000, including physical capital investment, harambee capital investment, and human capital investment. A breakdown of total savings by institution is given in Table 6.15. Farm households contribute the most to local savings, followed by town households, KDCU, rural nonfarm households, and government respectively.

Rest of the world

A summary of exports from and imports to the region appears in Table 6.16. As noted, the rest of the world includes both the rest of Kenya and the rest of

11. The marginal expenditure propensities have been estimated using the extended linear expenditure system (ELES) of Lluch, Powell, and Williams, 1977.

Table 6.12. *Household incomes, Kutus region, Kenya 1987 (000 KSh)*

Income source	Rural nonfarm	(%)	Small farm	(%)	Large farm	(%)	Low education	(%)	High education	(%)	Total	(%)
Land	173	(0.75)	2,614	(4.80)	10,333	(6.37	113	(1.26)	573	(1.86)	13,806	(4.94)
Capital services	3,442	(14.96)	14,005	(25.71)	40,778	(25.15)	1,591	(17.72)	7,311	(23.75)	67,127	(24.03)
Hired labor	5,816	(25.28)	3,743	(6.87)	18,232	(11.24)	1,038	(11.56)	2,488	(8.08)	31,317	(11.21)
Family labor	10,760	(46.77)	24,412	(44.81)	78,584	(48.46)	5,105	(56.87)	16,982	(55.17)	135,843	(48.62)
RoK[a] hired labor	2,684	(11.67)	7,979	(14.65)	12,797	(7.89)	0	(0.00)	289	(0.94)	23,749	(8.50)
RoK other	130	(0.57)	1,726	(3.17)	1,431	(0.88)	1,130	(12.59)	3,139	(10.20)	7,556	(2.70)
Total	23,005	(100.00)	54,479	(100.00)	162,155	(100.00)	8,977	(100.00)	30,782	(100.00)	279,398	(100.00)
Per household	34.29		30.45		57.34		21.22		35.34			
Per capita	6.43		4.59		6.06		4.51		11.04			
Avg per household	42.45											
Avg per capita	5.95											

[a]RoK = rest of Kenya.

Table 6.13. *Household expenditure and savings, Kutus region, Kenya, 1987 (000 KSh)*

	Rural nonfarm	(%)	Small farm	(%)	Large farm	(%)	Low ed town	(%)	High ed town	(%)	Total	(%)
Expenditure	17,963	(78.08)	45,880	(84.22)	128,575	(79.29)	8,392	(93.49)	24,639	(80.04)	225,449	(80.69)
Savings	3,015	(13.11)	4,046	(7.43)	18,725	(11.55)	416	(4.63)	5,372	(17.45)	31,574	(11.30)
Harambee capital	13	(0.06)	506	(0.93)	3,436	(2.12)	13	(0.14)	151	(0.49)	4,119	(1.47)
Human capital	2,014	(8.75)	4,047	(7.43)	11,419	(7.04)	155	(1.73)	622	(2.02)	18,257	(6.53)
Total	23,005	(100.00)	54,479	(100.00)	162,155	(100.00)	8,976	(100.00)	30,784	(100.00)	279,399	(100.00)

Table 6.14. *Average (aep) and marginal expenditure propensities (mep), Kutus region households, 1987*

Activities	Rural nonfarm households aep	mep	Small farm households aep	mep	Large farm households aep	mep	Low ed town households aep	mep	High ed town households aep	mep
Food crops	0.08	0.02	0.15	0.07	0.12	0.04	0.05	0.02	0.01	0.01
Livestock	0.01	0.01	0.06	0.06	0.06	0.05	0.00	0.00	0.00	0.01
Farm-based nonfarm	0.00	0.00	0.05	0.06	0.04	0.02	0.00	0.00	0.00	0.00
Manufacturing	0.04	0.01	0.02	0.00	0.02	0.02	0.02	0.02	0.02	0.03
Retail	0.40	0.40	0.36	0.43	0.40	0.43	0.63	0.64	0.49	0.37
Transport	0.06	0.10	0.05	0.03	0.03	0.02	0.04	0.03	0.05	0.07
Services	0.02	0.04	0.02	0.03	0.01	0.02	0.01	0.00	0.04	0.06
Housing services	0.14	0.14	0.06	0.08	0.04	0.06	0.14	0.16	0.07	0.07
Financial services	0.00	0.00	0.04	0.06	0.04	0.04	0.00	0.00	0.02	0.03
Government services	0.00	0.01	0.00	0.00	0.00	0.00	0.00	0.00	0.00	0.01
Harambee capital	0.00	0.00	0.01	0.01	0.02	0.03	0.00	0.00	0.00	0.00
Human capital	0.09	0.08	0.07	0.08	0.07	0.08	0.02	0.02	0.02	0.03
Capital	0.13	0.15	0.07	0.08	0.12	0.15	0.05	0.07	0.17	0.22
RoW[a] activities	0.04	0.04	0.02	0.02	0.03	0.03	0.03	0.02	0.07	0.09
RoW other	0.01	0.01	0.00	0.00	0.01	0.01	0.01	0.01	0.02	0.01
Total	1.00	1.00	1.00	1.00	1.00	1.00	1.00	1.00	1.00	1.00

Note: These are the marginals estimated a la ELES (Lluck, Powell, Williams, 1977) and then "adjusted."
[a] RoW = rest of world.

Table 6.15. *Regional savings by institution, Kutus region, 1987 (000 KSh)*

	Capital	(%)	Harambee capital	(%)	Human capital	(%)	Total	(%)
Rural nonfarm	3,015	(7.51)	13	(0.32)	2,014	(11.03)	5,042	(8.06)
Small farm	4,046	(10.08)	506	(12.28)	4,047	(22.17)	8,599	(13.75)
Large farm	18,725	(46.64)	3,436	(83.42)	11,419	(62.55)	33,580	(53.71)
Low-ed town	416	(1.04)	13	(0.32)	155	(0.85)	584	(0.93)
High-ed town	5,372	(13.38)	151	(3.67)	622	(3.41)	6,145	(9.83)
KDCU	5,112	(12.73)	0	(0.00)	0	(0.00)	5,112	(8.18)
Government	3,464	(8.63)	0	(0.00)	0	(0.00)	3,464	(5.54)
Total	40,150	(100.00)	4,119	(100.00)	18,257	(100.00)	62,526	(100.00)

Table 6.16. *Regional imports and exports, Kutus region, Kenya, 1987 (000 KSh)*

	Exports	Imports	Net
Commodities	207,969	181,905	26,064
Labor	23,749	9,851	13,898
Other factors	7,556	47,518	(39,962)
Total	239,274	239,274	0

the world outside Kenya. As can be seen from Table 6.16, the region is a net exporter of goods and labor and a net importer of other factor income. The bulk of other factor imports consists of local business profits and capital factor payments that leave the region and accrue to outside interests. These facts regarding regional trade in labor and capital factor income help to explain why one local official reported that "Kutus is a great place to do business but not so good a spot to find work."

Conclusions

This chapter has provided an empirical description of the Kutus regional economy. As demonstrated, the local economy is dominated by agricultural activities, especially the production of coffee, maize, and beans, and livestock products. As noted, however, the production of these major primary sector products is potentially constrained on the supply side by limited water resources, seasonal shortages of labor, and the increasingly restricted availability of land. The town economy is closely tied to the agricultural sector, processing and trading agricultural output and supplying intermediate goods to primary-sector producers. In addition, town activities play an important role in producing and distributing consumer goods to the local population. Town activities are also nontrivial producers of export goods and services. In general, town production is seen to be operating under conditions of excess capacity.

Households in the area are marked by a significant diversity in terms of income sources. In total, approximately half of local households have at least two major sources of income. Moreover, rural–urban income linkages are especially important for household welfare. Almost two-thirds of farm households are engaged in some type of town business activity and around one-third of town-based households are involved in farming. Households, in the aggregate, are net exporters of labor.

In sum, the economy is characterized by a complex set of production, value-added, and consumption linkages. As demonstrated, the SAM is an ideal tool for the study of such economic diversity at the local level.

7

Household nutrition and economic linkages: A village social accounting matrix for West Java, Indonesia

KATHERINE RALSTON

Improving nutrition is a high development priority in Indonesia. The Indonesian government does not directly subsidize consumer prices for this purpose, but it invests considerable effort in monitoring nutritional status and uses nutritional improvement as one criterion for evaluating the impact of economic policies.[1] Any accurate and useful evaluation depends on a clear understanding of which households are vulnerable to malnutrition, the source of household incomes, and likely avenues for household income growth.

The study presented here uses a social accounting matrix (SAM) framework to analyze the relationship between household nutrition and economic linkages in a West Javan village. Households in this village are grouped according to dietary energy consumption to identify sources of income for households of different nutritional status as a starting point for exploring the nutritional implications of village income change.

Survey data to estimate the SAM were collected by the author. The survey focused on household economic activities and on nutritional status at both household and individual levels from April 1988 to March 1989. The sample included 49 households (about 5 percent of the village population). Interviews were conducted with all working-age members of the household. The survey was carried out under a Cornell Food and Nutrition Policy Program technical

Katherine Ralston is an economic analyst at the Economic Research Service, U.S. Department of Agriculture.

1. The central and local governments also operate a number of consumer-oriented and nutritional programs such as rice price stabilization, infant-weighing, promotion of home gardens and oral rehydration, Vitamin A clinical testing, supplementation and fortification, and disaster relief, including food distribution and short-term employment.

assistance contract with the Indonesian Ministry of Health, funded by a World Bank loan.

The village setting, survey, and household classifications

Cibageur[2] is located in the district of Sukabumi, West Java province. It is about one hour by public transport from the district capital and about three hours from the national capital city of Jakarta. Its geography places it between the productive wetlands and high population densities that run through the middle of Java and the more sparsely populated dry highlands of the southern coast. The village contains both kinds of land, but is on predominantly dry, hilly land.

The lowland section of the village is close to the local market center, which lies at the intersection of two paved roads. The upland area is difficult to reach, involving a one- to two-hour hike up a narrow path. Transportation within the village is slow, but for an economy with a very low wage rate this is not a major impediment to economic transactions. In fact, a surprising range of commodities is transported into and out of the village on foot, including food, building materials, bicycles, and furniture. Motor transportation to larger population centers is available at the crossroads. The crossroads market center serves two other villages in addition to Cibageur. The three villages were part of a larger village which was subdivided administratively in 1982. Thus, the administrative boundaries of Cibageur are not economic boundaries; households near the village borders trade extensively with neighboring villages.

The village received a large number of immigrants following the 1965 anti-communist purge, when a tea plantation in the village was confiscated from its owner and partially opened for settlement. The remainder of the tea plantation's land was taken over by a cacao plantation, which rents out unplanted land to village residents and employs labor from the village.

Economically, the village relies mainly on agriculture, including both wet rice and dry-land crops such as groundnuts and cassava. Fruits, vegetables, and timber make up important supplementary production. Many households also engage in nonfarm enterprises such as small retail shops or door-to-door sales, prepared foods, and production of furniture, brooms, and woven bamboo walls. A small number of households operate more capital-intensive enterprises such as mechanical rice milling and minibus transportation. Other employment can be found working on family farms, on the plantation adjacent to the village, in local factories, or carrying harvested crops, construction

2. The name of this village has been changed for protection of privacy.

materials, and other goods into and out of the village. A small fraction of village households have more formal employment in the civil service, and some receive pensions from military service.

Cibageur as a representative village

Although every village has its unique characteristics, Cibageur reflects economic patterns found in much of rural Java, and to a lesser extent, other parts of Indonesia.

Studies of the rice-producing lowlands suggest a steady movement from agricultural labor into off-farm work, including commuting or migration to the cities (Hart, 1986). Hart notes the difficulty of determining from national-level data whether this movement reflects the "push" of lower employment opportunities in agriculture or the "pull" of higher wages in nonagricultural jobs.

Studies by Hayami and Kikuchi (1982) and by Collier, Wirodi, Makali, and Santoso (1988), based on repeated surveys of several villages in lowland Java, provide a village-level view of trends in labor demand. Both studies note that labor demand in rice production not only has failed to keep up with population growth, but has actually decreased due to technological changes that include the use of hand tractors for land preparation and the sickle in harvesting. Labor institutions have shifted away from an open-harvest system, in which anybody could assist in the harvest in return for a share, to various closed-harvest arrangements, in which only invited workers are allowed to participate. Hayami's and Kikuchi's study suggests a decline in the share of harvest received by harvesters during 1968–78, while Collier, Wirodi, Mikali, and Santoso's study shows that the real agricultural wage (in kilograms of rice per hour) increased from 1980 to 1987. Given increases in yields, Hayami suggests that actual payments to labor may have increased during the earlier period as well. The rise in wages could be taken as evidence that increases in nonagricultural labor demand have outpaced the release of labor from agriculture. However, the existence of unemployment and underemployment suggests that the slack has not been absorbed, and that labor market imperfections maintain wages above the market clearing level: Not everyone who gets pushed out of agriculture succeeds in finding equally or more attractive off-farm work.

Agricultural labor opportunities are limited by geography as well as by technology. The predominance of dry hilly land makes rice production a relatively small part of village agriculture. However, Cibageur is close enough to the urban economy to send surplus labor to the rapidly growing town of Sukabumi and to the capital city of Jakarta. The real wage, measured in 1989, is comparable with the level found in many villages by Collier et al. (1988). Off-farm employment includes activities with high returns, such as shopkeeping and light manufacturing, as well as activities with low returns, including some food processing operations. High-return activities are evidence of links to the urban economy, whereas participation in low-return activities suggests that slack labor is not completely absorbed by off-farm work.

Cibageur, because of its intermediate proximity to urban markets, is typical of the environment of a large fraction of the population of Java. The development of Cibageur's links to the urban economy probably lags behind that of villages closer to large cities; village–town links will spread to an increasing number of villages as the urban-oriented economy expands. Cibageur's upland geography and its relatively late entry into the urban economic sphere make this village representative of parts of Indonesia outside of Java, as well.

The village survey

The data that serve as a basis for this research are from a survey conducted during January through March 1989, in conjunction with a study of economic determinants of intrahousehold food distribution. The survey sample consists of forty-nine households drawn from a stratified random sample, designed to proportionally represent three subvillages.

The survey included a current recall component, in which households were interviewed every fifteen days for three months. A second component, spread over several interviews, was a retrospective survey to obtain enough information to estimate economic flows for a full year. The detailed bimonthly recall questionnaire recorded expenditures on food and other household goods, changes in major food stocks, time allocation of all household members, earnings from employment and household enterprises, and payments for all inputs and taxes. The retrospective survey covered the nine-month period preceding the start of the survey. The year represented in the SAM begins in April 1988, following the rice harvest, and includes special purchases for the Moslem holiday of Idul Fitri. The end of the rice harvest and Idul Fitri purchases serve as useful boundary points for the village's annual economic cycle, and they were easily remembered by households when they reconstructed their economic histories.

The nine-month history included information on inputs, production, and labor use for all agricultural plots, changes in livestock and crop inventory, debt, and asset ownership. Households were asked to describe major changes in earnings from wages and nonfarm enterprises for the previous nine months – for example, which months they had worked at which job, whether enterprises had been started or stopped, and whether prices of intermediate inputs for enterprises had changed. For household expenditures, one form was used to enumerate purchases of clothing, other durables, and construction; a separate form was used to record major changes in spending patterns for food and frequent nonfood purchases such as lantern fuel and soap. Household expenditures were totaled by multiplying three-month expenditures on frequently purchased items by four and adding durable purchases recorded in the three-month current survey as well as in the nine-month retrospective survey.

The study was organized around the need to develop a trusting and informative relationship between enumerator and household. This was important not only to obtain the detailed information just described, but also to gather qualitative data that were useful for constructing and interpreting the SAM and for understanding intrahousehold resource distribution. Thus, each enumerator was assigned only seven households. The budget allowed for seven enumerators, resulting in a total of forty-nine households. The enumerators were female graduates of the Bogor Agricultural Institute who spoke Sundanese, the local language. The option of hiring local residents was considered but not chosen, since it appeared that residents might be more willing to discuss their household finances with an outsider than with a neighbor.

The survey was pretested in two other villages before the interviews at Cibageur began. Participants in the survey and all pretests gave informed consent, and confidentiality was carefully protected. Sampled households were encouraged to feel free not to participate, and one sampled household did decline. Participants received a gift each month during the survey worth about 5,000 Rp or rupiah (U.S. $3.00), equal to four or five times the daily agricultural wage.

Three sampled households were identified by village officials as members of "forbidden organizations" (Communists and fundamentalist Moslems), who were not allowed to be interviewed. These households were replaced from a list of alternates that had been prepared as part of the random sample. This could have introduced some bias, because these households may have been more likely to be poor due to social stigma.

The enumerators spent several days getting to know the households before formal interviews began. As the survey progressed, there were also opportunities to correct errors in responses. This was especially important where landholdings were concerned; over time, as participants became more willing to give complete information, inconsistencies emerged. Having become very familiar with the households, the enumerators believed that the recorded responses were of good quality in most areas. This was less true for data on savings, for data needed to estimate imports and exports (such as location of purchases), and for destination of sales.

Household classifications based on a nutritional indicator

Since this study focused on households and their links to the village economy, it is important to clarify how household boundaries were drawn. A household was defined as a group of individuals eating largely from the same budget. In cases where two generations lived under the same roof but considered themselves to be eating from separate budgets, the two "budget groups" were treated as separate households. The village census from which the sample was drawn generally listed such groups separately as well.

In order to focus the analysis on nutritional implications of policy scenarios, a nutritional indicator was used to classify households. While a nutritional indicator is endogenous and thus will change as a result of simulated policies, the baseline measure can be used to identify characteristics of households at risk of malnutrition and to estimate the effect of policies on these households.

The nutritional indicator used in this case was the level of dietary energy consumption. An indicator based on dietary energy consumption will identify households at risk of malnutrition due to insufficient consumption of a fairly balanced diet.[3] This indicator reflects household food consumption, thus masking individual malnutrition due to inequalities in intrahousehold distribution. In a separate study of this village (Ralston, 1992), intrahousehold calorie distribution is examined explicitly. Calorie consumption was lower, ceteris paribus, for female children under eighteen than for male children. Calorie consumption increased with both male and female labor contributions to the household, and this increase was greater for female children. Thus, rural development policies may affect intrahousehold calorie allocations as well as household calorie consumption. Policies that directly or indirectly increase labor contributions of female children can increase female calorie consumption.

The nutritional indicator was derived as the average daily energy consumption per adult equivalent unit. Total energy consumption for the household was estimated from the energy content of foods purchased, drawn from household stocks, grown on the household's own farm, or received as gifts over a three-month period. This average was divided by the number of adult equivalent units to adjust for household size and composition. The use of adult equivalent units rather than simple household size accounts for the fact that households with different age-sex compositions have different energy requirements, even before differences in activity levels are considered. The number of adult equivalent units per household is calculated based on the energy requirement scale from the World Health Organization (WHO) (1973).

---

3. While nutrients such as protein and vitamins are also important, evidence suggests that by increasing food consumption to a level that meets energy requirements, other nutrient requirements will also be met for most of the population (Latham, 1984). This is not true in cases where the diet is imbalanced nutritionally, leading to nutrient deficiency diseases such as blindness caused by vitamin A deficiency, goiter and cretinism from iodine deficiency, and iron-deficiency anemia. In these cases, nutrition education, fortification, and targeted dietary supplements are likely to be more effective than income-related policies.

Table 7.1. *Daily energy intake by household group*

	% of sample	Average (KCal/day)	Range (KCal/day)
Low-calorie households	29	1,823	1,278–2,211
Medium-calorie households	35	2,478	2,282–2,649
High-calorie households	36	3,379	2,717–4,776

This scale compares energy requirements for different age-sex categories based on a moderate activity level.[4]

The division of households into groups was based on the household composition-adjusted energy consumption. Economic characteristics of the groups are closely linked to group nutritional characteristics. As the subsequent comparison of household groups will suggest, differences in energy consumption are probably partly accounted for by differences in activity levels, but the lowest energy consumption group is most likely vulnerable to undernutrition.

The lower cutoff for the highest group is 2,680 kilocalories. This figure is derived as the calorie requirement for a fifty-five-kilogram reference male (aged eighteen to thirty years) engaged in subsistence agriculture activities, according to the WHO methodology. The basal metabolic rate (BMR, the minimum energy expenditure at rest) for the reference male is 1,520 kilocalorie, and subsistence agriculture activities are assumed to lead to an average energy expenditure of 1.76 times the BMR, or 2,675 kilocalorie (see WHO, 1985, pp. 71–78). The upper cutoff for the lower group is 85 percent of this level, or 2,274 kilocalorie. The use of these two cutoff points results in three household groups with relevant nutritional distinctions as well as a sufficient sample size in each group to obtain reasonably comfortable estimates. Table 7.1 reports the average energy levels and ranges for the three groups.

Characteristics of household groups

A comparison of the three household groups reveals large income differences. These income disparities can be traced to differences in access to land, physical capital, government jobs, migrant remittances, and pensions. Fur-

---

4. Note that while the index is adjusted for household composition, it is not adjusted for activity levels. Direct adjustments of this type were beyond the scope of this study. While data are available for hours allocated to different activities, they cannot be accurately translated into energy expenditure without appropriate calorimetric equipment. As a result, a high value for the index could represent adequate energy consumption for a high activity level, while a low value could represent adequacy for a low activity level.

thermore, the relationship between calorie consumption and income is not monotonic. This may be due to differences in energy requirements among the three groups.

Table 7.2 shows that the low-calorie households are the poorest (524,000 Rp per year), the medium-calorie households are the richest (1,536,000 Rp per year), and the high-calorie households are at an intermediate income level (1,021,000 Rp per year). Income sources (Tables 7.2 and 7.3) and landholdings (Tables 7.4, 7.5, and 7.6) reveal distinct patterns in income sources for the three groups.

Medium-calorie households benefit from higher asset levels, access to government jobs, and pensions. On average, they own both more wet rice land and more dry land than the other two groups, although average ownership is not large even for this group (0.15 hectare for rice land, 0.38 for dry land). These asset levels are reflected in high returns to own-enterprise labor, which generates 53 percent of this group's income. The medium-calorie group also is the only one with income from physical capital, such as minivan rental and fuel-powered rice milling. Earnings from government jobs and pensions contribute substantially to the medium-calorie group's income.

High-calorie households do almost as well in terms of income from farming, and they receive substantial migrant remittances, although they earn relatively little income from hired labor. They control more wet rice land (0.29 hectare) and almost as much dry land (0.51 hectare) as the medium-calorie households (with 0.18 hectare for rice land and 0.56 for dry land). Total returns to own-enterprise labor are almost as high as for the medium-calorie group, at 607,000 Rp. Migrant remittances by themselves (232,000 Rp) are nearly equal to the sum of pensions and physical capital returns for the medium-calorie group. Hired labor contributes only 12 percent to these households' income on average. Government and high-wage private-sector jobs provide the bulk of such earnings.

Low-calorie households have very small landholdings and must rely largely on hired-labor income, although they have some small enterprises. They control an average of only 0.07 hectare of rice land and 0.33 of dry land, and crop activities generate an average of only 62,000 Rp per year. This group earns some income (54,200 Rp) from low-capital enterprises such as palm-sugar production and snack preparation. But the bulk of income for this group comes from wage work in agriculture (29,500 Rp), low-wage jobs such as construction (121,000 Rp), and high-wage jobs such as minivan operation (128,300 Rp). Agriculture and low-wage jobs pay about 1,000 to 2,000 Rp per day, whereas high-wage jobs pay about 3,000 to 5,000 Rp per day.

Age and geographic comparisons between the low-, medium-, and high-calorie groups can be seen in Table 7.7. Some of these differences may be associated with differences in income and wealth levels. In particular, low-calorie households are young, suggesting the possibility that some may have

Table 7.2. *Average total household income (share) by source,*
1000 Rp (%)

	Low-calorie household	Medium-calorie household	High-calorie household
Land	2.4 (0.5)	2.8 (0.2)	4 (0.4)
Physical capital	0 (0)	92.2 (6)	0 (0)
Animal capital	12.1 (2.3)	3.7 (0.2)	53.5 (5.2)
Hired labor	317.7 (60.7)	370.4 (24.1)	123.4 (12.1)
Own-enterprise labor	166.5 (31.8)	816.3 (53.2)	608 (59.6)
Migrant remittances	25 (4.8)	95 (6.2)	231.9 (22.7)
Pensions	0 (0)	155.3 (10.1)	0 (0)
Total income	523.7 (100)	1535.6 (100)	1020.8 (100)

Table 7.3. *Sources of labor income by household group, 1000 Rp (%)*

	Low-calorie household	Medium-calorie household	High-calorie household
Own enterprise labor			
Rice	7.2 (2)	66.4 (6)	109.0 (15)
Nonrice	57.1 (12)	328.7 (28)	267.0 (36)
Livestock	19.4 (4)	15.4 (1)	84.0 (11)
Low capital	54.2 (11)	51.0 (4)	108.2 (15)
High capital	0.0 (0)	176.8 (15)	0.0 (0)
Hired labor			
Agriculture	29.5 (6)	17.8 (2)	22.7 (3)
Low wage	121.1 (25)	163.8 (14)	11.0 (2)
High wage	128.3 (26)	129.4 (11)	42.4 (6)
Government	0.0 (0)	238.7 (20)	86.3 (12)
Total	484.2 (100)	1,286.7 (100)	731.4 (100)

Note: Low-capital enterprises include the retail sector (small shops and door-to-door peddling), low-capital food processing (cooking snacks), and light manufacturing (brooms, furniture, and woven bamboo walls). High-capital enterprises include high-capital food processing (rice milling) and transportation (minibus). Agricultural labor includes work on other farms. Low-wage labor (1,000–2,000 Rp per day) includes work in the plantation, work in nearby factories, and hired employment in local construction, retail, low-capital food processing, light manufacturing, and wood gathering. High-wage labor (3,000–5,000 Rp per day) consists of work in the transportation sector (driving the minibus) and high-capital food processing. Government jobs include teaching, working in the clinic, and working for the village or subdistrict government.

Table 7.4. *Average land owned, rented, and controlled (hectares)*

	Low-calorie household	Medium-calorie household	High-calorie household
Wet rice land			
Owned	0.04	0.15	0.1
Rented/sharecropped	0.02	0.03	0.2
Total controlled	0.07	0.18	0.29
Dry land			
Owned	0.23	0.38	0.29
Rented/sharecropped	0.1	0.18	0.22
Total controlled	0.33	0.56	0.51

Table 7.5. *Distribution of land ownership (%)*

	Low-calorie household	Medium-calorie household	High-calorie household	All households
Wet rice land				
More than 1 ha	0	5.9	0	2
Between 0.25 and 1 ha	0	0	22.2	8.2
Between 0.1 and 0.25 ha	21.4	29.4	16.7	22.4
Between 0.05 and 0.1 ha	14.3	11.8	11.1	12.2
Less than 0.05 ha	14.3	29.4	16.7	20.4
Own no land	50	23.5	33.3	34.7
Total	100	100	100	100
Dry land				
More than 1 ha	0	11.8	11.1	8.2
Between 0.25 and 1 ha	21.4	5.9	33.3	20.4
Between 0.1 and 0.25 ha	42.9	11.8	16.7	22.4
Between 0.05 and 0.1 ha	0	17.6	11.1	10.2
Less than 0.05 ha	14.3	17.6	11.1	14.3
Own no land	21.4	35.3	16.7	24.5
Total	100	100	100	100

low incomes simply because they have not yet accumulated or inherited assets. Interestingly, female household heads are only slightly more prevalent among the low-caloric households. Geographically, high-caloric households are most likely to live in the lowland section of the village, which is consistent with their greater participation in wet rice cultivation.

The nonmonotonic relationship between income and energy consumption among household groups may be due to differences in energy consumption, which are not accounted for in the estimation of per-adult-equivalent energy consumption. Although actual differences in energy expenditure would be

Table 7.6. *Distribution of total land controlled (%)*

	Low-calorie household	Medium-calorie household	High-calorie household	All households
Wet rice land				
More than 1 ha	0	5.9	5.6	4.1
Between 0.25 and 1 ha	7.1	5.9	16.7	10.2
Between 0.1 and 0.25 ha	21.4	41.2	27.8	30.6
Between 0.05 and 0.1 ha	14.3	11.8	22.2	16.3
Less than 0.05 ha	28.6	23.5	11.1	20.4
Control no land	28.6	11.8	16.7	18.4
Total	100	100	100	100
Dry land				
More than 1 ha	7.1	11.8	16.7	12.2
Between 0.25 and 1 ha	35.7	41.2	61.1	46.9
Between 0.1 and 0.25 ha	42.9	29.4	22.2	30.6
Between 0.05 and 0.1 ha	0	5.9	0	2
Less than 0.05 ha	14.3	5.9	0	6.1
Control no land	0	5.9	0	2
Total	100	100	100	100

Table 7.7. *Village demographics*

	Low-calorie households (N = 14)	Medium-calorie households (N = 17)	High-calorie households (N = 18)
Female-headed households (%)	6.7	5.5	5.2
Family size	5.3	4.1	2.9
Household heads 40 and under (%)	71	47	39
Household heads over 40 (%)	29	53	61
Households in lowland section (%)	14	35	50
Households in moderate upland section (%)	57	30	33
Households in isolated upland section (%)	29	35	17

difficult to estimate accurately, the sources of income for the three groups offer some clues about possible energy expenditure patterns. The fact that high-calorie households cultivate a greater area of rice, work that is labor-intensive, may contribute to higher energy expenditures. Similarly, the fact that several medium-calorie household heads receive pensions and work in government jobs may contribute to lower average energy expenditures for this group relative to the high-calorie group.

The high-calorie and medium-calorie households probably have adequate

Table 7.8. *Consumption and own production*

	All households	Low-calorie household	Medium-calorie household	High-calorie household
Rice				
Total production (1,000 Rp)	9,384	1,019	3,437	4,931
Total consumption (1,000 Rp)	6,774	1,567	2,080	3,127
Own-farm consumption (1,000 Rp)	2,191	684	500	1,006
Marketed surplus ratio (%)	0.77	0.33	0.85	0.8
Self-sufficiency ratio (%)	1.39	0.65	1.65	1.58
Self-supply ratio (%)	0.32	0.44	0.24	0.32
Nonrice crops				
Total production (1,000 Rp)	49,005	4,687	22,714	21,604
Total consumption (1,000 Rp)	7,399	1,861	2,272	3,266
Own-farm consumption (1,000 Rp)	2,907	436	788	1,684
Marketed surplus ratio (%)	0.94	0.91	0.97	0.92
Self-sufficiency ratio (%)	6.62	2.52	10	6.62
Self-supply ratio (%)	0.39	0.23	0.35	0.52

Note: Marketed surplus is the fraction of total production not consumed directly on farm. Self-sufficiency is the ratio of total production to total consumption. Self-supply is the fraction of total consumption actually met by own-farm production.

nutrient intake. High-calorie households all consume more than the energy requirement for subsistence farming activities. The medium-calorie households consume at least 85 percent of the subsistence farming requirement, and almost all consume more than the energy requirement for moderate activity (2,350 kilocalorie). The low-calorie households appear to be the only group vulnerable to malnutrition. All households in this group consume less than 85 percent of the energy requirement for subsistence farming activities and less than the requirement for more moderate activity as well.

Village factor and commodity markets

Food. Village markets are relatively diverse and well developed; yet subsistence food production encompasses a nonnegligible fraction of total production. Furthermore, not all households are equally linked to the market. Table 7.8 gives the marketed surplus ratio (fraction of production not consumed directly by the household), self-sufficiency (total production divided by total consumption), and self-supply (direct own-farm consumption divided by total consumption) for rice and other crops. Low-calorie households have the lowest marketed surpluses for rice as a result of low levels of rice land ownership and control. Thus, they benefit least from a producer price increase in rice.

While the low-calorie group has the lowest self-sufficiency, representing the level of consumption that could be met by own-production, it has the highest level of self-supply, or total consumption actually met by own-production. Other households sell and repurchase rice to a much higher degree, perhaps to take advantage of quality differences.

On average, the degree of interaction with the rice market is high. The village has a marketed surplus rate of 77 percent, and a self-supply rate of only 32 percent. Even the poorest households are not completely withdrawn from the market.

Labor. The labor market offers some diversity but few chances for income security. Land preparation tasks are generally performed by men, who receive a daily wage and a meal. The wage paid for land preparation was approximately 1,000 Rp (about sixty cents in 1989) for a five-hour day. With the value of the meal included, the wage was about 1,300 Rp. Transplanting and weeding are performed by women, who are paid a share of the crop after it is harvested. In the survey year, workers compensated in-kind earned the equivalent of about 200 Rp per hour. Although in-kind earnings valued at market prices are comparable to the hourly cash wage, the women receive no meal, must wait for payment, and must share the yield risk with the farm operator.

Other local opportunities for wage labor include local construction, the nearby plantation, and factories. There also is a broad range of self-employment activities, which include small-scale food processing, such as snack preparation and palm-sugar production; light manufacturing of woven bamboo walls, furniture, brooms, and baskets; and marketing through small shops, door-to-door sales, and town–village trade. Implicit wage rates for these activities, calculated as returns to labor per hour, average close to the agricultural wage, but they are highly variable over time, depending on fluctuations in sales.

During the survey year, returns to labor in small-scale food processing ranged from 40 to 220 Rp per hour and monthly earnings ranged from 9,000 to 40,000 Rp ($5.40 to $24.00 in 1989). Hourly returns in light manufacturing ranged from 113 to 285 Rp, and monthly earnings ranged from 5,000 to 27,000 Rp ($3.00 to $16.20). Retail sales, which require some operating capital, averaged about 300 Rp per hour, and anywhere from 6,000 to 80,000 Rp ($3.60 to $48.00) per month, depending on sales.

Labor tying, through lending to workers in exchange for reliable availability, has been reported in other parts of West Java (Hardjono, 1987). In Cibageur, households did not report any credit arrangements with employers, although the survey was not designed to focus on this arrangement, and Hardjono (1987) noted that her respondents were reluctant to discuss this institution. It may well be that the markets for credit and labor in this village

Table 7.9. *Proportion of labor hired by household group*

	Low-calorie household	Medium-calorie household	High-calorie household
Agriculture	0.08	0.37	0.55
Wood	1	0	0
Retail	0.81	0.19	0
Construction	0.06	0.23	0.71

do not leave the same niche for labor tying as an institution. Credit is available from local traders, so households are not dependent on employers for loans. Further, the small amount of rice land in this village relative to labor availability reduces the peak season labor demand problem for employers.

Labor is often provided on a volunteer basis, both to family and friends and to village projects. Labor "gifts" were reported frequently in rice production. These arrangements were mostly among relatives and/or friends who provided labor to one another without cash or share of harvest payment. However, workers under this arrangement were usually given a large meal with expensive ingredients such as chicken and fancier vegetables. Such labor may have been exchanged for labor in return, but probably often was not; many of the relatives and friends offering assistance controlled smaller plots of land than the household receiving the labor contribution. The village government also organizes volunteer labor one or two days per week for small projects.

The role of each group on the demand side of the direct labor market is shown in Table 7.9. The high-calorie group is by far the most important employer of agricultural and construction labor, while the low-calorie group is a more important employer in retail and wood products.

Land. Simple land rental is rare, but sharecropping is common, with several different arrangements depending upon the owner's responsibility for inputs. Sharecropping among extended-family members was common but not dominant: Roughly one-third of sharecropping arrangements was conducted with parents. The local plantation also sharecropped land out to households.

A small amount of land, 1 hectare out of the total of 400 hectares in the village, was available for use by village officials in lieu of salary. A small amount of communal land, about 2 hectares, was also available for use by households.

Landownership in the village is skewed, although the extent of landlessness in the village is less severe than in other parts of the country. Only 2 percent of the sample households own over one hectare of rice land, while most households own less than a quarter of a hectare. Holdings of the less valuable dry land are larger, but the pattern is similar: 8 percent of households own more than one hectare while over half own less than one-quarter of a hectare. Ten percent of the sample households own about 57 percent of the rice land and, similarly, 10 percent of the households own 55 percent of the dry land owned by village residents. This does not include land owned by the plantation, which accounts for a large fraction of the dry land in the village. Eighteen percent of households own no land, but only one household in the sample does not have access to land at least in the form of a sharecropping arrangement (it is headed by a teacher).

Credit/savings. The local markets for credit and asset sharing are relatively well developed. Traditional credit sources offer small- to medium-sized loans. Small-scale purchase credit (on the order of $10 to $20) is available from vendors who sell goods and then collect monthly payments. Households also may borrow rice for repayment after the harvest. The nominal interest rates on these loans are as high as 100 percent, since each kilogram of rice borrowed must be repaid with two kilograms. However, the price of rice can decline by as much as 50 percent following the harvest, leaving the real interest rate much lower. Larger-scale credit ($100 and up) is available through pawning of land or livestock. The implicit interest rate in these arrangements is equal to the productive value of the land or animals, which are held by the lender until the loan is repaid. A traditional futures market also serves a credit function; a farmer may sell a crop before it is harvested at a discounted price. Commercial state-controlled banks offer credit for agricultural inputs as well as larger loans for investment in land, vehicles, or equipment. Savings tend to be invested in traditional instruments such as livestock and land.

Another traditional form of savings is the local "savings lottery." Members contribute savings each week, and each week one member takes the pot to use for large purchases such as furniture. While this form of savings pays no interest, it protects members from theft and substitutes for self-discipline in the same way that "Christmas accounts" once functioned in the United States. Savings also may be deposited at the subdistrict bank branch, which accepts deposits of any amount but pays interest only on certificates of deposit with a minimum balance of $500 to $600.

The availability of small credit is an effective tool for increasing demand for durable goods such as clothing and furniture. Likewise, agricultural credit plays an important role in facilitating input use. However, a lack of access to larger investment loans is a barrier to small enterprise formation by the poor. A government rural development program provides loans and assistance with marketing for specific small operations such as poultry production. Funds for these projects are limited, however, and the projects target individual villages.

Village institutions

Households and families. The household structure has important distributional implications for the village economy. A nuclear family unit consisting of two parents and their children was the most common household type in the village, but roughly 20 percent of the households fell into other categories, including polygamous families,[5] multiple generations living together, and female-headed households.

Young families often live with the bride's parents until they can afford to build their own home. They also live with the bride's parents when the bride delivers her first child, even if they have their own home. Surveyed households in such an arrangement stressed as a point of pride that they maintained separate budgets and cooked food separately, although this division is undoubtedly flexible. In another multigenerational living arrangement, older parents sometimes live with their grown children; the parent (often widowed) provides baby-sitting and other household services and sometimes allows the younger family to farm land. Extended families living together make up 14 percent of the village households and are more common in the low-calorie group (28 percent of low-calorie households). Some of these households overlap with female-headed households: Almost one-third of the extended families were headed by widowed daughters living with their widowed mothers. Even when not living together, extended families provide a great deal of mutual assistance in the form of labor and food; gifts of food are common and, while usually not large, they may play an important role in assisting poorer members of the family.

Female-headed households may result from death of the male head or divorce, although in this village it appears to be rare for a family to remain in this state. Only 6 percent of the sample households were headed by women, and there was no difference in this rate across household groups. Divorce is not uncommon in West Java as a whole, and Cibageur is no exception. According to local interpretation of the Moslem marriage contract, wives may ask for a divorce if they are not being supported well enough, and this causes much anxiety for new husbands. Wives with children retain possession of the home if it was acquired after the marriage. Even so, the difficulty of supporting a family alone leaves a divorced woman dependent on her parents or on the prospect of remarriage. Still, the ability to leave a

5. This village included an estimated 4 percent of husbands with two wives (up to four are permitted, but no one with the inclination was wealthy enough for more than two). Under these arrangements, each wife and her children live in their own domicile, and the husband divides his time and income between his families. The division of a husband's income places an extreme burden on the first wife, and one such wife in the survey sample reported that she could remain in the marriage only because she had inherited land from her parents; otherwise she would be forced (and permitted by local interpretation of Islamic law) to divorce her husband to seek a husband who could support her.

marriage gives West Javan women more options than their counterparts in South Asia.

Rules for inheritance and marriage also leave women in a much better position than in other parts of Asia. Daughters inherit land equally with their brothers. Families of brides receive bride-price payments from the groom's family, and these payments go largely toward the expense of the wedding and establishment of the new couple's household. Daughters are thus not seen as a large future expense as in South Asia, where dowry payments are required from the bride's family.

Village government. The official village organizations are generally structured as part of a hierarchy designed by the central government and replicated in every village, although their charitable and labor-organizing functions reflect older cultural traditions. They are a vehicle to implement programs designed and funded by higher levels of government. Although they could also serve as organizational structures for locally designed projects, their capacity for self-finance is very limited.

Village and higher-level government functions are divided as follows. The village government collects land taxes from village residents, which are used to purchase materials for small infrastructure projects, such as small bridges. Estimated tax collections for the village during the survey year totaled 5 million Rp (U.S. $3000 in 1989), an average of 5,000 Rp per household. Village residents contribute volunteer labor one day per week for these projects.

The provincial government, working through district and subdistrict governments, is responsible for larger infrastructure funding for roads and school buildings and for salaries for village officials and schoolteachers. The provincial government collected an estimated 4 million Rp in school fees and spent over 34 million Rp for schoolteacher salaries in the survey year. Thus, village education is heavily subsidized by higher level government, at an average of about 50,000 Rp per primary-school-aged child per year. Village government salaries are also subsidized: The salaries of village officials, totaling an estimated 13 million Rp, far exceed village tax revenues.

The village has three administrative subvillages, each with an appointed head. These officers are the link between the bureaucracy and village residents. They disseminate information from the village government and organize their neighbors for village activities. In addition, they are responsible for maintaining lists of residents, keeping track of "blacklisted" residents (former members of the Communist or Islamic fundamentalist parties), identifying poor families for targeted public works employment, and initiating requests for emergency assistance.

Local leaders are elected every five years. Candidates are nominated to the dominant party, GOLKAR (Working Group), as well as to two other legally permitted parties, the PDI (Democratic Party of Indonesia) and PPP (a moderate Moslem party). Although campaign activities by the two smaller parties are significantly restricted, they win a small number of votes. In this village, the local officials were relatively wealthy but were not the wealthiest village residents. The wealthiest residents (including the one household with running water) appeared to have considerable informal influence, both in advising leaders on decisions and in developing popular support for local development efforts.

Religious institutions. Local mosques play an important role in village life. Each subvillage in Cibageur has its own mosque. This building serves not only as a religious gathering place but also as a meeting place for local discussion. Residents make weekly contributions, which are used to furnish the mosques with such items as mats and an amplifier, to fund new buildings (with matching funds from higher-level government), and to provide emergency assistance for families.

Other institutions. The village chapter of the Family Welfare Organization is composed of women who volunteer to assist in nutrition activities by the health clinic and carry out other activities, including encouraging women to accumulate savings for small-enterprise capital. In this village there are also wealthy and influential individuals who have no official status in either the village government or the mosque, but who are consulted by officials and give powerful motivational speeches on behalf of government policy. These individuals have stronger links to business and culture outside the village (one had children attending college in the United States).

The village SAM structure and estimation

The Cibageur village SAM organizes the village economy into five sets of accounts, labeled activities (1), factors (2), institutions (3), capital (4), and outside (5) (see Table 7.10). Activities outside the market are included in the SAM as if households purchased the output of these activities from themselves, with imputed expenditure and imputed incomes included in the relevant accounts.

The first nine activity (set 1) accounts are agricultural, covering production of wet rice (1.1), dry rice (1.2), maize (1.3), tubers (1.4), soybeans (1.5), groundnuts (1.6), vegetables (1.7), tree crops (1.8) and livestock and fish ponds (1.9). The next seven activity accounts cover nonagricultural activities, including construction (1.10), retail (1.11), small-scale food processing (1.12), large-scale food processing (1.13), light manufacturing (1.14), transportation (1.15), and production of primary (wood) products (1.16). Livestock includes chickens, ducks, goats, and sheep, as well as larger animals such as

Table 7.10. *Social accounting matrix outline*

	1. Activities 1.1 ... 1.18	2. Factors 2.1 ... 2.5	3. Institutions 3.1 ... 3.6	4. Capital accounts 4.1 ... 4.6	5. Outside 5.1 ... 5.5	6. Total
1. *Activities*	(1,1)		(1,3)	(1,4)	(1,5)	(1,6)
1.1 Rice				Crop Stocks		
1.2 Dry rice						
1.3 Maize						
1.4 Tubers						
1.5 Soybeans						
1.6 Groundnuts						
1.7 Vegetables	Village Input-output Table		Consumption	Animal and Physical Capital Purchases	Local exports Indonesia exports	Total sales
1.8 Tree crops						
1.9 Lvstk/fish						
1.10 Constr						
1.11 Retail						
1.12 Low fdproc						
1.13 Hi fdproc						
1.14 Lt mfg						
1.15 Transport						
1.16 Primary			Teachers			
1.17 Education						
1.18 Health						
2. *Factors*	(2,1)	(2,3)			(2,5)	(2,6)
2.1 Land	Value-added in village production	Relatives' labor	Civil servants	Plantation labor	Local labor	Total land, labor, and capital Value added
2.2 Phys capital						
2.3 Anim capital						
2.4 Hired labor						
2.5 Own-enterprise labor						

Row items	(·,1)	(3,2)	(3,3)	(3,4)	(3,5)	(3,6)
3. Institutions 3.1 Migrants 3.2 Low calorie 3.3 Medium calorie 3.4 High calorie 3.5 Religious 3.6 Village govt		Payment to households for factors Use of govt land	Migrant remittances to households Religious tax / Govt tax	Land saving Purchase / Borrow Educational expenditures	Migrant remittances Indonesia / World Pensions	Total migrant remittances Total household income Total receipts
4. Capital 4.1 Physical 4.2 Land 4.3 Human 4.4 Animal 4.5 Inventory 4.6 Financial			(4,3) Household savings Household human Capital savings			(4,6) Total saving
5. Outside 5.1 Exogenous govt 5.2 Plantation 5.3 Local imports / Indonesia imports 5.4 Indonesia 5.5 World	(5,1) Local imports Indonesia imports	(5,2) Use of land Payments to outside factor owners	(5,3) Household local imports Household Indonesia imports Household govt exp Migrant rel remittances exp	Physical capital imports / Land purchased from outside Investment totals	(5,5) Town / World Totals	(5,6) Local imports Indonesia imports
6. Total	Total payments	Total payments to factors				Total row = Total column

cattle and water buffalo. Almost all households at least raise chickens, and most raise small ruminants as well. Only one household owns water buffalo. Construction includes home building as well as construction of small livestock shelters. Retail activities include door-to-door trading, marketing of goods outside the village, and small village shops. Small-scale food processing includes palm-sugar production as well as preparation of snacks and meals for sale in local shops. Large-scale food processing consists of a mechanical rice milling operation. Transportation includes two minivans, which are licensed to run a route to and from the nearest town (Sukabumi). Wood products include both firewood and lumber for local construction and export. The last two accounts, education (1.17) and health (1.18), are service activities covering teachers and traditional health providers.

The factor account (2) is broken down to reflect payments to land (2.1), physical capital (2.2), animal capital (2.3), hired labor (2.4), and own-enterprise labor (2.5). Payments to land are primarily through sharecropping. Payments to physical capital include rental of pesticide sprayers (in the case of agriculture) and rental payments for a minivan (in the case of transportation). Payments to animal capital consist of rental payments for animal traction. Payments to hired labor include both wage labor and labor compensated with a share of the harvest, where the harvest share is evaluated at the farm-gate price. Payment to own-enterprise labor represents returns to labor from a household's farm or other enterprise; it also includes returns to the household's own land in agriculture.

Institutions include migrants (3.1), low-calorie, medium-calorie, and high-calorie household groups (3.2, 3.3, and 3.4), the mosque (3.5), and endogenous government (3.6). Migrants include both migrants to other parts of Indonesia (mainly the capital, Jakarta) as well as international migrants to Saudi Arabia and Kuwait. The endogenous government account covers fee-for-service activities such as education. Since both revenues and expenditures for these services increase with household income, this account is placed in the endogenous section of the SAM as another village institution. The remainder of government activities, including taxation and development expenditures, are reflected in an exogenous account (5.1). The religious institution (3.5) collects contributions from households and uses them to hire labor and purchase equipment. In addition, this institution collects fees for religious education and for crop prayers and, in turn, hires from the education sector.

The capital accounts include investments in physical capital (4.1), land (4.2), human capital (4.3), animals (4.4), inventory (4.5), and savings (4.6). Physical capital includes buildings, vehicles, agricultural tools, and large food processing equipment. Human capital includes all expenditures on education. Inventory refers to storage of crops by the households, as well as crops that have not yet been harvested.

Since the village trades in goods and factors with areas in Indonesia as well as the rest of the world, the outside account is disaggregated as well. A plantation (5.2) hires labor from the village, rents unplanted land to village residents, and exports cacao to the rest of Indonesia. The local trade account (5.3) encompasses the nearest villages. Indonesia (5.4) covers the remainder of Indonesia, and the world (5.5) includes all other countries. In general, local imports are used to meet the gap between consumption and production, and local exports are the channel for generating village surplus. Imports from the rest of Indonesia consist of imported inputs such as agricultural chemicals, and exports to the rest of Indonesia include crop surplus and lumber. There are no direct imports from the rest of the world to the village, but several migrants from the village send remittances from other countries, primarily Saudi Arabia and Kuwait.

The village survey data were used to estimate account flows for each cell in the SAM. The SAM was balanced by setting imports and exports equal to the difference between production and consumption. Household accounts were balanced by setting savings equal to the difference between income and expenditure. While some data were available on imports, exports, and savings, these data were felt to be less reliable than data on production, consumption, and income.

Because of the high level of integration with the surrounding economy, the calculation of flows in and out of the village required some further assumptions. Imported inputs were assumed to come from the rest of Indonesia, since they are not produced locally. Imports of commodities required to match reported supply and reported consumption were assumed to be imported from the local area, since they are all produced locally.

The survey sample covered about 5 percent of the total village population. Thus, the reported transactions were multiplied by twenty to estimate flows for the entire village. Estimates of plantation sales were not inflated, since this information was available for the whole plantation from the plantation manager.

The estimated village SAM and villagewide linkages

The estimated SAM clearly illustrates the three dominant characteristics of the village economy, which influence all other economic linkages: The economy is very open, production is dominated by agriculture, and household income is dominated by returns to hired labor and own enterprise labor.

The linkages within the village economy are first of all constrained by the openness of the village. Although exports serve as an important source of income, the high import content of many activities reduces the total impact of exogenous income changes on the economy. Overall, imports account for 39 percent of total final demand, with imported commodities making up 14.6 percent and imported intermediates making up 24.5 percent. Imported rice is

Table 7.11. *Social accounting matrix coefficients and flow totals*

	1. Activities								
Purchases from	1.1 Rice	1.2 Dry rice	1.3 Maize	1.4 Tubers	1.5 Soybeans	1.6 Peanuts	1.7 Veg etc	1.8 Treecrops	1.9 Livestock
1. Activities									
1.1 Rice	0.0235	0	0	0	0	0	0	0	0.0672
1.2 Dry rice	0	0.0668	0	0	0	0	0	0	0
1.3 Maize	0	0	0.0632	0	0	0	0	0	0
1.4 Tubers	0	0	0	0.1268	0	0	0	0	0
1.5 Soybeans	0	0	0	0	0.0018	0	0	0	0
1.6 Groundnuts	0	0	0	0	0	0.0438	0	0	0
1.7 Vegetables	0	0	0	0	0	0	0.0526	0	0
1.8 Tree crops	0	0	0	0	0	0	0	0.0126	0
1.9 Lvstk/fish	0.0012	0.0016	0.0011	0.0011	0	0.0003	0.0002	0	0
1.10 Constr	0	0	0	0	0	0	0	0	0.0002
1.11 Retail	0	0	0	0	0	0	0	0	0
1.12 Low fd proc	0	0	0	0	0	0	0	0	0
1.13 Hi fd proc	0	0	0	0	0	0	0	0	0
1.14 Lt mfg	0	0	0	0	0	0	0	0	0
1.15 Transp	0	0	0	0	0	0	0	0	0
1.16 Primary	0	0	0	0	0	0	0	0	0
1.17 Education	0	0	0	0	0	0	0	0	0
1.18 Health	0	0	0	0	0	0	0	0	0
2. Factors									
2.1 Land	0.054	0.0154	0.0136	0.0074	0.1981	0.0109	0.0016	0	0
2.2 Phys cap	0.0036	0	0	0	0	0	0	0	0.1334
2.3 Anim cap	0.716	0.005	0.1609	0.226	0	0.011	0.1373	0.0002	0.001
2.4 Hire lab	0.194	0.4072							
2.5 Own-ent lab	0.0683	0.0092	0.6859	0.5807	0.8	0.9329	0.755	0.9714	0.3497

168

3. Institutions									
3.1 Migrants	0	0	0	0	0	0	0	0	0
3.2 Low cal	0	0	0	0	0	0	0	0	0
3.3 Med cal	0	0	0	0	0	0	0	0	0
3.4 High cal	0	0	0	0	0	0	0	0	0
3.5 Religious	0	0	0	0	0	0	0	0	0
3.6 End govt	0	0	0	0	0	0	0	0	0
4. Capital									
4.1 Physical	0	0	0	0	0	0	0	0	0
4.2 Land	0	0	0	0	0	0	0	0	0
4.3 Human	0	0	0	0	0	0	0	0	0
4.4 Animal	0	0	0	0	0	0	0	0	0
4.5 Inventory	0	0	0	0	0	0	0	0	0
4.6 Financial	0	0	0	0	0	0	0	0	0
5. Outside									
5.1 Ex govt	0.5197	0	0	0	0	0	0	0	0
5.2 Plantation	0.0642	0.3271	0	0	0	0	0.052	0	0
5.3 Local imp	0	0.1677	0.0753	0.058	0	0.0011	0.0012	0.0158	0.4485
5.4 Indonesia	0	0	0	0	0	0	0	0	0
5.5 World	0	0	0	0	0	0	0	0	0
6. Total	1.00	1.00	1.00	1.00	1.00	1.00	1.00	1.00	1.00
Flow totals (Rp)	239,747,808	49,107,943	14,095,840	108,920,980	2,174,240	189,590,790	48,847,860	52,005,820	121,370,647

169

Table 7.11. *(cont.)*

Purchases from	1. Activities								
	1.10 Constr	1.11 Retail	1.12 Sm fdproc	1.13 Lg fdproc	1.14 Lt mfg	1.15 Transp	1.16 Firewood	1.17 Educ	1.18 Health
1. Activities									
1.1 Rice	0	0.0023	0.0284	0	0	0	0	0	0
1.2 Dry rice	0	0	0	0	0	0	0	0	0
1.3 Maize	0	0	0	0	0	0	0	0	0
1.4 Tubers	0	0.0045	0.1419	0	0	0	0	0	0
1.5 Soybeans	0	0	0	0	0	0	0	0	0
1.6 Groundnuts	0	0	0.1597	0	0	0	0	0	0
1.7 Vegetables	0	0	0	0	0	0	0	0	0
1.8 Tree crops	0	0.007	0.1597	0	0	0	0	0	0
1.9 Lvstk/fish	0	0.1132	0.0213	0	0	0	0	0	0
1.10 Constr	0	0	0	0	0	0	0	0	0
1.11 Retail	0.0979	0.0034	0	0	0	0	0	0	0
1.12 Low fd proc	0	0	0	0	0	0	0	0	0
1.13 Hi fd proc	0.0571	0.0039	0	0	0	0	0	0	0
1.14 Lt mfg	0	0.0135	0	0	0	0	0	0	0
1.15 Transp	0.2014	0.0442	0	0	0.1444	0	0	0	0
1.16 Primary	0	0	0	0	0	0	0	0	0
1.17 Education	0	0	0	0	0	0	0	0	0
1.18 Health	0	0	0	0	0	0	0	0	0
2. Factors									
2.1 Land	0	0	0	0	0	0	0	0	0
2.2 Phys cap	0	0	0	0	0	0.2388	0	0	0
2.3 Anim cap	0	0	0	0	0	0	0	0	0
2.4 Hire lab	0.1091	0.0376	0	0	0	0.2086	0.4563	1	1
2.5 Own-ent lab	0.0722	0.0413	0.0753	0.5903	0.2307	0	0.5437	0	0

3. Institutions									
3.1 Migrants	0	0	0	0	0	0	0	0	0
3.2 Low cal	0	0	0	0	0	0	0	0	0
3.3 Med cal	0	0	0	0	0	0	0	0	0
3.4 High cal	0	0	0	0	0	0	0	0	0
3.5 Religious	0	0	0	0	0	0	0	0	0
3.6 End. govt	0	0	0	0	0	0	0	0	0
4. Capital									
4.1 Physical	0	0	0	0	0	0	0	0	0
4.2 Land	0	0	0	0	0	0	0	0	0
4.3 Human	0	0	0	0	0	0	0	0	0
4.4 Animal	0	0	0	0	0	0	0	0	0
4.5 Inventory	0	0	0	0	0	0	0	0	0
4.6 Financial	0	0	0	0	0	0	0	0	0
5. Outside									
5.1 Ex. govt	0	0	0	0	0	0	0	0	0
5.2 Plantation	0	0	0	0	0.6249	0	0	0	0
5.3 Local imp	0.1091	0.008	0.4137	0.4097	0	0.5525	0	0	0
5.4 Indonesia	0.3532	0.721	0	0	0	0	0	0	0
5.5 World	0	0	0	0	0	0	0	0	0
6. Totals	1.00	1.00	1.00	1.00	1.00	1.00	1.00	1.00	1.00
Flow totals (Rp)	80,811,160	334,676,660	81,021,620	110,024,000	10,740,200	127,700,000	94,969,400	40,533,660	1,920,000

Table 7.11 *(cont.)*

| Purchases from | 2. Factors | | | | | 3. Institutions | | | | | |
	2.1 Land	2.2 Phys cap	2.3 Anim cap	2.4 Hired lab	2.5 Own-ent lab	3.1 Migr	3.2 Low cal	3.3 Med cal	3.4 High cal	3.5 Religion	3.6 End govt
1. Activities											
1.1 Rice	0	0	0	0	0	0	0.2741	0.1154	0.1454	0	0
1.2 Dry rice	0	0	0	0	0	0	0.0703	0.0282	0.0332	0	0
1.3 Maize	0	0	0	0	0	0	0.0069	0.0099	0.0024	0	0
1.4 Tubers	0	0	0	0	0	0	0.0082	0.0017	0.0046	0	0
1.5 Soybeans	0	0	0	0	0	0	0.0003	0.0001	0	0	0
1.6 Grooundnuts	0	0	0	0	0	0	0.0046	0.0057	0.0106	0	0
1.7 Vegetables	0	0	0	0	0	0	0.0582	0.0237	0.0685	0	0
1.8 Tree crops	0	0	0	0	0	0	0.026	0.0108	0.024	0	0
1.9 Lvstk/fish	0	0	0	0	0	0	0.0747	0.0367	0.064	0	0
1.10 Constr	0	0	0	0	0	0	0.0911	0.0149	0.1497	0	0
1.11 Retail	0	0	0	0	0	0	0.3223	0.2054	0.4042	0	0
1.12 Low fd proc	0	0	0	0	0	0	0.1212	0.0623	0.0804	0	0
1.13 Hi fd proc	0	0	0	0	0	0	0.0003	0.0007	0.0007	0	0
1.14 Lt mfg	0	0	0	0	0	0	0.0063	0.006	0.0021	0	0
1.15 Transp	0	0	0	0	0	0	0.0075	0.0006	0.001	0	0
1.16 Primary	0	0	0	0	0	0	0.0812	0.0277	0.0502	0	0
1.17 Education	0	0	0	0	0	0	0	0	0	0.2286	0.9933
1.18 Health	0	0	0	0	0	0	0.0002	0.0001	0.0005	0	0
2. Factors											
2.1 Land	0	0	0	0	0	0	0	0	0	0	0
2.2 Phys cap	0	0	0	0	0	0	0	0	0	0	0
2.3 Anim cap	0	0	0	0	0	0	0	0	0	0.4913	0
2.4 Hire lab	0	0	0	0	0	0	0	0	0	0	0
2.5 Own-ent lab	0	0	0	0	0	0	0	0	0	0	0

3. Institutions											
3.1 Migrants	0	0	0	0	0	0	0	0	0	0	0
3.2 Low cal	0.0302	0	0.1011	0.3422	0.0858	0.057	0	0	0	0	0
3.3 Med cal	0.044	1	0.037	0.4844	0.5111	0.263	0	0	0	0	0
3.4 High cal	0.066	0	0.5731	0.1709	0.4031	0.68	0	0	0	0	0
3.5 Religious	0	0	0	0	0	0	0.011	0.0036	0.0038	0	0
3.6 End govt	0.0548	0	0	0	0	0	0	0	0	0	0
4. Capital											
4.1 Physical	0	0	0	0	0	0	0.0098	0.0026	0.0091	0	0
4.2 Land	0	0	0	0	0	0	0	0.0354	0	0	0
4.3 Human	0	0	0	0	0	0	0.0156	0.0048	0.0029	0	0
4.4 Animal	0	0	0	0	0	0	0.0113	0.008	0.059	0	0
4.5 Inventory	0	0	0	0	0	0	0.0468	0.0764	0.0977	0	0
4.6 Financial	0	0	0	0	0	0	−0.2621	0.2963	−0.222	0	0
5. Outside											
5.1 Ex govt	0	0	0	0	0	0	0.0142	0.0231	0.008	0	0
5.2 Plantation	0.805	0	0	0	0	0	0	0	0	0	0
5.3 Local imp	0	0	0	0	0	0	0	0	0	0	0.0067
5.3 Local imp	0	0	0.2888	0.0024	0	0	0	0	0	0	0
5.4 Indonesia	0	0	0	0	0	0	0	0	0	0.2801	0
5.5 World	0	0	0	0	0	0	0	0	0	0	0
6. Total	1.00	1.00	1.00	1.00	1.00	1.00	1.00	1.00	1.00	1.00	1.00
Flow totals (Rp)	21,820,940	31,352,260	33,592,460	259,960,750	543,010,180	122,800,000	146,628,902	522,105,263	367,496,995	6,334,220	39,347,660

173

Table 7.11 (*cont.*)

| Purchases from | 4. Capital | | | | | | 5. Outside | | | | | 6. Flow total |
	4.1 Phys	4.2 Land	4.3 Human	4.4 Animal	4.5 Inventory	4.6 Financial	5.1 Ex gov	5.2 Plant	5.3 Local	5.4 Indonesia	5.5 World	
1. Activities												
1.1 Rice	0	0	0	0	0.8349	0	0	0	0	0	0	239,747,808
1.2 Dry rice	0	0	0	0	0.1044	0	0	0	0	0	0	49,107,943
1.3 Maize	0	0	0	0	0.0053	0	0	0	0	0.0081	0	14,095,840
1.4 Tubers	0	0	0	0	0	0	0	0	0	0.1104	0	108,920,980
1.5 Soybeans	0	0	0	0	0.0527	0	0	0	0	0.0029	0	2,174,240
1.6 Groundnuts	0	0	0	0	0.0024	0	0	0	0	0.2205	0	189,590,790
1.7 Vegetables	0	0	0	0	0.0003	0	0	0	0	0	0	48,847,860
1.8 Tree crops	0	0	0	0	0	0	0	0	0	0.0251	0	52,005,820
1.9 Lvstk/fish	0	0	0	1	0	0	0	0	0	0	0	121,370,647
1.10 Constr	0.7601	0	0	0	0	0	0	0	0	0	0	80,811,160
1.11 Retail	0	0	0	0	0	0	0	0	0.0766	0	0	334,676,660
1.12 Low fd proc	0	0	0	0	0	0	0	0	0.0021	0.1532	0	81,021,620
1.13 Hi fd proc	0	0	0	0	0	0	0	0	0	0	0	110,024,000
1.14 Lt mfg	0	0	0	0	0	0	0	0	0	0	0	10,740,200
1.15 Transp	0	0	0	0	0	0	0	0	0.0203	0.1623	0	127,700,000
1.16 Primary	0	0	0	0	0	0	0	0	0.0567	0	0	94,969,400
1.17 Education	0	0	0	0	0	0	0	0	0	0	0	40,533,660
1.18 Health	0	0	0	0	0	0	0	0	0.0054	0	0	1,920,000
2. Factors												
2.1 Land	0	0	0	0	0	0	0	0	0.0147	0.0147	0	21,820,940
2.2 Phys cap	0	0	0	0	0	0	0	0	0	0	0	31,352,260
2.3 Anim cap	0	0	0	0	0	0	0	0	0	0	0	33,592,460
2.4 Hire lab	0	0	0	0	0	0	0.1374	0.1882	0	0	0	259,960,750
2.5 Own-ent lab	0	0	0	0	0	0	0	0	0	0	0	543,010,180

	4.1 Physical	4.2 Land	4.3 Human	4.4 Animal	4.5 Inventory	4.6 Financial	5.1 Ex. govt	5.2 Plantation	5.3 Local imp	5.4 Indonesia	5.5 World	Flow totals
3. Institutions												
3.1 Migrants	0	0	0	0	0	0	0	0	0	0.0237	1	122,800,000
3.2 Low cal	0	0	0	0	0	0	0	0	0	0	0	146,628,902
3.3 Med cal	0	0	0	0	0	0.5264	0	0	0	0	0	522,105,263
3.4 High cal	0	0	0.2456	0	0	0	0	0	0	0	0	367,496,995
3.5 Religious	0	0	0.7544	0	0	0	0	0	0	0	0	6,334,220
3.6 End govt	0	0	0	0	0	0.3361	0	0	0	0	0	39,347,660
4. Capital												
4.1 Physical	0	0	0	0	0	0	0	0	0	0	0	6,126,500
4.2 Land	0	0	0	0	0	0	0	0	0	0	0	18,500,000
4.3 Human	0	0	0	0	0	0	0	0	0	0	0	5,895,000
4.4 Animal	0	0	0	0	0	0	0	0	0	0	0	27,545,000
4.5 Inventory	0	0	0	0	0	0	0	0	0	0	0	82,644,600
4.6 Financial	0	0	0	0	0	0	0	0	0	0	0	34,673,818
5. Outside												
5.1 Ex. govt	0	0	0	0	0	0	0	0	0	0.1173	0	100,279,560
5.2 Plantation	0.1698	0	0	0	0	0	0.8118	0	0	0.0271	0	36,815,840
5.3 Local imp	0.0702	1	0	0	0	0	0	0.8241	0	0	0	309,397,652
5.4 Indonesia	0	0	0	0	0	0	0	0	1	0.1494	0	709,435,910
5.5 World	0	0	0	0	0	0	0	0	0	0	0	106,000,000
6. Total	1.00	1.00	1.00	1.00	1.00	1.00	1.00	1.00	1.00	1.00	1.00	
Flow totals	6,126,500	18,500,000	5,895,000	27,545,000	82,644,600	34,673,818	100,279,560	36,815,840	309,397,652	709,435,910	106,000,000	

the most important item in commodity trade, making up 50 percent of total commodity imports and 52 percent of final demand for rice.

The estimated SAM illustrates the magnitude of the role of agriculture in the economy. Final demand for crops and livestock is 822 million Rp ($493,000 in 1989), 48 percent of total final demand for all sectors. Wet rice alone accounts for 14 percent of total final demand, tubers account for 6 percent, groundnuts for 11 percent, and livestock for 7 percent. Retail accounted for 19 percent of total final demand, large-scale food processing for 6 percent, and transportation for 8 percent.

It is also clear from the SAM how important labor is in the Cibageur economy. Returns to own-enterprise labor and hired labor make up 90 percent of total village value-added, with returns to own-enterprise labor accounting for 61 percent, and returns to hired labor accounting for 29 percent.

An important implication of the large role of agriculture is that agricultural growth is likely to be limited due to land constraints. Wet rice land is fully utilized in the village, so increases in production can only come from yield increases, which may not be associated with large increases in employment. Dry land sharecropping from the cacao plantation can be increased only temporarily, while the plantation is not fully planted.

In the sections that follow, the linkages among sectors of the village economy are explored in more detail, and their implications for sources of economic growth are discussed.

Production linkages

Table 7.11 presents the estimated SAM coefficients, calculated as the fraction of each column's total payments paid to each row. As is typical of agricultural villages, the input–output matrix (columns 1.1 through 1.18, rows 1.1 through 1.18) is sparse, with few linkages between activities. Crop activities purchase seeds from themselves and a small amount of dung from livestock, but make no other purchases from other activities. Similarly, livestock purchases animals from itself and a small amount of medicine from the local retail sector. Of the nonfarm activities, construction is slightly more strongly linked to other village sectors, purchasing local lumber, woven bamboo walls from light manufacturing, and nails from the retail sector. The input–output coefficients associated with these purchases total over 0.35, with purchases of lumber alone representing almost two-thirds of that total, with an input–output coefficient of 0.20. The retail sector purchases from a number of other activities, including rice, tubers, tree crops, livestock, small-scale food processing, light manufacturing, transportation, and wood products. However, the total input–output coefficients for purchases from these sectors is only 0.18, less than the total for construction. Small-scale food processing is the most strongly linked sector on the production side, purchasing from rice, tubers, groundnuts, tree crops, and livestock. The input–output coefficients associated with these purchases total over 0.51. Of the remaining nonfarm activities, purchases from other activities are virtually nil, except for light-manufacturing purchases of inputs from the wood products sector.

While agriculture's linkages to other activities are weak, payments to labor are high, as shown in SAM columns 1.1 through 1.18, rows 2.4 through 2.5. Coefficients for payments to hired labor are moderate to high for wet rice (0.19), dry rice (0.40), maize (0.16), and tubers (0.23), while returns to own-enterprise labor are very high, as a fraction of total output, for all crops other than rice and dry rice, with coefficients between 0.58 and 0.97. Payments to land are highest for rice, as are payments to animal capital.

Imports from the region (row 5.3) and from the rest of Indonesia (row 5.4) are high for many activities. In addition to the high import ratio for rice mentioned earlier, other high-leakage sectors are transportation and rice milling, which import fuel from the rest of Indonesia.

Factor payments and other household income

Columns 2.1 through 2.5 of the SAM show the payments from each factor to household groups. Migrant remittances (column 3.1) and pension payments (column 5.1, row 3.3) also contribute to household income.

Returns to own-enterprise labor make up the bulk of these payments, accounting for 61 percent of total village value-added, although this varies widely by household group. The SAM coefficients show that low-calorie households account for 8.6 percent of these returns; medium-calorie households, 51.5 percent; and high-calorie households, 40.3 percent. As a fraction of total household income (which includes migrant remittances and pensions in addition to value-added), own-enterprise labor makes up 32 percent for low-calorie households, 53 percent for medium-calorie households, and 60 percent for high-calorie households.

Returns to hired labor make up another 29 percent of value-added, so that the two labor categories alone add up to 90 percent of total value-added. Here also, medium-calorie households capture nearly half (48.4 percent) of these returns, with 34 percent going to low-calorie households, and only 17 percent going to high-calorie households. Hired labor represents a higher proportion of total income for low-income households than for any other group (60 percent).

Returns to animal capital, physical capital, and land make up 3.7 percent, 3.5 percent, and 1.4 percent, respectively, of total value-added. Again, returns vary widely by household group. Over half (57.3 percent) of returns to animal capital accrue to high-calorie households, and all payments to physical capital are earned by medium-calorie households. While high-calorie households earn the largest share of payments to land in the village, only 14 percent of land payments are captured by village households at all; most of the remainder is paid to the local plantation under sharecropping arrangements.

Migrant remittances contribute an amount equivalent to an additional 13.8 percent of village value-added to household incomes. Sixty-eight percent of all remittances accrue to high-calorie households, to make up 23 percent of these households' total incomes. Pensions represent the equivalent of only 0.6 percent of village value-added, although they provide 10 percent of the total income of medium-calorie households, the only households collecting pensions.

Household expenditures and investments

SAM columns 3.2 through 3.4 report the fraction of household income paid to each sector.

Expenditure patterns of each household group reveal some significant differences in linkages with the village economy. The most important distinction of the medium-calorie households is that, during the survey year, they were the only group with positive savings. While all households invested in physical, human, and animal capital and crop inventories, low- and high-calorie households drew down on assets while medium-calorie households accumulated savings over and above investment in other instruments.

After accounting for savings and investment, the two largest expenditure categories are retail and rice, although for high-calorie households construction appears as a large item. Other significant categories are small-scale food processing and livestock. The high-calorie group outspends other households on retail, both as an average total and as a fraction of total income.[6] This expenditure category is weakly linked to the village economy, since over 70 percent of retail volume is imported. The medium-calorie group spends more on rice on average, although the low-calorie group spends more as a fraction of its total income. Rice also has a high import content (52 percent), and shares of hired-labor and own-enterprise-labor value-added for this sector are low (19 and 7 percent, respectively).

The food expenditure patterns are somewhat misleading if taken as indicators of diet. For example, the high-calorie group spends more than the medium-calorie group on livestock products, even though the medium-calorie group has a higher average income and would be expected to spend more income on meat. Dividing average household expenditures by the average number of total adult equivalent units per household does not change this

6. Furthermore, the marginal propensity for the low-calorie households to consume rice is higher than the average propensity; thus, increases in income for this group not only improve energy consumption but generate a link to the rest of the village economy through rice production. Returns to hired labor from rice production accrue disproportionately to poor households, which in turn consume more rice, creating more linkages with the village economy.

Table 7.12. *Marginal propensities to consume by household group*

	Low calorie	Medium calorie	High calorie
1.1 Rice	0.126	0.007	0.069
1.2 Dry rice	0.026	0.002	0.014
1.3 Maize	0.00000191	0.00000144	0.00000111
1.4 Tubers	0	0	0
1.5 Soybeans	0	0	0
1.6 Groundnuts	0.00000181	0.00000171	0.00000130
1.7 Veg etc.	0.017	0.017	0.117
1.8 Tree crops	0.00000245	0.000000363	0.00000245
1.9 Livestock	0.16	0.015	0.114
1.10 Construction	0	0	0
1.11 Real	0	0	0
1.12 Low food proc	0.201	0.019	0.143
1.13 High food proc	0	0	0
1.14 Light mfg	0	0	0
1.15 Transportation	0.00000274	0.000000221	0.00000177
1.16 Wood	0.00000413	0.000000354	0.000000277
1.17 Education	0	0	0
1.18 Health	− 0.026	0.002	0.004

Notes: Marginal propensities were estimated from a quadratic consumption function. Paddy rice and dry-land rice are not distinguished in consumption, so the marginal propensity to consume rice was spread accross the two categories according to their proportions of total rice consumption in the village. Coefficients that were not statistically significant from zero are reported as zero. The negative effect of total income on health for low-calorie households (the poorest) may be due to improvements in diet and sanitation with increases in income.

apparent anomaly, because the high-calorie households average only 2.3 adult equivalent units while medium-calorie households average 3.3. Low-calorie households average 4.1 adult equivalents, lowering their relative position even further. However, high-calorie households are far more likely to supply meat from on-farm livestock, which appears in the livestock account, whereas the medium-calorie group is more likely to purchase imported meat, which appears in the retail sector.

Columns 4.1 through 4.6 of the SAM show the distribution of each investment account. Although the high savings rate of medium-calorie households is clearly desirable, these savings do not have a direct impact on the village economy, because they are deposited in a bank outside the village. They are available to some extent for loans to village residents, but profits from those loans do not stay in the village. The financial account thus represents an important leakage from the village when compared with other savings instruments and investments like crop inventory and livestock, which are purchased from the village.

Village exports and other exogenous accounts

Columns 5.1 through 5.5 of the SAM show purchases by each exogenous account, including the government, the plantation, local exports, exports to the rest of Indonesia, and exports to the rest of the world.

Total commodity exports from the village to the local area and to the rest of Indonesia sum to 537.7 million Rp (about $322,000 in 1989). This amounts to 32 percent of total final demand. The major exporting activities are groundnuts (29 percent of commodity exports), large-scale food processing (20 percent), transportation (23 percent), and tubers (14 percent). Other, smaller, exporting sectors include maize, soybeans, retail, lumber, and health. An additional 17 million Rp enters the village as remittances from migrants in the rest of Indonesia, and 106 million Rp is remitted from migrants abroad.

The plantation hires village labor, as does the government. The government also pays pensions to households of retired soldiers; these payments go directly to medium-calorie households, the only group receiving such pensions. The linkages among the exogenous accounts themselves include the estimated exports of the plantation to the rest of Indonesia, as well as payments to balance exogenous accounts. The exogenous government account subsidizes the endogenous fee-for-service government account to cover the gap between fees and services. Local imports from the rest of Indonesia balance the gap between local imports and local exports. The rest of Indonesia imports from the rest of the world. Finally, the exogenous government account requires a balancing payment from the rest of Indonesia to cover the gap between taxes collected and payments to hired labor, pensioners, and the endogenous government.

Conclusion: Identifying prospects for growth

The social accounting matrix provides a useful framework for analyzing the linkages among sectors of the village economy. The SAM summarizes the sources of income for households of different types, and it reveals likely mechanisms to increase incomes for each type of household through interactions among activities, factors, and households. Although it is fairly open, the village economy is an important economic unit. The majority of hired-labor demand by agriculture and other enterprises and an important part of final demand are satisfied from within the village. The village is an important economic unit from a policy perspective as well, since many rural development programs are targeted to individual villages.

Village export patterns point to a key growth bottleneck for an economy structured around supplying urban centers. The scope for increases in agricultural exports is severely limited by land constraints given existing technologies. Some dry land for maize and tuber production will be available for a few years until the plantation is fully planted to cacao, but production increases thereafter will be limited to yield increases. Nonagricultural exports, including large-scale food processing and transportation, are capital intensive and have high import contents. Incomes from those sectors accrue primarily to wealthy households, whose expenditure patterns result in high direct and indirect income leakages.

There are some important prospects for growth, however. Poultry and aquaculture activities (grouped with livestock in this SAM) are areas of the food sector that are less limited by land constraints and have a large potential for income growth given the village's proximity to urban markets. Small broiler poultry operations have been shown to have low investment requirements, rapid capital turnover, and high profits when veterinary and marketing assistance are provided. Fish ponds, which many households in the village have already started, may have a similar potential, although start-up costs are somewhat higher. Loans and technical assistance for these activities targeted to households in the low-calorie group could be an important vehicle for improving their relative economic position and nutrient intake.

Other prospects for growth include increased migrant remittances, job opportunities within commuting distance, and an increase in local light manufacturing. The village's proximity to Jakarta and to the growing town of Sukabumi gives residents access to a large market for unskilled labor in construction. The proximity to growing urban areas also gives the village access to markets for local light manufactures (i.e., furniture), which provide an opportunity to generate value-added by processing raw materials before exporting them from the village.

The low-calorie group can benefit in relative terms from these changes only if its relative participation in these activities increases. This could be accomplished through targeted loans and training for furniture manufacture and targeted job-placement assistance. These programs already exist within the central government's Department of Manpower; however, they have not yet reached this village. Interestingly, investment in local roads (which the village is already pursuing) could have mixed implications for the low-calorie group. If road construction facilitates exports and marketing, it could increase employment. However, motorized transportation will displace the low-income workers who earn wages carrying loads over village trails by foot.

The efforts of the Indonesian nutrition community to make nutritional improvement a criterion for the success of economic development can help focus attention on the poor, who are most vulnerable to malnutrition. The village SAM reveals that improving incomes for the poor is likely to benefit the village economy, because poor households have stronger expenditure linkages with the village economy and spend a higher fraction of incremental income on goods with a low import content.

8

The village CGE: Basic model and estimation

This chapter presents the basic village CGE model that we estimate for the Senegalese village of Keur Marie; the Indian, Mexican, and Javan villages; and the Kenyan village-town. After a discussion of the basic village and village-town model, the model structure and parameters are compared across the four villages and village-town. The chapter concludes with a summary of the programming and estimation of the models.

The village CGE

Our village CGEs are rooted in a model of a diversified household-farm economy (or, in the Senegalese case, compound-farm economy) engaged in staple production but also potentially in a portfolio of other income activities. As in the neoclassical household-farm model (Barnum and Squire, 1979; Singh, Squire, and Strauss, 1986), households maximize utility derived from leisure and income obtained by allocating their labor and other factors to production and work activities inside and outside the village.

The village and the households within it are price takers with respect to most goods. Active trade in goods among households is evidence that few households are constrained to be completely self-sufficient. That is, most goods can be considered as tradables at the household level. We refer to such goods as *household tradables*. These are goods whose prices are determined by markets outside the household, either inside or outside the village. Chapters 3 through 7 document the openness of village economies: A large share of village supplies of goods is "imported" from outside markets, and often a significant part of production is "exported" from the village. These findings

182

reveal the importance of tradables in village economies. Goods whose prices are determined outside the village are referred to as *village tradables*.

We depart from the standard neoclassical household-farm model by not assuming that all goods are household tradables. For example, hired labor is not a perfect substitute for family labor in household production activities; in general, it is costly to separate labor from management on household-farms (e.g., see Bardhan, 1988). In this spirit, family labor and hired labor appear as separate factor inputs in village production functions. There is a missing market for family labor, in the sense that there is not perfect substitutability between family and market supply of this critical input. The household faces a constraint of balancing its total (fixed) supply of time with its demand for time in leisure and income activities, including migration.

The allocation of family time between leisure and income activities is guided by the shadow value (opportunity cost) of family time, equal to the marginal utility of leisure, and by the marginal utility of income. Lacking a perfect substitute for family labor, households face trade-offs between consumption (i.e., leisure) and production, implying that the consumption and production sides of the household-farm models nested within our village CGEs must be solved simultaneously instead of recursively. (For a theoretical treatment of agricultural households with missing markets, see Singh, Squire, and Strauss, 1986; and de Janvry, Fafchamps, and Sadoulet, 1991.) In our models, domestic and foreign migration opportunities influence the endogenous price of family time.[1]

Fixed *village* prices for household tradables imply that excess demands (supplies) can be imported into (exported from) the village at prices determined by outside markets. In the case of hired labor, the exogenous wage assumption may reflect a Lewis-type (1954) surplus labor environment within the village, resulting in a perfectly elastic hired labor supply. The coexistence of this fixed wage with an endogenous wage for family labor is logically consistent, given imperfect substitutability between the two factor inputs in household-farm production. It is also consistent with a real world in which households have differential access to migrant labor markets, which can profoundly affect the opportunity cost of family time in village activities.

Not all household tradables are village tradables. In most versions of our models, goods and factors besides family labor, physical capital, and land are treated as tradables. However, two of the experiments in Chapter 9 explore the implications of endogenous village prices: an endogenous hired-worker wage and an endogenous price for staples. High transactions costs may force villages to be self-sufficient in some goods and factors. Unless there is a surplus of wage labor within the village or a nearby source of labor that can

---

1. As in most neoclassical household-farm models, we assume physical capital and land are fixed in the short run. Hence, they are treated as household nontradables as well.

be imported into the village at low cost, excess demand for hired labor will tend to exert upward pressure on village wages.

High transactions costs often cut local LDC economies off from outside goods markets. In many instances, goods that economists generally consider to be tradable are, in practice, nontradable, because of poor access to markets due to backward and inefficient marketing and transportation infrastructures. In Mexico, for example, despite a government-guaranteed price for corn that was more than double the world price in the early 1990s, most corn farmers did not market their crop. Isolated by high transactions costs, many local corn economies groped for their own equilibrium prices and quantities, influenced tangentially, if at all, by the policy price. At the same time, Mexico's *ejido* (land reform) laws inhibited the functioning of land markets and converted what would have been market rental rates on land into household-specific shadow rents.

Given the potentially critical importance of endogenous prices and resource constraints in local economies, the scope for using fixed-price models for policy and market analysis may be limited. The approach outlined here makes it possible to introduce various combinations of household and village nontradables into micro economywide models.

The basic village model

Households are assumed to maximize a utility function of the form

$$U = U(X_i, X_l) \quad i = 1, \ldots, I \text{ goods} \tag{1}$$

where X_i denotes household demand for good i and X_l is the demand for leisure. Utility is maximized subject to four constraints:

$$\textit{a cash-income constraint: } \sum_{i=1}^{I} P_i \, X_i = \Pi + er^*REMITS + P_V \, VS + \overline{Y} \tag{2}$$

where P_i is the village price of good i; Π is net income from household-farm production; *REMITS* denotes remittances from internal and international migrants; *er* is the exchange rate used to convert remittances to the local currency (equal to 1 for domestic remittances and the international exchange rate for remittances from abroad); P_V is the local price of tradable input V (e.g., wage labor); *VS* is the household's supply of this input; and $\overline{Y}$ is exogenous income;

$$\textit{production technologies: } Q_i = Q_i(FL_i, V_i, K_i) \tag{3}$$

where Q_i is output of good i, FL_i is family labor input into activity i, V_i is a vector of tradable inputs (including hired labor), and K_i denotes capital inputs;

$$a \text{ family time constraint: } X_l + \sum_{i=1}^{I} FL_i + MIG + LS \leqslant \overline{T} \tag{4}$$

where $\overline{T}$ represents the family's total time endowment; and

$$\text{remittance functions: } REMIT_d = \phi_d(MIG_d) \tag{5}$$

where MIG_d is family migration to destination d (d = foreign or domestic).

The first-order conditions for utility maximization require that the marginal value product (output price times the marginal product Q_{V_i}) equals the price for all tradable inputs V_i:

$$P_i Q_{V_i} = w_V \tag{6}$$

For family labor,

$$P_i Q_{FL_i} = \omega/\lambda \tag{7}$$

where Q_{FL_i} is the marginal product of family labor, ω denotes the marginal utility of family time, and λ is the marginal utility of income. Conditions (7) imply that family labor is allocated to village production activities up to the point where the marginal effect on household income equals the opportunity cost of family time (i.e., the family wage). They also imply that households spread their scarce labor time across production activities to equalize marginal value products of family labor. The marginal utility of family time equals the marginal utility of leisure (U_{X_l}):

$$U_{X_l} = \omega \tag{8}$$

Households allocate their time to migration until the family wage equals the marginal returns to migration in the form of remittances, denoted R_{MIG_d}.[2]

$$R_{MIG_d} = \omega/\lambda \tag{9}$$

Utility maximization implies that each commodity i is demanded at the level where the marginal utility of consuming the good equals the opportunity cost, in terms of lost utility from alternative uses of scarce family income. The opportunity cost of consumption is the price of the good weighted by the marginal utility of income:

$$U_{X_i} = \lambda p_i \tag{10}$$

---

2. Disutility (e.g., high psychic costs) of migration may result in a lower level of migration than implied by this condition. It could be incorporated into the model by including migration as a separate argument in the utility function, with a marginal utility of migration less than zero. In the present model, migration affects household-farm utility in only two ways: positively, by generating remittance income (the left-hand side of condition [9]); and negatively, by competing with other income activities and leisure for scarce family time (the right-hand side of [9]); the opportunity cost of migration is the family wage.

The household's cash income and time constraints are assumed to be binding; that is,

$$\Pi + er^*REMITS + P_V \, VS + \overline{Y} - \sum_{i=1}^{I} P_i \, X_i = 0 \tag{11}$$

$$X_I + \sum_{i=1}^{I} FL_i + MIG + LS = \overline{T} \tag{12}$$

The first-order conditions for utility maximization outlined here are similar to those for household-farm models with incomplete labor markets (e.g., Singh, Squire, and Strauss, 1986; de Janvry, Fafchamps, and Sudoulet, 1991; Lopez, 1986). However, the villagewide model incorporates household-farms into a local general-equilibrium framework. Four sets of conditions (13 through 16) ensure that the decisions of our households yield an equilibrium solution to the village model. The first set of conditions consists of the material-balance equations

$$Q_i = C_i + G_i + I_i + MS_i \tag{13}$$

where C_i is the total consumption demand for good i, summed across households; G_i and I_i are total government and investment demands for sector-i output; and MS_i denotes net village marketed surplus. Conditions (13) stipulate that the local markets for all goods clear. For tradables, these conditions determine village net marketed surplus (exports minus imports) for each sector. Because the village includes both net sellers and net buyers of locally produced goods, the existence of marketed surplus for some households does not imply a marketed surplus for the village. For nontradables ($MS=0$), Condition (13) determines endogenous village (or village-town) market-clearing prices.

Village input market equilibrium requires a balance between factor supplies (summed across households, plus imported factors VM) and demands (summed across production activities, plus any exogenous demands).[3] These factors do not include family labor, for which there is a missing village market. (Excess demand for family labor in the village is ruled out by household-specific time constraints.) The second set of conditions, for factor markets, are:

$$\sum_{h=1}^{H} VS_h + VM = \sum_{i=1}^{I} V_i \tag{14}$$

---

3. Exogenous demands include any government demand (e.g., for labor in public works projects) or, in the case of the Indian village, temple demand for production factors, including hired labor.

Because physical capital and land inputs are assumed to be fixed in the short run, condition (14) applies only to hired labor.[4] In the case of an exogenous wage (elastic supply), this condition determines total hired-labor demand. In the case of a fixed village supply of wage labor (endogenous wage), it determines the village wage.

The third condition requires equilibrium in the local capital market:

$$I = \sum_{i=1}^{I} I_i = \sum_{h=1}^{H} S_h(Y_h) \tag{15}$$

where $S_h(Y_h)$ denotes household-specific savings levels.[5] Village investment demand is obtained from an investment-shares matrix that converts sectoral investment demands (shares of sector output) into demands for village investment-goods sector outputs. We adopt the neoclassical assumption that investment is endogenous in our villages and village-town. Condition (15) does not include a village analogue to what appears as foreign borrowing in national CGE models. That is, it requires villages to self-finance their investments. This is usually a reasonable assumption, given missing or incomplete credit markets that characterize LDC rural economies. However, it can easily be relaxed by allowing households to borrow from the outside world, when applicable.

Finally, village trade with the outside world must balance:

$$\sum_{i=1}^{I} P_i \, MS_i + \sum_{h=1}^{H} \sum_{d=1}^{D} REMIT_{h,d} = 0 \tag{16}$$

A fundamental difference between our village models and a conventional country CGE is that there may be more than one "rest-of-the-world" for a village. There are at least two rest-of-the-worlds in the Mexican, Kenyan, and Javan models. The first is the rest of the country of which the village is part, which constitutes a common-currency trade unit with the village. The second is the foreign world, separated from the village by an exchange rate. The Mexican and Javan villages and Kenyan village-town interact with the foreign world through migration, for which payment usually is received in foreign currency. In the Javan case, there are two Indonesian rest-of-the-worlds (a local market and the rest of the country) and one rest-of-the-world outside Indonesia. There also may be multiple government accounts,

---

4. Supply–demand equilibrium for intermediate inputs is implied by the material balance constraints (13).

5. Savings imply a two-step process in which household-farms first allocate their full income to savings and consumption and then maximize a utility function of the form of equation (1). For simplicity, we treat savings in our models as determined by fixed savings propensities that differ across household groups.

including local and state, provincial, or federal governments. Governments generally play a minimal role in our villages and village-town.

There is no reason to expect village exports and imports to balance for individual rest-of-the-world accounts. For example, income remitted by international migrants typically is used to finance imports of goods from the rest of the country – not directly from abroad. However, the value of total village imports and exports (including migrant labor) must equal. This equality is implied by the other equations in the model, and thus equation (16) represents the redundant or left-out equation in the village CGE system. There is also no reason to expect that outside government revenues from a village and expenditures in the village will balance. When the former (latter) are greater, government activity generates a positive (negative) income leakage from the village.

The only role for international exchange rates in our models is to convert international migrant remittances into the currency of the country of which the village is part, because labor is the only export for which our villages receive payment in foreign currency. The exchange rate is fixed in all of our experiments:

$$er = \overline{er} \tag{17}$$

In the three cases where there is income from international migration, the village (or village-town) generates foreign exchange for the nation to which it belongs by exporting migrant labor abroad.

The choice of functional forms

Moving from the theoretical model outlined here to a village economywide model requires selecting functional forms for utility, production, and migration. For our applications we specify Cobb-Douglas utility and production functions and a remittance function of the form:

$$REMIT_d = MIG_d{}^{\eta_d} \tag{18}$$

where η_d is the elasticity of remittances with respect to family time allocated to migration. Separate remittance functions were estimated for each household-farm group. Differences in migration response across households reflect differential access to domestic and international migrant labor markets.

These functional forms are simple and computationally tractable, and most of their parameters can easily be estimated from the data contained in village SAMs. For example, the exponents of the Cobb-Douglas production function are equal to the shares of factors in sector value-added. Cobb-Douglas utility functions imply linear demand functions. The use of simple production and utility functions makes it relatively easy to trace through the effects of policy and market changes on village production, incomes, and expenditures. It makes the results of our policy experiments relatively easy to decipher rather than appearing as output from a "black box." This is a particularly attractive feature of the models, we think, when it comes to presenting them to a fairly broad audience and when it comes to interpreting the results from comparative village experiments.

There are trade-offs between simplicity, on the one hand, and the restrictiveness of functional forms, on the other. The drawbacks to using a Cobb-Douglas functional form in consumption and production applications are well known (Deaton and Muellbauer, 1980; Chambers, 1988; Heathfield and Wibe, 1987). They have some potentially important implications for our policy and market experiments. For example, a Cobb-Douglas utility function rules out a backward-bending labor-supply response in a standard consumer household model. Nevertheless, it does not rule out a negative effect of (exogenous) wages on hired-labor supply in a villagewide model. A case in point is our migrant remittance experiment for the Javan village, which reveals evidence of a backward-bending migration supply curve. An increase in returns to village households from migration has two effects: a substitution effect encouraging families to reallocate their time from other activities to migration, and an income effect that drives up the marginal utility of leisure. The income effect dominates in the Javan case, leading to less migration.

Cobb-Douglas production functions constrain all factor inputs to be substitutes within individual production activities. However, they do not constrain factor inputs to be substitutes across activities. Substitutability of factors within individual activities does not imply positive cross-price effects on factor demand in a village general-equilibrium model or, for that matter, in a model of a diversified household-farm. For example, an increase in the wage for hired workers induces households to shift their production away from labor-intensive activities. This may reduce the demand for family labor, even though family and hired labor are assumed to be (imperfect) substitutes in individual Cobb-Douglas production functions.

Less restrictive functional forms can easily be incorporated into villagewide economic models. In current work, especially studies focusing on individual rather than comparative village or village-town models, we are incorporating more general specifications, including constant elasticitity of substitution (CES) production functions and almost-ideal demand system (AIDS) demand functions. The estimation of these functions is somewhat more demanding (though not at all intractable) computationally and also with regard to data, but it is fruitful to explore the sensitivity of village economywide models to the choice of functional forms. We encourage readers who plan to estimate villagewide models to experiment with alternative functional forms, following the lead of both household-farm and CGE modelers.

An intravillage comparison of model structure and parameters

The heterogeneity of results from the policy experiments presented in the next chapter results from the considerable diversity in production, factors, and institutions that characterizes our five villages.

This section compares estimated parameters across the village and village-town models. This is equivalent to comparing the structures of the five economies as depicted in the SAMs presented in Chapters 3 through 7. With few exceptions, the parameters in our models were calculated directly from SAM coefficients.

Table 8.1 reveals that the five villages cover a broad spectrum in terms of per capita incomes and income diversification. The correlation between income and diversification within households is disputed in the development economics literature. Empirical studies in Asia and Latin America tend to find a negative correlation between per capita income and diversification, while the limited research from sub-Saharan Africa, where credit and risk obstacles impede efforts by poor households to diversify income sources, suggests a positive correlation (e.g., see Reardon, Delgado, and Matlan, 1992). There appears to be a relatively high correlation between income and diversification within our villages and village-town. At one end of the spectrum are the Senegalese village of Keur Marie and the Indian village, with very low average annual per capita incomes ($105 and $124, respectively) and relatively undiversified economies. The Indian village economy consists of seven production sectors plus internal migration, of which the top three account for 91 percent of total village income and the largest (staples) accounts for 73 percent. The Senegalese village has six production sectors plus internal migration, of which the largest three account for 86 percent of income. As we shall see, these two villages are less integrated into local and regional product markets on the input and output sides than the other two villages or the village-town.

At the other extreme are the Javan and Mexican villages and the Kenyan village-town. The Javan and Kenyan cases have relatively high average per capita incomes ($462 and $350, respectively). They also are the most diversified of all our villages, both in terms of the number of income sources (fifteen sectors plus internal and international migration in the Javan case; eight sectors plus migration in the Kenyan case) and in terms of the concentration of income among these sources (the top three sources account for 76 and 61 percent of income in these villages, with the largest shares being 34 and 25 percent, respectively). The Javan village and Kenyan village-town economies are relatively commercialized and integrated into regional product markets.

The anomaly is the Mexican village, which, largely as a result of high-paying international migration, has the highest average per capita income of

Table 8.1. *Average income and diversification in the four villages and village-town*

	Average annual per capita income	Income sources (no.)	Percentage share in total income of	
			3 largest sources	Largest source
Java	462	17	76	34
Kenya	350	9	61	25
Mexico	700	7	78	48
India	124	8	91	73
Senegal	105	7	86	30

all five economies ($700). In terms of diversification, however, the Mexican village economy more closely resembles the low-income Senegalese village, with only five production sectors plus internal and international migration. Seventy-eight percent of total village income comes from the three largest income sources, and the largest single source (livestock) accounts for just under one-half of total income.

Village and regional markets

Subsistence staple production is a fundamental feature of all four villages and the village-town. Many households engage in production exclusively for subsistence; others produce some staple surplus to market inside or outside the village. Transactions costs in LDC rural areas tend to be household-specific; hence, some households transact in outside markets while others do not (de Janvry, Fafchamps, and Sudoulet, 1991). This is likely to be the case with regard to marketing surplus outside the village or village-town, where market information, access, and transportation play a critical role. Transactions costs are less likely to be a problem in local staple markets, however.

Households that do not market their output outside the village or village-town frequently trade in local markets. For example, although the Mexican village lacks a central marketplace, an active trade in maize and other goods takes place on doorsteps and in *tienditas*, small stores typically consisting of a window cut into an exterior wall of the storekeeper's house. It is not uncommon for a woman to take small quantities of maize from the storage place in the house to a village store to exchange for flour, lard, soap, or other items. It is rare, however, for men to market their corn harvests; only 16 percent of farmers reported doing so in the survey year. Those who sell grain outside the village own their own trucks, which almost always are gifts from family migrants in California. Those who do not export their surplus from the village cite the high cost of transporting their crop to the nearest government

Table 8.2. *Integration with outside markets* (shapes of output)

	Senegal	India	Mexico	Kenya	Java
Staples					
Exports	0	.37	.16	.05	0
Imports	0	.34	.12	.05	.61
Agricultural					
Exports	.82	N.A.	N.A.	.52	.72
Imports	.13	N.A.	N.A.	.09	.02
Nonagricultural products					
Exports	.27	.28	.08	.29	.29
Imports	.94	.52	.71	.46	.49
Livestock					
Exports	0	.16	.38	.09	0
Imports	0	.38	.13	.04	.49
Migrant remittances as share of					
Total commodity exports	.60	.05	.72	.15	.23
Gross village product	.46	.05	.31	.12	.14

Notes: Exports and imports as shares of total supplies, by sector, and migrant remittances as shares of commodity export earnings and gross village product. Sectoral aggregation is as follows:
Senegal: staples: millet; ag. exports: peanuts. nonag: services and commerce.
India: staples: dryland farming; nonag.: services, village nonag. production, retail, government production.
Mexico: staples: basic grains; ag. exports: livestock; nonag.: renewable resource extraction, handicrafts, commerce.
Kenya: staples: food; ag. exports: coffee; nonag.: rural nonfarm, manufacturing, retail, transport, services.
Java: staples: rice, dry land rice; ag. exports: maize; nonag.: see Table 8.3.

purchase point more than 32 kilometers away. Increasingly, surplus maize is used as an input in local livestock production.

Table 8.2 summarizes village and village-town integration with outside markets. Subsistence staple production is reflected in generally low export shares for staples, ranging from 0 percent in Senegal and Java to 37 percent in India. Nevertheless, the villages and village-town interact actively with the outside world in nonstaple markets, and in some cases they also rely on outside markets to satisfy some of their staple demand. Sixty-one percent of total rice supply in the Javan village is obtained outside the village. The import share for the Indian village is 34 percent. The Mexican village and Kenyan village-town depend only slightly on staple imports. Only in the Senegalese village are transactions with outside staple markets completely absent on both the production and consumption sides. Transactions with outside markets for livestock products tend to mirror those with staple markets.

In contrast to staples and livestock products, village supplies of nonagricultural goods rely heavily on imports, with import shares ranging from 46 percent in the Kenyan village-town to 94 percent in the Senegalese village. Agroexports are important in three cases – the Senegalese and Javan villages and the Kenyan village-town. The Senegalese village exports peanuts, the Javan village maize, and the Kenyan village-town coffee.

The bottom panel of Table 8.2 reveals the importance of labor exports in the village and village-town economies. The ratio of migrant remittances to total commodity exports ranges from lows of 5 and 15 percent in India and Kenya to highs of 60 and 72 percent in Senegal and Mexico. In the two most migration-dependent villages, migrant remittances are equivalent to 31 to 46 percent of the gross village product (GVP).

Production and factors

Tables 8.3 and 8.4 summarize the production sectors, factors of production, and factor productivities in the five villages. These tables reveal a continuum of complexity in terms of the diversity of production structures. The Javan village has by far the most complex production structure of the villages in this study, with three staple sectors, five export sectors, a livestock sector, and eight nonagricultural sectors that include some light manufacturing as well as services (Table 8.3). At the other extreme, the Indian, Mexican, and Senegalese villages have few sectors (five to six), and two of these villages (India and Mexico) have no agricultural export sectors.

Factors of production and their productivity in different village production activities are summarized in Table 8.4. The list of production factors in a village model reflects both the factor-market institutions in the village and the interests of the researcher who constructed the model. The basic factor list includes family labor, hired labor, physical capital, and land. The Indian model, however, reflects a research focus on the sexual division of labor, with separate male and female categories of family and hired labor. It also lacks a land factor, instead incorporating land rents into a family capital account that includes net farm profits. These factor categories primarily reflect modeling choices. The Indian model also contains farm servant and salaried labor categories, which in large part are not relevant to other village settings. It includes public and private credit as explicit factor inputs, which reflects both a modeling choice and the fact that credit plays an important role in the production strategies of households in this village. The factor categories are most complex in the Senegalese village, where households and compounds play distinctive roles in village production, and where land institutions are both diverse and an explicit research focus.

Table 8.3. *Production sectors in the village and village-town models*

Village	Staples	Commodity group		
		Agricultural exports	Other agriculture	Nonagricultural sectors
Java	Rice (wet) Rice (dry) Vegetables	Maize Tubers	Livestock and fish	Retail Food processing Light manufacturing Transportation Primary Education and health Religion Services
Kenya	Food	Coffee	Livestock	Rural nonfarm Manufacturing Retail Transport Services
India	Dry-land farming Wetland farming	—	Livestock	Services Village production Retail Government production
Mexico	Basic grains	—	Livestock	Renewable resources Handicrafts Commerce
Senegal	Millet	Peanuts	Livestock Other crops	Services Commerce

Table 8.4 reveals differences in factor productivity and hired labor use among the five villages and among production activities within the villages. The numbers in the table are factor shares in value-added, which under the assumption of profit maximization are equal to the exponents of the Cobb-Douglas production function. Not surprisingly, production is most hired-labor-intensive in the most commercialized village (Java), where the hired-labor share in value-added is .52 in wet rice production and .93 in dry rice production. By contrast, the hired-labor share in staples is only .06 in the Mexican village and .04 in the Senegalese village. In all villages except Java, family factors play a dominant role in staple production. In the Mexican village, the family-labor share of value-added in maize production is 34 percent, while in the Senegalese village, manager, house, and compound labor account for 31 percent of staple value-added. By contrast, family labor accounts for less than 20 percent of value-added in wet rice production and 2 percent in dry rice production in the Javan case. These differences in value-added shares may be explained partly by differences in methods used to

Table 8.4. *Production factors and value-added shares models*

Village and factor	Commodity group			
	Staples	Agricultural exports	Livestock	Nonagricultural sectors
Java				
Family labor	Rice (wet) .184 Rice (dry) .021 Vegetables .847	.873	.786	.445
Hired labor	Rice (wet) .523 Rice (dry) .932 Vegetables .151	.104	.002	.462
Land	Rice (wet) .146	.023	0	0
Physical capital	Rice (wet) .010	0	0	.094
Animal capital	Rice (wet) .138	0	.212	0
Kenya				
Family labor	.512	.805	.236	Rural nonfarm .701 Manufacturing .505 Retail .738 Transportation .474 Services .132
Hired labor	.028	.046	—	Rural nonfarm .119 Manufacturing .149 Retail .058 Transportation .099 Services .549
Land	.290	.033	.054	0
Physical capital	.171	.291	.710	Rural nonfarm .180 Manufacturing .346 Retail .204 Transportation .427 Services .319
India				
Family labor	Male 0.069 Female 0.029	0	0	0
Hired labor	Male 0.048 Female 0.084	0	0	Male services 0.045 Village 0.021 Production retail 0.023
Farm servant Labor	0.026	0	0.104	0
Salaried	0	0	0	Government production 0.984
Capital	0.068	0	0	0
Family capital	0.615	0	0.704	Services 0.767 Village production 0.936 Retail 0.573

Table 8.4. *(cont.)*

| Village and factor | Commodity group | | | |
	Staples	Agricultural exports	Livestock	Nonagricultural sectors
Credit	Private 0.006 Public 0.039	0	0 0.060	0 Services 0.013 Village production 0.004 Retail 0.004
Mexico				
Family labor	0.341	—	0.105	Renewable resources 0.573 Handicrafts 0.606 Commerce 0.600
Hired labor	0.067	—	0	Renewable resources 0.172 Handicrafts 0.125
Land	0.399	—	0.635	Renewable resources 0.171
Capital	0.194	—	0.260	Renewable resources 0.083 Handicrafts 0.269 Commerce 0.400
Senegal				
Manager labor	0.104	0.050	Other crops 0.122	0
House labor	0.175	0.153	Other crops 0.099	0
Compound labor	0.030	0.039	Other crops 0.088	0
Village labor	0.039	0.015	Other crops 0.013 Livestock 0.026	0
Imported labor	0.005	0.002	Other crops 0.001	0
Nonagricultural labor	0	0	Livestock 0.864	Services 1.0 Commerce 1.0
Land				
Secure	0.546	0.382	Other crops 0.135	0
Moderately secure	0.013	0.057	Other crops 0.310	0
Insecure	0.004	0.164	Other crops 0.233	0
Borrowed	0.085	0.138	0	0
Grazing	0	0	Livestock 0.109	0

allocate value-added between family labor and land rents in the village models. Nevertheless, the combined contribution of family labor and land to value-added in grain production is considerably lower in the Javan case (33 percent) than in the other four villages (54 to 96 percent). Hired-labor use in agricultural exports and in nonagricultural sectors is also highest in the Javan case (10 and 46 percent, respectively) and lowest in the Senegalese case (1.5 and 0 percent, respectively). Livestock production utilizes almost no hired labor in any of the five villages.

The distribution of value-added between hired labor and other factors has important implications for our policy experiments. When family labor is in short supply or has a high opportunity cost in other activities, output response in labor-intensive sectors depends critically on households' ability to expand their production using hired labor. This, in turn, is reflected in the hired-labor output elasticities in Table 8.4. In sectors that rely heavily on family inputs (labor, land, and physical capital), whose total supplies are fixed in the short run, output response may be limited, particularly if the shadow prices of these resources are high. In light of this, we would expect, for example, to find a higher output elasticity for staples in Java than in Mexico, Senegal, or India, where staple production is relatively family-labor-intensive and (especially in the Mexican case) where income opportunities for family migrants abound.

Household incomes and expenditures

The income and expenditure side of the village models has important implications for assessing the impacts of policy changes on poverty and inequality, on the marketed surplus of village production and regional trade linkages, and on village savings and investment. Where villages are price takers in regional commodity markets, consumption linkages with village production are minimal. However, leisure demand competes with village production for scarce family time, and market failures resulting from high transactions costs with outside commodity markets create rich consumption linkages in our villages and village-town.

Distribution of factor income and remittances

Village factor value-added is the largest component of household farm income. The household distribution of land and capital value-added reflects primarily the distribution of land and capital assets, both of which are concentrated in large- and medium-landholding households. The distribution of family-labor value-added reflects both family labor endowments and the returns to this labor in village production activities. It also reflects possible differences across households in the opportunity cost of family labor in the village. Labor migration may pull family labor out of village production if

Table 8.5. *Distributions of village value-added across household groups*

Village and factor	Household group			
	Subsistence	Smallholder	Largeholder	Other
Java[a]				
Family labor	8.6	51.1	40.3	
Hired labor	34.3	48.6	17.1	
Land	21.6	31.4	47.1	
Capital	6.1	59.0	34.9	
Kenya[b]				
Family labor	7.9	18.0	57.8	16.3
Hired labor	18.6	12.0	58.2	11.2
Land	1.3	18.9	74.8	5.0
Capital	5.1	20.9	60.7	13.3
India[c]				
Farm labor	8.7	24.6	64.5	2.2
Hired labor	24.4	28.1	7.2	40.3
Land	6.6	13.1	77.3	3.0
Capital	14.6	22.2	41.8	21.4
Mexico				
Farm labor	2.1	48.5	49.4	
Hired labor	8.1	25.1	66.7	
Land	5.7	48.3	46.0	
Capital	6.4	48.3	45.3	
Senegal[d]				
Farm labor	25.5	32.7	41.8	
Hired labor	23.6	52.2	24.1	
Land	11.1	43.8	45.1	
Capital				

[a] Household groups are low-calorie, medium-calorie, and high-calorie intake, respectively. Capital includes animal plus physical capital.
[b] Smallholder and landless group includes salaried households. Mediumholder group includes subsistence households. Other households include urban groups.
[c] Male and female labor categories combined. Hired labor includes servants. Land includes "family capital" category.
[d] Family labor includes manager, compound, and house labor. Hired labor includes village labor category.

the returns to migration (marginal remittances) are high and/or if the productivity of family labor in village activities is low for some households.

Family-labor value-added is most equally distributed in the least commercialized village (Senegal), and it is unequally distributed in all others (Table

Table 8.6. *Household distribution of migrant remittances*

Village	Subsistence	Smallholder	Largeholder	Other
Java	5.7	26.3	70.3	
Kenya	9.0	31.0	45.5	14.5
India	3.3	0.0	78.3	18.4
Mexico	6.2	41.7	52.1	
Senegal	0.2	11.4	88.4	

Note: Domestic plus foreign remittances.

8.5). The share of this factor income going to the largeholder group ranges from a low of 42 percent in the Senegalese village to a high of 64 percent in the Indian village. The share accruing to the smallholder and landless group ranges from a low of 2.1 percent in the Mexican village to a high of 26 percent in the Senegalese village. Hired-labor value-added is more equally distributed than family-labor value-added in all five villages. More than one-fifth of this factor income goes to smallholder and landless households in all but the Mexican village, where hired-labor value-added, like family-labor value-added, is concentrated in medium- and largeholder households.

Migrant remittances do not compensate for unequal distributions of village value-added. Landless household groups generally lack access to relatively lucrative migration activities. Table 8.6 shows the distribution of internal and/or international migrant remittances across households in our villages. Landless households receive only a small share of remittances, from a low of 0.2 percent in Senegal to a high of 9 percent in the Kenyan village-town. Smallholder households capture the largest share of remittances in the Mexican village. The share accruing to largeholder households ranges from 45 percent in Kenya to 88 percent in Senegal. Unequal access to migration opportunities is particularly striking in the case of the Senegalese village, which has the lowest degree of interaction with regional and national markets of the five villages we studied.

Expenditures

Household expenditure patterns shape the impact of income changes on marketed surplus, trade linkages, and village savings and investment. When some commodities are village nontradables, they also influence the effect of income changes on endogenous village prices, and thus on production. Because expenditure patterns vary across household groups in the same village, a given income change can have very different consequences, depending upon how it is distributed.

Table 8.7. *Savings propensities and budget shares by commodity and household group*

Village and commodity group	Household group			
	Subsistence	Smallholder	Largeholder	Other
Java				
Staples	34.5	30.2	23.6	
Agricultural exports	4.0	5.1	4.0	
Other agriculture	6.4	6.6	6.1	
Nonagricultural	55.1	58.1	66.3	
Savings propensity	8.4	13.0	17.3	
Kenya				
Staples	10.3	19.6	16.2	
Agricultural exports	0	0	0	
Other agriculture	0.9	8.1	8.3	
Nonagricultural	88.8	72.3	75.5	
Savings propensity	21.9	20.1	24.5	18.4
India				
Staples	69.5	69.8	69.3	
Agricultural exports				
Other agriculture	6.4	7.9	7.9	
Nonagricultural	24.1	22.3	22.8	
Savings propensity	1.7	−7.3	35.3	
Mexico				
Staples	22.6	6.2	7.9	
Agricultural exports				
Other agricultural	20.7	11.1	14.8	
Nonagricultural	56.7	82.7	77.3	
Savings propensity	9.0	1.0	27.7	
Senegal				
Staples	70.2	40.0	24.0	
Agricultural exports	0.4	2.9	2.4	
Other agriculture				
Nonagricultural	2.8	1.1	1.8	
Savings propensity	1.4	4.0	4.1	

In general, the shares of staple demand in household budgets are highest in the smallholder and landless group, and they are lowest in the highest income and most commercialized villages, where nonstaple items are more likely to compete with staples in household budgets (Table 8.7). The staple shares for subsistence households range from a low of 10 percent in the Kenyan village to a high of 70 percent in the Senegalese village. The lowest staple budget shares are in medium- and largeholder Mexican households (6.2 and 7.9 percent, respectively). The Mexican village has a high degree of integration with outside markets on the factor side (labor migration) and in consumption. It is typical of a "commuter" village, in which labor "exports" finance market consumption demands. These differences in staple demands imply that a given change in income will tend to have a greater impact on marketed surplus of staples (and, if staples are village nontradables, on staple prices) in the poorest and least commercialized villages and in the smallest landholding groups.

The budget shares of nonagricultural goods are highest in the most commercialized villages and in Mexico. The consumption demand for these goods is satisfied primarily by imports to the village, but it is more likely to be met through local production in the Javan and Kenyan cases, where nonagricultural sectors are relatively well developed. Even there, however, village imports play a key role in satisfying local consumption demands, because nonagricultural production tends to rely heavily on inputs purchased from outside the local economy. Trade linkages, therefore, are potentially large.

Savings rates are uniformly highest in the largeholder households, but they vary widely across villages. The within-village disparity in savings rates is greatest in India (from −7.3 percent in the mediumholder group to 35 percent in the largeholder group). However, savings propensities for smallholder and landless groups in Kenya (20 to 22 percent) are higher than largeholder savings propensities in both Java and Senegal (17 and 4 percent, respectively). More regressive distributions of income gains will tend to have the most favorable effect on savings in the Indian, Mexican, and Senegalese cases. Equitable distributions of income gains will tend to have the lowest cost in terms of lost savings in the Javan and Kenyan cases.

Summary and conclusions

Our village economywide modeling integrates microeconomic, household-farm modeling into a computable general-equilibrium framework. In this sense, it represents a marriage of household-farm and CGE approaches. The structure of the base model is the same for all four villages and the Kenyan village-town. This is to facilitate comparisons of model results across the five applications. Nevertheless, the models reflect all of the striking structural differences among villages and between these and the village-town revealed in the SAMs presented in Chapters 3 through 7. These include differences in production activities; household groups and institutions; village resource constraints; production factors and production function parameters; expenditure patterns of different household-farms, compounds, and other village institutions; and interactions with the outside world. These differences were highlighted in this chapter by comparing model parameters among our five village and village-town applications.

The village models were solved using Minos5, a nonlinear programming algorithm in GAMS developed by Murtagh and Sanders (1983). This produced the base solution for each of our five models. Separate experiment files were set up for each of the sixteen policy simulations presented in the next chapter. They use the base models as the starting points for each simulation, and they generate output tables reporting percentage differences between the experiment results and the base solutions. These output files were used to construct all of the tables in Chapter 9. Our interpretation of simulation results from the five models will emphasize structural differences among villages in explaining diverse villagewide impacts of policy, market, and environmental shocks.

9

Policy simulations

This chapter presents findings from five sets of experiments carried out using our village CGE models. They explore the villagewide and village-town–wide impacts of changes in output prices and product markets, technologies and ecologies, income transfers, labor markets, and international economic environments (exchange rates). For each experiment, we first explain how the experiment was carried out using the village CGE, and we then examine the effects of the policy, market, or environmental change on production, factor demands and prices, the level and distribution of household-farm incomes, and expenditure linkages outside the village. The experiments are useful for understanding the economic structure of our five villages and the villagewide implications of policy, market, or environment-induced changes. We believe they also provide insight into the likely effectiveness of alternative policies at achieving specific development goals.

The total impact of an exogenous shock on a village variable involves both direct and indirect effects. The indirect effects are conveyed by village prices and shadow prices. For example, our first experiment simulates the villagewide impact of an increase in the (exogenous) staple price. The direct effects in this experiment include an increase in staple prices for consumers (thereby reducing staple consumption) and an increase in the marginal value product (i.e., profitability) of labor and other factors in staple production. In combination, these two direct effects increase the supply and reduce the demand for staples, pushing up the marketed surplus of staples.

This, however, unleashes a variety of indirect effects that wend their way through our villages and village-town. Higher profits from staple production boost village incomes, affecting households' demand for goods and leisure. Increased demand for family time in staple production and in leisure drives up the family "shadow wage," or opportunity cost of family time. A changing family wage spreads the effects of the staple-price change into other village production activities and into migration. If prices besides the family wage are endogenous (e.g., hired-worker wages in experiment 2, and an endogenous staple price in experiment 4), they, too, transmit effects of the exogenous shock across households, production activities, and migration. Economic theory usually offers little guidance as to the magnitude or sign of the total impacts of exogenous shocks when prices of some factors or goods are endogenous to villages or households.

Price and market experiments

Our price and market experiments explore the sensitivity of village economies to changes in prices of staples and agricultural exports in different market environments. They simulate the effects of a 10 percent increase in the price of the major staple and of village agricultural export, respectively. Results of these experiments may be expressed as elasticities by dividing the numbers in the tables by ten.

Overall, this set of experiments reveals a high own-price elasticity of supply for staples in the most diversified and high-income village group (Java, Kenya, and Mexico). Substitution across sectors enables diversified villages to channel resources into staple production from nonstaple production or migration as the terms of trade for staples improve. Cross-price supply effects – that is, the effect of changes in the staple price on the production of nonstaples – are also stronger in these villages. The high-income group exhibits stronger production linkages that transmit price increases in one sector (e.g., grains) to other sectors (e.g., livestock, for which grains are an input). By contrast, the nondiversified and less commercialized villages have fewer production linkages and face sharply diminishing returns to labor in staple production, which absorbs most of the family labor prior to the price change. This limits the supply response to price changes in the two poorest villages.

Despite lower production elasticities, the effect of staple price changes on household incomes in the poorest villages is relatively large, due to a high correspondence between income from staple production and total income where incomes are not highly diversified away from staple production. Thus, we find the interesting result that the relative effects of staple-price policy on farm incomes are *greater* in the villages where the staple supply response is *lower.*

The supply response is considerably more elastic for agricultural exports, although here, too, elasticities are higher in the more developed villages. In more commercial settings, export price changes translate into large changes in household income.

Separate staple-price experiments were run using the base model, in which hired-worker wages were assumed to be fixed, and using the same model with an endogenous-wage specification. The exogenous-wage specification (the usual assumption in neoclassical household-farm models) generally increases the (positive) own-production effect and reduces the (negative) cross-production effect of the staple-price change. This is because the availability of a hired, though imperfect, substitute for family labor at a fixed market wage lessens the trade-off between leisure and production and between staple and nonstaple production. Households usually increase their demand for hired labor in response to the staple-price increase in the endogenous-wage model, too. This drives up wages, however, which in turn dampen the supply response. (Braverman and Hammer [1986] find a similar result in their microeconomic household-farm model with endogenous wages.)

Nevertheless, the impact of wage assumptions in our policy experiments also depends on the family- and hired-labor intensities of the sector favored by the price change (staples) relative to the other sectors. For example, if nonstaple sectors are relatively labor-intensive, then a reduction in nonstaple production, whose relative profitability falls, may free up more labor than the increase in staple production absorbs. Because of these general equilibrium feedback effects in village factor markets, the effect of the staple-price increase on family-labor migration is not necessarily negative, as generally would be the case in a recursive, household-farm model. If nonstaple production is relatively hired-labor-intensive, then a shift from nonstaple to staple production may free up hired labor. In the endogenous-wage experiment, this could *reduce* the shadow price of hired labor, increasing the positive effects of a staple-price increase on staple production and dampening the negative effects on nonstaple sectors. The effect of introducing endogenous wages for hired workers into the staple-price experiment, therefore, cannot be determined a priori.

Experiment 1: Staple prices

The results of the staple-price experiments appear in Tables 9.1 (base model) and 9.2 (endogenous-wage model). Table 9.1 reveals high own-price elasticities of staple supply in Java, which is production-diversified, in the Kenya village-town model, and in Mexico, which is diversified through migration. In these villages, the 10 percent increase in staple price is associated with a 7 to 14 percent increase in staple output. By contrast, in India and Senegal the increase is on the order of 4 percent. The cross-price elasticities (measuring effects on other production sectors) are negative or zero, as expected. They are strongest in Java, where resources are pulled out of livestock production, and in Kenya, where resources are withdrawn from nonagricultural production.

Table 9.1. *Staple price experiment*

	Percentage changes				
	Senegal	India	Mexico	Kenya	Java
Household-farm production					
Staple	3.82	4.07	7.45	14.24	13.75
Agricultural exports	−0.99	0.00		0.01	−0.32
Livestock	0.00	−1.41	−0.27	0.00	−5.54
Nonagricultural	0.00	−0.59	−1.18	−4.75	−0.90
Labor demand					
Family	4.92	0.32	2.86	0.21	−0.10
Hired	1.68	8.90	6.27	−0.31	6.18
Total	3.82	0.81	3.12	0.11	1.93
Shadow prices					
Family labor	3.16	11.06	0.59	0.00	0.01
Hired labor					
Physical capital		14.76	1.03	0.52	7.13
Land	6.79		1.00	21.74	22.74
Household-farm incomes					
Nominal	4.00	8.30	1.00	1.27	1.94
Real	0.54	1.22	0.21	−0.17	0.06
Income by household group (real)					
Subsistence	−0.44	1.05	−1.49	−0.70	1.80
Mediumholder	1.07	0.75	0.36		−0.55
Largeholder	0.40	1.96	0.25	−0.04	0.24
Nonfarm		−6.10		−0.76	
Household consumption					
Leisure	−0.44	−1.26	−0.54	0.00	0.01
Staples	−4.94	−1.20	−8.21	−7.83	−3.80
Manufactures	3.70	8.71	1.00	1.23	2.07
External linkages					
Migration	−0.93	−3.94	−1.47	0.01	−0.02
Marketed surplus	1142.24	25.54	32.78	70.52	−1.88[a]
Intermediate trade[b]	−0.03	6.76	−0.08	−6.00	3.62
Final trade	4.18	43.67	1.75	42.71	1.89
Total trade	1.66	9.48	0.81	0.35	3.46

[a] Negative in the base. A negative percentage change indicates that the variable increased (i.e., became closer to zero or positive) from the negative base. A value in excess of −1 indicates that the variable turned positive. A positive percentage indicates that the variable decreased from the negative base.
[b] Trade = net imports.

Table 9.2. *Endogenous wage experiment*

	Percentage changes				
	Senegal	India	Mexico	Kenya	Java
Household-farm production					
Staple	3.29	1.63	7.00	14.25	7.86
Agricultural exports	−1.14			0.05	2.32
Livestock	−2.14	−1.25	−0.25	0.00	−4.76
Nonagricultural	−1.84	−0.88	−2.56	−4.67	−5.86
Labor demand					
Family	4.72	0.27	2.26	0.25	−0.01
Hired					
Total	3.11	0.26	2.09	0.20	−0.01
Shadow prices					
Family labor	2.98	9.05	0.44	0.00	−0.22
Hired labor	1.59	14.16	4.57	−0.14	1.31
Physical capital		12.45	0.85	0.59	3.75
Land	6.40		0.88	21.75	21.15
Household-farm incomes					
Nominal	3.82	8.23	0.84	1.32	0.54
Real	0.37	1.16	0.05	−0.11	−1.32
Incomes by household group (real)					
Subsistence	−0.76	3.50	−1.60	−0.65	−1.14
Mediumholder	0.82	1.52	0.20		−2.03
Largeholder	0.32	0.57	0.07	0.02	−0.37
Nonfarm		−5.82		−0.69	
Household consumption					
Leisure	−0.42	−1.06	−0.51	0.00	−0.01
Staples	−5.14	−0.81	−8.35	−7.78	−5.25
Manufactures	3.54	9.10	0.84	1.29	0.72
External linkages					
Migration	−0.75	−3.52	−1.08	0.01	0.54
Marketed surplus	1099.14	16.93	32.02	70.45	−0.33[a]
Intermediate trade[b]	−0.04	5.35	0.09	−5.96	−1.12
Final trade	3.83	39.99	2.01	42.60	16.03
Total trade	1.51	7.91	1.02	0.37	0.45

[a] Negative in the base. A negative percentage change indicates that the variable increased (i.e., became closer to zero or positive) from the negative base. A value in excess of −1 indicates that the variable turned positive. A positive percentage indicates that the variable decreased from the negative base.
[b] Trade = net imports.

Table 9.1 reports widely varying changes in family- and hired-labor demand in response to the price change. The changes in total family-labor demand range from a low of -0.1 percent in Java to a high of 4.9 percent in Senegal. The Indian village achieves its moderate increase in staple supply primarily by increasing its demand for hired labor. In three of the five villages, the exogenous wage and the substitutability between family and hired labor result in a large increase in hired-labor demand – from just over 6 percent in Java and Mexico to nearly 9 percent in India. The exogenous-wage specification permits an increase in hired-labor demand for staple production without substantially reducing hired-labor demand in other sectors.

Not surprisingly, the staple price increase generally raises the shadow prices of family labor (the family wage), land, and capital. The availability of hired labor at a fixed wage checks the upward pressure on the shadow price of family labor while exerting upward pressure on the shadow prices of fixed factors (land and capital). The change in the family wage is negligible in Java and Kenya. Here, the sectors most adversely affected by the staple-price increase – livestock and nonagricultural production, respectively – are the most labor-intensive (with family-labor value-added shares on the order of .7 to .8), and staple production is least family-labor-intensive (.02 and .51, respectively).

The increase in the shadow value of family labor results in decreases in migration in Mexico and India (-1.5 and -3.9 percent, respectively). Migration also decreases in Senegal (-0.9 percent). There is a slight *increase* in migration in Kenya, however, because of the decline in the family wage. This finding illustrates the complexity of regulating rural out-migration through agricultural price policy.

The staple-price change results in substantial differences in income gains across the five villages and a negative real-income change for at least one household group in each village. The largest nominal income gain occurs in India (8.3 percent); that is, the elasticity of total income with respect to the staple price there is close to unity. At the other extreme, the elasticity is only around 0.1 in the Mexican village. This low correspondence between changes in the staple price and total income reflects a high degree of income diversification and a relatively high opportunity cost of family resources in staple production. In real terms, total income *decreases* in the Kenyan village-town, where many households do not produce staples. The effect of the price change on the flow of hired-labor value-added into different household groups also shapes these real income effects.

The household group-specific income elasticities with respect to the staple price (not shown) are positive in all of the household groups appearing in Table 9.1, but in seven of the sixteen groups it changes sign when calculated in real terms. In Mexico, real incomes in subsistence households decline by 1.5 percent, while real incomes in medium and largeholder households increase slightly. The largest real-income decline is for salaried households in India, which do not benefit from the price change on the production side but lose as consumers. All household groups lose in real terms in the Kenyan village-town. In Java, where subsistence households are important suppliers of hired labor to staple production, the real-income gain is positive for subsistence and largeholder households but negative for mediumholder households. The largest real-income gain from the staple price change is in Indian largeholder households (2 percent), followed closely by Javan subsistence households (1.8 percent). These findings reveal a complex pattern of real-income effects in economies where many households are net buyers of staples.

Leisure demand decreases in India, Senegal, and Mexico, which suggests that the negative effect of an increased opportunity cost of leisure outweighs the positive effect of higher total income on leisure demand in those three settings. There is almost no change in leisure demand in Java and Kenya, however, where real total income gains from the staple-price change are small or negative and where the effect on the shadow price of family labor is also small.

The effects of the staple-price change on production and consumption linkages outside the village vary considerably from village to village. Other things being the same, when the staple sector relies more heavily on modern inputs, the potential for the price increase to generate positive production linkages outside the village is greater. However, where resources to support increased staple production are withdrawn from sectors that utilize modern inputs, there is a negative linkage which dampens or may reverse the positive linkage from staples. The production linkages with the outside world are positive and large in Java and India, negative and large in Kenya, and small in Mexico and Senegal.

The effect of the price change on marketed surplus and total imports depends also on final demand. The change in final demand for staple and nonstaple goods is shaped by a direct own-price or cross-price effect, by changes in household income, by the distribution of income changes across household groups, and by household expenditure and savings propensities. Staple demand decreases in all five villages. Because staple supply elasticities are positive, the marketed surplus of staples increases. The relative magnitudes of these increases vary considerably across villages. They depend both on the supply and demand changes and on the initial marketed surplus levels, which are small or negative in some cases (e.g., in Senegal and Java). Total imports reflect both production and consumption linkages between the village and the outside economy. In our staple-price experiment, trade linkages are positive and large in Java and India, and positive and small in Senegal, Mexico, and Kenya.

Experiment 2: Endogenous-wage staple price

The assumption of a fixed wage usually is justified in the household-farm economics literature by the observation that individual producers are price takers in local and regional markets. Price changes, however, affect large numbers of producers simultaneously. Because of this, the fixed-wage assumption actually corresponds to a Lewis-type world of labor surplus. If surplus labor is not available within or outside the village, an increased demand for hired labor to raise staple production will exert upward pressure on local wages, other things being equal. This, in turn, is likely to dampen the positive effect of the price change on staple production and magnify the negative effect on competing sectors, for whom labor costs increase. It also increases the value of wage earners' principal asset, potentially increasing the flow of value-added into wage-earner households.

Table 9.2 generally confirms these expectations. Compared with that of the exogenous-wage case, the supply effect of the staple-price change is substantially lower in Java and India, slightly lower in Mexico and Senegal, and virtually unchanged in the Kenyan village-town. The change in the wage rate relative to the base ranges from −0.1 percent in Kenya to 14 percent in India. Increased wages significantly reduce the elasticity of staple-labor demand with respect to the price change (not shown). For example, this elasticity drops from 2.4 to 1.4 in Java, from 1.8 to 0.5 in India, and from 2.0 to 1.4 in Mexico. It also increases (in absolute-value terms) the (negative) elasticity of labor demand in competing sectors (not shown). For example, the percentage decrease in labor demand in nonagricultural production in Java is seven times greater (−7.2 percent) in the endogenous-wage experiment. A similar pattern is evident for India, Senegal, and Mexico. As a result, the price change usually has a greater negative effect on nonstaple production in these four villages. The impact of the staple-price change on migration becomes positive in Java, and it stays negative in Senegal, India, and Mexico.

The increase in wage rates produces favorable real-income results for subsistence and mediumholder households in India and for all groups in Kenya. In Senegal, Mexico, and Java, however, the contractionary effect of wage increases on production results in lower real incomes relative to the fixed-wage experiment.

The implications of the endogenous-wage specification are quite small in the Kenyan village-town model. The similarity of outcomes in the two experiments for Kenya might suggest that labor-supply constraints on production are less binding there. Sectors that compete with staples in the village-town, however, are relatively labor-intensive. Thus, small decreases in production in those sectors release relatively large amounts of labor for staples, counteracting any upward pressure on wages.

Experiment 3: Agricultural export price

The effects of a 10 percent increase in the price of village agricultural exports were explored for the three villages that produced a major agricultural good for outside markets. India, Java, and Mexico lack a major export crop sector. In Mexico, however, 44 percent of livestock output is sold outside the village. The effects of a 10 percent increase in livestock prices were explored in the Mexican case.

Table 9.3 reports the results of the export-price experiment. Overall, they reveal a very high supply response to price changes in the export crop sector in the most developed setting, the Kenyan village-town, where output increases 89 percent. Substantial increases in the use of family and hired labor are required to support this production. The impact on production in the competing sectors is relatively small in Kenya, where agricultural exports are somewhat less labor-intensive and nonagricultural production is most labor-intensive. A high opportunity cost of family factors in export production is evident in increases in the shadow price of family labor and especially in the shadow value of land (from 6 to 15 percent).

Supply elasticities are relatively low in Mexico and Senegal (1 to 3 percent). Very low marginal products of labor inputs limit the supply response in these villages. In both of these cases, the increase in the export price exerts upward pressure on the shadow value of family labor (1.2 and 1.9 percent, respectively). Hired-labor demand increases in Senegal but decreases in Mexico, because livestock production does not use hired labor there. In both these villages, family labor is withdrawn from competing activities and from migration, which decreases by 2 to 3 percent.

The impact of the export price increase on household incomes depends on the distribution of value-added from the agricultural export and competing activities across households. The impact on household real incomes is influenced also by the consumption patterns of different household groups – in particular, their propensity to spend income on the export crop. This propensity is generally low – with the exception of animal products in Mexico – so that the nominal- and real-income effects are more similar in this than in the staple-price experiments. The export price change produces a dramatic increase in household incomes in Kenya and small increases in Senegal and Mexico. In the two villages with export crops, the nominal- and real-income effects are positively correlated with farm size. The income effects are more uniform across household groups in Mexico, where the availability of common (*ejido*) grazing lands makes livestock investment a viable means of storing wealth for households with few landholdings.

The reallocation of family resources toward export crop production and the resulting income effects generate positive demand linkages outside the village

Table 9.3. *Agricultural export price experiment*

	Percentage changes		
	Senegal	Mexico	Kenya
Household-farm production			
Staple	−0.99	−0.70	−0.99
Agricultural exports	3.01		88.70
Livestock	0.00	1.16	−0.12
Nonagricultural	0.00	−2.43	−0.90
Labor demand			
Family	2.71	1.03	37.98
Hired	0.41		9.31
Total	1.92	0.79	32.61
Shadow prices			
Family labor	1.90	1.24	0.38
Hired labor			
Physical capital		8.23	26.21
Land	5.96	10.69	14.52
Household-farm incomes			
Nominal	2.50	5.17	26.67
Real	2.26	3.78	26.67
Income by household group (real)			
Subsistence	3.93	3.35	25.16
Mediumholder	3.66	4.22	
Largeholder	1.07	3.39	27.14
Nonfarm			24.28
Household consumption			
Leisure	−0.23	2.17	−0.29
Staples	2.95	5.21	26.44
Manufactures	2.26	5.20	26.76
External linkages			
Migration	−2.33	−3.02	−0.94
Marketed surplus	−462.51	−5.71	−51.67
Intermediate trade[a]	0.72	0.33	7.78
Final trade	2.22	7.83	220.16
Total trade	1.32	3.97	35.48

[a] Trade = net imports.

in all three cases. These linkages are relatively small on the production side. The increases in demand for intermediate production inputs from outside the village range from less than 1 percent in the case of Mexican livestock (which is not commercial-input-intensive) to 7.7 percent for Kenyan coffee.

Final imports increase in both villages and the village-town, reflecting a strengthening of outside linkages as a result of intensifying export crop production.

Experiment 4: Export price experiment with agricultural nontradables

Experiment 4 explores the villagewide impact of increasing cash-crop prices when other agricultural goods are village nontradables. It is identical to the previous experiment except that the village and village-town economies are constrained to be self-sufficient in staples. This experiment is a villagewide analogue to the agricultural-household experiment in de Janvry, Fafchamps, and Sadoulet (1991), in which individual households producing the cash crop are constrained to be self-sufficient in staples. In our village and village-town models, we allow trade in staples among village households but not between the village and the outside world.

The direct effect of higher cash-crop prices is to draw family resources into cash-crop production and out of competing activities, including staples. However, higher incomes from cash crops increase village demand for staples. The combination of lower staple output and higher staple demand creates a scarcity of staples in the local economy. This drives up the local price of staples. One effect of rising staple prices is to draw family resources back into staple production.

This dampens the cash-crop supply response and increases competition for scarce family resources with other activities, including tradables production, migration, and leisure.

The implications of a missing outside market for staples are best understood by comparing Tables 9.3 and 9.4. In both villages and in the village-town, the impact of a higher cash-crop price on staple production changes sign, rising from -0.99 to 0.38 in Senegal, from -0.70 to 1.57 in Mexico, and from -0.99 to 3.86 in Kenya. The missing staple market reduces the cash-crop supply response substantially in Senegal and Kenya but only slightly in Mexico, where livestock exports do not compete significantly with staples for family time. Staple prices rise from a low of 3 percent in Mexico to a high of 4.5 percent in Kenya. These findings highlight the influence of food markets on cash-crop supply response. They also suggest that when villages are constrained by a lack of access to outside staple markets (i.c., high transactions costs in food markets), technological advances in food production may be critical to increasing the supply elasticity of cash crops.

Nontradables create new income linkages within the villages and village-town. Despite lower cash-crop production, the impact of the cash-crop price on household nominal incomes is higher when outside staple markets are missing. The effect on total real incomes, however, is small; as consumers,

Table 9.4. *Agricultural export-price experiment when staples are village nontradables*

	Senegal	Mexico	Kenya
Household-farm production			
Staple	0.38	1.57	3.86
Agricultural	2.46		58.01
Livestock	1.23	1.09	8.95
Nonagricultural	−3.91	−2.80	−7.03
Labor demand			
Family	4.66	1.90	21.00
Hired	0.00	0.10	4.00
Total	3.07	1.76	17.74
Shadow prices			
Family labor	3.09	1.43	0.21
Physical capital		8.49	24.27
Land	8.62	10.92	19.60
Staples	4.39	3.07	4.53
Household-farm incomes			
Nominal	4.12	5.47	17.48
Real	2.33	3.82	14.24
Income by household group (real)			
Subsistence	1.18	2.86	12.75
Mediumholder	3.86	4.31	
Largeholder	3.35	3.44	13.99
Nonfarm			14.59
Household consumption			
Leisure	−0.40	1.97	−0.15
Staples	0.38	2.36	12.38
Manufactures	3.76	5.50	17.50
External linkages			
Migration	−2.55	−3.48	−0.53
Marketed surplus	N.A.	N.A.	N.A.
Intermediate trade[a]	−27.10	0.25	−3.47
Final Trade	4.31	8.31	197.76
Total trade	−14.53	4.19	22.05

[a] Trade = net imports.

villagers lose due to local staple-price inflation. In Senegal and Mexico there is a redistribution of real income from subsistence to medium- and largeholder farms. In the Kenyan village-town, nonfarm households are hit hard by the staple-price increase; the effect of the cash-crop price rise on their real incomes drops from 24 to 14 percent.

The implications of local nontradables for migration and trade are mixed. The village staple-market constraint reduces migration in Senegal and Mexico, as staples compete with labor exports for scarce family time. This effect is outweighed in Java by the negative effect of a missing staple market on the supply of cash crops. There, the impact of the cash-crop price increase on migration remains negative, but it is smaller in absolute value. Because food imports into the villages are now ruled out, the cash-crop price no longer affects village marketed surplus. Overall, missing food markets tend to reduce trade linkages between our villages and the outside world.

Experiment 5: Agricultural subsidies

This experiment explores the effect of a 10 percent agricultural output subsidy in the form of a negative value-added tax on crop production. This differs from the staple-price experiment in that the magnitude of the initial effect of the subsidy is sensitive to the value-added content of the sector prices.

The results of the subsidy are summarized in Table 9.5. As in the staple-price experiment, the own-supply elasticity is relatively large in the three most developed villages, ranging from 0.6 in Mexico to 1.2 in Kenya. It is on the order of 0.3 in the Indian and Senegalese villages. The competing agricultural sectors – crops, agricultural exports, and, in the Indian, Mexican, and Kenyan cases, livestock – are adversely affected by the subsidy as family resources flow away from these activities and into relatively more profitable staple production. The virtual wage for family labor increases in all five villages, reducing migration by between 0.1 and 9.6 percent. The migration effect is smallest in Java and Kenya, where the agricultural subsidy favors a less family-labor-intensive production activity.

The income effects of the production subsidy vary greatly across the five villages. Total nominal- (equals real-) income increases in all cases as a result of the subsidy. The increase is highest in the Indian, Senegalese, and Kenyan cases (2.9 to 6.5 percent) than in the Javan and Mexican cases (0.7 and 1.4 percent).

The impact of the subsidy on incomes is distributed unequally across household groups. The distribution of impacts depends on both the value-added composition of the affected production activities and on the way in which value-added is distributed across households. In some cases (India, Mexico, and Kenya), largeholder households benefit relatively more from the staple subsidy than do subsistence households. In Senegal and Java, however, the reverse is true. Poor households benefit from the subsidy to the extent that their family- and hired-labor value-added from staple production increases. They lose, however, to the extent employment in the adversely affected sectors dries up. Wealthy households are less adversely affected by the loss of employment activities in the sectors that compete with staples for

Table 9.5. *Agricultural subsidies experiment*

	Percentage changes				
	Senegal	India	Mexico	Kenya	Java
Household-farm production					
Staple	3.33	2.56	6.28	11.78	6.92
Agricultural exports	−1.07			−0.23	−2.65
Livestock		−0.76	−0.09	−0.01	−0.26
Nonagricultural	0.00		−1.59	−0.11	−0.33
Labor demand					
Family	3.82	0.16	2.28	3.01	−2.41
Hired	1.52	6.32	4.91	0.71	5.59
Total	3.03	0.51	2.49	2.58	0.18
Shadow prices					
Family labor	4.72	2.86	0.80	0.05	0.07
Hired labor					
Physical capital					8.84
Land	2.09				21.68
Household-farm incomes					
Total	2.90	6.45	1.36	2.89	0.69
Income by household group (real)					
Subsistence	5.87	6.04	1.17	2.75	3.19
Mediumholder	4.33	6.20	1.37		0.23
Largeholder	1.43	7.11	1.36	3.17	0.35
Nonfarm		0.55		2.02	
Household consumption					
Leisure	−0.32	−0.58	0.33	−0.02	0.25
Staples	3.58	6.71	1.34	2.96	1.01
Manufactures	2.54	6.74	1.36	2.88	0.83
External linkages					
Migration	−3.00	−9.64	−1.98	−0.11	−0.18
Marketed surplus	−25.89	−5.32	10.47	28,05	5.82[a]
Intermediate trade[b]	−0.05	1.53	−0.74	0.02	2.74
Final trade	9.74	4.23	8.47	0.63	−2.33
Total trade	2.00	−0.02	0.54	−2.74	2.28

[a] Negative in the base. A negative percentage change indicates that the variable increased (i.e., became closer to zero or positive) from the negative base. A value in excess of −1 indicates that the variable turned positive. A positive percentage indicates that the variable decreased from the negative base.
[b] Trade = net imports.

family resources, but often they are more likely to be engaged in nonstaple production. The income gains are most evenly distributed across farm households in India (around 6 to 7 percent for the three farm groups), although salaried households, predictably, gain little from the production subsidy (0.5 percent). The income gains are also relatively equally distributed in Mexico, although here they are small (1.2 to 1.4 percent). In Kenya, largeholder incomes rise 3.2 percent and subsistence incomes increase 2.7 percent.

The effect of the staple subsidy on leisure demand is complex. On the one hand, because leisure is a normal good, increases in income increase the demand for leisure. On the other hand, a rise in the shadow price of family time increases the opportunity cost of leisure. Leisure demand increases as a result of the subsidy in Java and Mexico (by 0.2 and 0.3 percent, respectively). It decreases (by 0.6 and 0.3 percent) in India and Senegal, and it is little changed in Kenya.

Trade linkage outcomes are sensitive to the own-price and cross-price supply effects of the subsidy, to income changes, and to household consumption patterns in the five villages. Where household incomes increase and nonstaple production falls, the demand for imports of nonstaples increases. The increase in staple production that is stimulated by the subsidy decreases net staple imports, but higher incomes stimulate staple demand. The overall effect on trade linkages is ambiguous. Net imports increase as a result of the subsidy in Senegal, Mexico, and Java, and they decrease in India and Kenya. Marketed surplus of staples decreases in Senegal, India, and Java, and it increases in the other two cases.

Overall, the results of our price experiments suggest that price policy alone is likely to be an ineffective vehicle to raise rural incomes and alleviate rural poverty. Large changes in staple prices translate into relatively small changes in rural incomes. For subsistence households that are net purchasers of staples, real incomes may decline when staple prices increase. The positive effect of higher staple prices on nominal income (e.g., through an increase in value-added from staple production) may be more than offset by the negative effect of a higher staple price on the consumption side.

Where farms exhibit sharply diminishing returns to factors in production (e.g., the Senegalese case), the supply response to prices is small. In these cases, technological change is likely to be far more effective at raising incomes than are price incentives. A sluggish income response to price changes can also be explained by market failures, which create trade-offs between the use of family resources in production and consumption activities. High transactions costs in staple or other markets can dampen the effect of policy changes on real incomes, and they can have important distributional implications. Finally, where village economies are highly diversified, relatively large changes in staple prices often translate into small changes in household-farm incomes, even when the effect is magnified by local income linkages. In this case, policies that narrowly focus on staple production in an effort to raise rural incomes and alleviate poverty are likely to fail. However, policies aimed at increasing cash-crop production while ignoring local food-supply constraints are also likely to have disappointing results.

Production experiments: Technologies and ecologies

Given the sharply decreasing returns to family inputs that characterize most developing-country agricultural systems, technological change is likely to have a more important impact on household-farm incomes and generate more income linkages than price policy. The positive impacts of both price policy and technological advance are mitigated, however, by the ecological decline endemic to many LDC rural areas, including those in which the adoption of new agricultural technologies has been greatest. Our second set of experiments explores the villagewide effects of productivity-enhancing technological change and of ecological deterioration, which reduces the area and/or efficiency of land in crop production.

Experiment 6: Technological change

Impacts of technological change in staple production were examined by increasing the technological shift parameter in the Cobb-Douglas production function for staples by 10 percent (Table 9.6). The immediate effect of this change is to increase the marginal productivity of family resources in staple production. This induces profit-maximizing household-farms to increase their allocation of resources to the staple sector. Hired labor is assumed to be available at the (fixed) local wage. However, the outward shift in demand for family labor, capital, and land destabilizes the village internally through a perceived scarcity of these factors. As a result, shadow prices of these factors increase. Inputs of capital and land in village production activities are assumed to be fixed in the short run. Family labor, however, is fluid across activities. Lacking a perfect hired substitute, families withdraw their labor from nonstaple activities in order to meet the increased demand for labor in staple production. The higher shadow value of family labor dampens the positive effect of the technological change on staple production.

The increases in staple production that result from the technological change are large relative to the effects of price policies reported earlier. This is especially true for the two least-developed villages, in which low productivity of family inputs limited the supply response to price increases. The supply elasticity with respect to output price was on the order of 0.4 in the Indian and Senegal villages (Table 9.1). The elasticity with respect to the technological change is 1.3 in India and 1.4 in Senegal. It ranges from 1.4 to 2.3 in the three highest-income villages.

Table 9.6. *Technological change experiment*

	Percentage changes				
	Senegal	India	Mexico	Kenya	Java
Household-farm production					
Staple	13.66	12.80	16.91	22.95	14.11
Agricultural exports	−1.07			−0.23	−2.65
Livestock	0.00	−0.75	−0.09	−0.01	−0.27
Nonagricultural	0.00		−1.59	−0.11	−0.33
Labor demand					
Family	3.82	0.16	2.28	3.01	−2.41
Hired	1.52	6.28	4.91	0.71	5.59
Total	3.03	0.51	2.49	2.58	0.18
Shadow prices					
Family labor	3.45	9.19	0.80	0.05	0.07
Hired labor					
Physical capital		10.65	1.83	1.91	8.84
Land	6.07		2.14	17.80	21.68
Household-farm incomes					
Nominal	2.90	6.41	1.36	2.89	0.69
Real	2.90	6.41	1.36	2.89	0.69
Income by household group (real)					
Subsistence	5.87	6.00	1.17	2.75	3.19
Mediumholder	4.33	6.17	1.37		0.23
Largeholder	1.43	7.06	1.36	3.17	0.35
Nonfarm		0.55		2.02	
Household consumption					
Leisure	−0.32	−0.58	0.33	−0.02	0.25
Staples	3.58	6.67	1.34	2.96	1.01
Manufactures	2.54	6.70	1.36	2.88	0.83
External linkages					
Migration	−3.00	−9.57	−1.98	−0.11	−0.18
Marketed surplus	1193.86	24.52	30.11	59.88	3.65[a]
(Net imports)					
Intermediate trade[b]	−0.03	6.18	−0.34	0.17	4.26
Final trade	2.89	31.68	2.38	23.41	−6.07
Total trade	1.13	8.06	0.97	3.20	3.31

[a]Negative in the base. A negative percentage change indicates that the variable increased (i.e., became closer to zero or positive) from the negative base. A value in excess of −1 indicates that the variable turned positive. A positive percentage indicates that the variable decreased from the negative base.

[b]Trade = net imports.

The increase in staple production is achieved in the Javan case primarily by using more hired labor, the demand for which increases by 6 percent. Some resources are withdrawn from agricultural export production, the output of which falls by 3 percent. The availability of hired labor and a shift of resources out of noncrop production enable households in this village to increase staple production without a sharp rise in the shadow value of family labor. As a result, the trade-off between staple production and (1) migration (which decreases only marginally) and (2) leisure (which increases slightly) is minimized, and total family-labor supply declines (by 2.4 percent). Households in the Javan village, here as in most other experiments, behave much like the traditional neoclassical farm household (Singh, Squire, and Strauss, 1986).

The trade-offs between leisure and migration, on the one hand, and staple production, on the other, are stronger in the other four villages. The trade-off is most pronounced in the two lowest-income villages. There, the increase in staple output is achieved at the expense of both migration and leisure. Family-labor supply increases by 3.8 and 0.2 percent, respectively, in Senegal and in India, where staple production is highly labor-intensive. Hired-labor demand also increases (by 1.5 and 6.3 percent); however, hired labor appears to be a relatively poor substitute for family labor in these cases. In the Mexican case, the staple-supply response is supported by hired labor (a 5 percent increase) and by a reduction in family migration (by 2 percent). Family leisure demand increases slightly. The increase in staple production in Kenya is accomplished through relatively small changes in hired-labor demand (0.7 percent), migration (-0.11 percent), and leisure (-0.02 percent), and through output reductions in nonstaple activities. In this village-town model, hired labor appears to be a limited substitute for family labor in staple production; the demand for hired workers increases by much less than the demand for family labor (0.7 percent).

The productivity change translates into real-income improvements for all household groups. Technological change dominates the staple-price policy in a Pareto sense: Net real-income gains are larger for all groups. The impact is most progressive in Senegal and Java, where subsistence households benefit more than the mediumholder and largeholder groups in relative terms. The income effects are largest in the least diversified, low-income villages. They are smallest, ranging from 1.2 to 1.4 percent, in the migration-diversified Mexican village. In Java, a high level of diversification in largeholder households together with a large hired-labor value-added component in staple production results in large income gains for subsistence households (3.2 percent) compared with medium- and smallholder households (0.23 and 0.35 percent, respectively).

Changes in household-farm incomes and in the composition of village production result in changes in demand for intermediate and final imports that vary widely across the five villages. The import linkages are largest in

India, where the demand for imports of intermediate and final goods increases by 6 and 32 percent, respectively. In Mexico and Senegal, where staple production uses few purchased intermediate inputs, the demand for intermediate imports declines slightly, while in the Javan case, where staple production is relatively intensive in purchased inputs, intermediate imports increase by 4 percent. Total net imports increase by 1 to 3 percent in these three villages.

The technological change has a large relative impact on final-good import demand in Kenya (23 percent), but this is somewhat misleading. Because of the high level of diversity of production to meet local consumption demand in this village-town model, baseline final-good imports are small. Combining villages and towns into a single model converts outside demand linkages (e.g., village demand for goods produced in the town) into internal linkages. By contrast, intermediate imports are large in the baseline. The combination of a large relative increase in final imports and a small relative increase in intermediate imports (0.17 percent) produces a modest increase in total imports (3 percent).

Overall, our findings illustrate the potential for technological change to generate both income growth within the village and trade linkages with regional and national markets.

Experiment 7: Ecological decline

Villagewide economic implications of ecological decline were explored by decreasing land inputs in all land-based activities by 10 percent. This corresponds to a notion of land inputs as efficiency units that decrease as land quality declines, or else to a reduction in the arable land area (e.g., as a result of soil erosion). Unlike our productivity experiment, the ecological decline experiment generates outcomes that are sensitive to the importance of land value-added in staples and other sectors and to the substitutability between land and other inputs in these activities. Because land value-added is not separated out from family-labor value-added in the Indian village, this case had to be excluded from our ecology experiment. The findings for the other four villages are summarized in Table 9.7.

The decrease in land inputs increases the shadow value of land and decreases the value of complementary inputs in the village. Production in the most land-intensive activities falls, and families reallocate resources toward less land-intensive and more labor-intensive production. In Senegal, Mexico, and Kenya, this means a decrease in all crop and livestock production and an increase in nonagricultural output. In Java, nonagricultural production increases, but there is also a shift of resources among agricultural production activities. Here, the land-intensive agricultural export activity is the victim of ecological decline: Output of the export crop declines by 6 percent, while staple production increases.

The reduction in agricultural production produces negative income link-

Table 9.7. *Ecology experiment*

	Percentage changes			
	Senegal	Mexico	Kenya	Java
Household-farm production				
Staple	−8.01	−6.13	−6.39	8.38
Agricultural exports	−8.78		−2.01	−6.46
Livestock	−10.00	−7.06	−0.74	0.38
Nonagricultural	8.60	0.19	0.05	0.47
Labor demand				
Family	−4.40	−2.13	−1.56	−0.48
Hired	−1.39	−3.48	−0.37	−0.98
Total	−3.37	−2.24	−1.34	−0.64
Shadow prices				
Family labor	−4.04	−1.33	−0.02	−0.10
Hired labor				
Physical capital		−5.26	−1.17	−0.89
Land	1.83	3.51	5.21	5.03
Household-farm incomes				
Nominal	−3.65	−3.44	−1.35	−0.58
Real	−3.65	−3.44	−1.35	−0.58
Income by household group (real)				
Subsistence	−6.64	−3.45	−1.28	−0.85
Mediumholder	−5.72	−3.55		−0.52
Largeholder	−1.78	−3.32	−1.44	−0.56
Nonfarm			−1.04	
Household consumption				
Leisure	0.37	−1.78	0.01	0.05
Staples	−4.43	−3.44	−1.36	−0.62
Manufactures	−3.23	−3.46	−1.34	−0.60
External linkages				
Migration	3.98	3.39	0.05	0.25
Marketed surplus	−426.66	−8.40	−15.69	−12.96[a]
Intermediate trade[b]	−0.50	0.26	−0.20	−0.31
Final trade	−4.27	−4.72	−11.02	−2.35
Total trade	−2.01	−2.15	−1.61	−0.49

[a] Negative in the base. A negative percentage change indicates that the variable increased (i.e., became closer to zero or positive) from the negative base. A value in excess of −1 indicates that the variable turned positive. A positive percentage indicates that the variable decreased from the negative base.
[b] Trade = net imports.

ages in the village. The flow of value-added to households that supply factors (land and complementary inputs) to the most land-intensive activities declines. This negative effect is only slightly mitigated by an increase in value-added from nonagricultural production. The impacts on household-farm incomes vary considerably across the four villages. The Javan village shows only a small total income change (− 0.6 percent). The income effect is larger in Mexico (− 3.4 percent), Senegal (− 3.6 percent), and the Kenyan village-town (− 1.3 percent).

Although total village income falls, the distributional effects of the ecological decline depend on the way in which value-added from the affected activities and migrant remittance income are distributed across the village household groups. In theory, some groups could benefit from the ecological decline if it resulted in a reallocation of village resources into activities that benefit them more than agricultural production. In practice, incomes fall in all household groups.

Ecological decline reduces the shadow value of family time. The reduction in the shadow value of family labor is largest (2 to 4 percent) in Mexico and Senegal. The lower family wage encourages a more intensive use of family labor in the least land-dependent village activities and in migration. Migration increases by over 3 percent in Mexico and by 4 percent in Senegal, as families reallocate resources away from the village.

The impacts on leisure demand vary, both in sign and magnitude. The decrease in the shadow price of family time reduces the opportunity cost of leisure, encouraging leisure consumption; however, the decrease in income discourages the demand for leisure as for other normal goods. The end result is a slight increase in leisure demand in Java, Kenya, and Senegal, and a slight decrease in Mexico.

Marketed surplus decreases in all but Java, and there are negative demand linkages for final-good imports from outside the villages. The decreases in final-good imports range from 2.3 percent in Java to 11 percent in Kenya. Intermediate imports also decrease in Java, Kenya, and Senegal, but they increase slightly in Mexico, where staple production is least intensive in modern inputs. Total net imports fall in all four villages.

Our ecology experiments produce a troubling finding with regard to the economic incentives for conservation. In the diversified economies that characterize these villages, the opportunity cost of investing in environmental quality can be high, as resources for environmental conservation must be pulled out of local production activities and migration, in which their shadow value is high. This is especially true where conservation is costly in terms of time and other family resources. A compensating high return to conservation investments is required in order to create incentives for this investment. Our experiments reveal, however, that in these diversified villages the relative income loss from environmental decline is small in most cases because households reallocate their resources to activities that are not highly dependent on land quality.

Income experiments

Income policies are frequently proposed as a quick-fix strategy to reduce poverty and stimulate growth through income linkages in rural areas. In a neoclassical world in which all prices are determined in outside markets, income transfers increase demand on the consumption side of household-farms without affecting the production side, where first-order conditions for profit maximization remain unchanged. The increase in rural household demand generates positive downstream growth linkages (Mellor, 1976; Hazell and Roell, 1983) and an increased rural demand for urban manufactures (Adelman, 1984). Migration unambiguously decreases.

Our villagewide models are designed to capture these trade-linkage effects of income transfers inside and outside the village. However, they also capture potential negative production side effects of income transfers, which result from the absence of a market for family labor and imperfect substitutability between family and hired inputs in the village. These production effects dampen, or in extreme cases may even reverse, the positive effect of transfers on rural incomes, poverty, and downstream growth.

The findings to be presented suggest that income transfers alone are usually a poor strategy to lift rural incomes and alleviate poverty. They, together with the productivity and price experiment results presented earlier, suggest that income transfers should be used only as one component of a more integrated strategy aimed at creating a basis for sustainable income growth by increasing the economic returns to family resources in production. Such a strategy requires a focus on technological change to increase the productivity of family resources, and rural-infrastructure development to increase the responsiveness of household-farms to market signals.

Since commodity prices are exogenous, the impacts of our transfer experiments operate solely through income. The most significant impacts of the transfers are on the marginal utility of leisure, on consumption patterns, and on the size distribution of village income. An increase in income raises the marginal utility of household leisure. If labor markets were neoclassical and hired labor a perfect substitute for family labor, the increase in the marginal utility of leisure would not affect production. In our model, however, it is not assumed that hired and family labor are perfect substitutes. The increase in the marginal utility of leisure leads to some substitution of hired for family labor. Migration is also reduced, and so are worker remittances. Nevertheless, the increase in the marginal utility of leisure leads to a decrease in production, which is most pronounced in family-labor-intensive sectors.

Since prices are exogenous, the only effects on consumption occur through differences in the distribution of factor and migration income across households and through differences in the demand patterns among village household groups. The income effect is less than the initial transfer, because part of the income increase is spent on leisure at the expense of village production and migration. Changes in income affect the final demand for goods and services in the village.

The changes in production and consumption influence linkages between the village and the rest of the economy. On the one hand, village production is reduced. This reduces the demand for intermediate-goods imports and the supply of exports to the regional and national economies. On the other hand, final demand for imports increases as incomes go up, but not proportionately, since there are changes in the composition of final demand by sector. A greater share of final demand must be satisfied by imports in view of the decline in village production. The overall impact of increased transfers to the village on the balance of village trade is therefore ambiguous in sign a priori.

Two types of income transfers will be examined: first, a consumer subsidy on staples and, second, direct income payments to subsistence, mediumholder, and largeholder households.

Experiment 8: Consumption subsidies

This experiment (Table 9.8) was modeled as a subsidy to households in the form of a 10 percent reduction in the consumer price of the principal staple crop, leaving the producer price unchanged. In a neoclassical household-farm model, the consumption subsidy would unambiguously increase household real incomes, leaving nominal incomes unchanged. The production side of the household-farm would be unaffected. In our village models, however, higher real incomes resulting from the subsidy increase the shadow value of family time. If a perfect substitute for family labor in village production is not available, this generates negative effects on production as well as on migration activities.

Household groups differ in their marginal propensities to consume staples. Because of this, the subsidy affects the real incomes of different household groups differently. The poorest groups, in which the largest share of income is spent on grain, benefit most from the consumption subsidy. The increase in real incomes of subsistence households is especially large (over 7 percent) in India and Senegal, the poorest villages. It is smallest in Java (1.2 percent) and intermediate in Kenya and Mexico (about 2 percent).

As a result of the increase in real income, the marginal utility of leisure and, therefore, the shadow value of family time rise. The elasticity of leisure with respect to real income (the percentage change in leisure divided by the percentage change in real income) is largest in Mexico (0.7) and Java (0.5); small (well under 0.1) in Senegal and India; and zero in Kenya, where the consumption subsidies are spread to nonagricultural households.

The increased shadow value of family time negatively affects production.

Table 9.8. *Consumption subsidy experiment*

	Percentage changes				
	Senegal	India	Mexico	Kenya	Java
Household-farm production					
Staple	−0.22	−0.47	−0.08	−0.02	−5.11
Agricultural exports	−0.18			−0.11	−1.63
Livestock	0.00	0.03	−0.02	−0.01	−0.16
Nonagricultural	0.00		−0.26	−0.05	−0.20
Labor demand					
Family	−0.75	−0.08	−0.28	−0.09	−2.25
Hired	−0.03	−0.23	−0.22	−0.03	−0.81
Total	−0.51	−0.09	−0.27	−0.08	−1.79
Shadow prices					
Family labor	0.56	−0.27	0.13	−0.02	0.0
Hired labor					
Physical capital		−0.39	−0.07	−0.05	−0.15
Land	−0.19		−0.03	−0.04	−0.69
Household-farm incomes					
Nominal	−0.88	−0.58	−0.13	−0.06	−1.39
Real	2.69	6.89	0.67	1.40	0.50
Income by household group (real)					
Subsistence	7.36	7.11	2.18	1.94	1.18
Mediumholder	3.72	7.26	0.50		0.71
Largeholder	1.12	6.64	0.66	1.59	−0.06
Nonfarm		7.43		0.99	
Household consumption					
Leisure	0.09	0.37	0.50	0.00	0.23
Staples	10.34	10.48	10.96	11.05	5.74
Manufactures	−0.98	−0.57	−0.13	−0.06	−1.39
External linkages					
Migration	−2.43	−8.60	−0.33	−0.05	−0.11
Marketed surplus	−1236.35	−21.40	−9.43	−20.48	14.73[a]
Intermediate trade[b]	−0.01	−0.23	−0.16	−0.07	−0.22
Final trade	−1.09	73.11	−0.09	11.13	−5.79
Total trade	−0.44	5.18	−0.13	1.39	−0.73

[a] Negative in the base. A negative percentage change indicates that the variable increased (i.e., became closer to zero or positive) from the negative base. A value in excess of −1 indicates that the variable turned positive. A positive percentage indicates that the variable decreased from the negative base.
[b] Trade = net imports.

The sectors that are most adversely affected are labor-intensive: staples in Java, India, and Senegal; agricultural exports in Java, Kenya, and Senegal; and nonagricultural production in Java and Mexico. The least affected activities are nonagricultural production in Senegal and livestock in Senegal, India, Mexico, and Kenya.

As a result of the reductions in village production and migration, the nominal incomes of households decline. In real terms, however, household incomes increase, as families benefit from lower consumer prices. The net effect of the consumption subsidy on real incomes depends on the interaction between the negative effect of the subsidy on village production and the positive effect of the subsidy on consumer purchasing power at given nominal incomes in different household groups.

The effects of the subsidy on village trade are complex. Intermediate-good imports decline in response to the contraction in village production. The net demand for final-good imports, however, increases in the Kenyan village-town and in India. As both staple prices for consumers and village value-added income fall, households in the other three villages shift their consumption away from import-intensive sectors in favor of village staples. The net effect on total imports is mixed: positive in Kenya and India, and negative in Senegal, Mexico, and Java. The combination of higher village staple demand and lower production results in a decrease in marketed surplus in all five cases.

Experiments 9–11: Income transfers

We carried out three income transfer experiments, one to each income group in the village. To make these experiments comparable within villages, the same absolute amount of income was transferred to each income group. To standardize across villages, the transfer in each village was set at 10 percent of the income of the village subsistence group. The results of the three income transfer experiments appear in Tables 9.9 through 9.11.

The mechanisms by which income transfers influence the village economy are similar to those in the consumption subsidy experiments, with the exception of price effects. Commodity prices for both producers and consumers are not affected by the income transfers. The income transfer increases the marginal utility of leisure in the target household group. This has a negative effect on village production, resulting in a reduced flow of value-added potentially to all household groups in the village. Quantitatively, the decreases in production are similar to those in the consumption subsidy experiments. They are fairly robust with respect to which household group is the direct recipient of the transfer. Across villages, negative production impacts generally are strongest (a maximum of 3.9 percent in staples) in the Javan village, with the Kenyan village-town running a distant second. These are the villages in which production activities are most diversified.

Table 9.9. *First transfer payment experiment: Subsistence households*

	Percentage changes				
	Senegal	India	Mexico	Kenya	Java
Household-farm production					
Staple	−0.07	−0.06	−0.05	−0.03	−3.88
Agricultural exports	−0.06			−0.14	−1.21
Livestock	0.00	0.00	−0.01	−0.01	−0.12
Nonagricultural	0.00	0.00	−0.17	−0.07	−0.15
Labor demand					
Family	−0.24	−0.01	−0.18	−0.13	−1.70
Hired	−0.01	−0.03	−0.14	−0.04	−0.61
Total	−0.16	−0.01	−0.18	−0.11	−1.35
Shadow prices					
Family labor	0.18	−0.04	0.09	−0.03	0.03
Hired labor					
Physical capital		−0.05	−0.04	−0.06	−0.11
Land	−0.06		−0.02	−0.05	−0.51
Household-farm incomes					
Nominal	0.84	0.89	0.44	1.87	0.37
Real	0.84	0.89	0.44	1.87	0.37
Income by household group (real)					
Subsistence	9.95	4.26	9.91	9.92	9.09
Mediumholder	−0.13	−0.03	−0.08		−1.05
Largeholder	−0.41	−0.10	−0.09	−0.07	−1.09
Nonfarm		−0.02		−0.07	
Household consumption					
Leisure	0.03	0.05	0.33	0.00	0.18
Staples	2.10	1.17	1.52	2.71	1.46
Manufactures	0.17	1.29	0.27	1.63	0.78
External linkages					
Migration	−0.77	−1.18	−0.22	−0.07	−0.08
Marketed surplus	−253.56	−2.41	−1.38	−5.10	6.59[a]
Intermediate trade[b]	0.00	−0.03	−0.11	−0.09	−0.17
Final trade	0.21	−9.85	0.48	−4.93	3.89
Total trade	0.08	−0.75	0.18	−0.72	0.21

[a] Negative in the base. A negative percentage change indicates that the variable increased (i.e., became closer to zero or positive) from the negative base. A value in excess of −1 indicates that the variable turned positive. A positive percentage indicates that the variable decreased from the negative base.
[b] Trade = net imports.

Table 9.10. *Second transfer payments experiment: Mediumholder households*

	Percentage changes				
	Senegal	India	Mexico	Kenya	Java
Household-farm production					
Staple	−0.07	−0.06	−0.05		−3.88
Agricultural exports	−0.06				−1.21
Livestock	0.00	0.00	−0.01		−0.12
Nonagricultural	0.00	0.00	−0.17		−0.15
Labor demand					
Family	−0.24	−0.01	−0.18		−1.70
Hired	−0.01	−0.03	−0.14		−0.61
Total	−0.16	−0.01	−0.18		−1.35
Shadow prices					
Family labor	0.18	−0.04	0.09		0.32
Hired labor					
Physical capital		−0.05	−0.04		−0.11
Land	−0.06		−0.02		−0.51
Household-farm incomes					
Nominal	0.84	0.89	0.44		0.37
Real	0.84	0.89	0.44		0.37
Income by household group (real)					
Subsistence	−0.05	−0.07	−0.08		−0.91
Mediumholder	3.18	5.07	1.04		1.76
Largeholder	−0.41	−0.10	−0.09		−1.09
Nonfarm		−0.02			
Household consumption					
Leisure	0.03	0.05	0.33		0.18
Staples	1.06	1.30	0.40		0.01
Manufactures	0.71	1.28	0.54		−0.13
External linkages					
Migration	−0.77	−1.18	−0.22		−0.08
Marketed surplus	−132.14	−2.66	−0.43		4.28[a]
Intermediate trade[b]	0.00	−0.03	−0.11		−0.17
Final trade	0.81	−11.02	0.80		0.32
Total trade	0.32	−0.84	0.33		−0.12

[a] Negative in the base. A negative percentage change indicates that the variable increased (i.e., became closer to zero or positive) from the negative base. A value in excess of −1 indicates that the variable turned positive. A positive percentage indicates that the variable decreased from the negative base.

[b] Trade = net imports.

Table 9.11. *Third transfer payments experiment: Largeholder households*

	Percentage changes				
	Senegal	India	Mexico	Kenya	Java
Household-farm production					
Staple	−0.07	−0.06	−0.05	−0.03	−3.88
Agricultural exports	−0.06			−0.15	−1.21
Livestock	0.00	0.00	−0.01	−0.01	−0.12
Nonagricultural	0.00		−0.17	−0.07	−0.15
Labor demand					
Family	−0.24	−0.01	−0.18	−0.13	−1.70
Hired	−0.01	−0.03	−0.14	−0.04	−0.61
Total	−0.16	−0.01	−0.18	−0.11	−1.35
Shadow prices					
Family labor	0.18	−0.04	0.09	−0.03	0.03
Hired labor		0.04			
Physical capital		−0.05	−0.04	−0.06	−0.11
Land	−0.06		−0.02	−0.05	−0.51
Household-farm incomes					
Nominal	0.84	0.89	0.44	1.87	0.37
Real	0.84	0.89	0.44	1.83	0.37
Income by household group (real)					
Subsistence	−0.05	−0.07	−0.09	−0.08	−0.91
Mediumholder	−0.13	−0.03	−0.08		−1.05
Largeholder	1.61	1.65	1.01	3.28	2.90
Nonfarm		−0.02		−0.07	
Household consumption					
Leisure	0.03	0.05	0.33	0.00	0.18
Staples	0.55	0.70	0.36	2.07	0.50
Manufactures	0.99	0.70	0.35	1.83	0.93
External linkages					
Migration	−0.77	−1.18	−0.22	−0.07	−0.08
Marketed surplus	−72.84	−1.51	−0.40	−3.91	5.06[a]
Intermediate trade[b]	0.00	−0.03	−0.11	−0.09	−0.17
Final trade	1.11	−6.40	0.52	−4.12	5.05
Total trade	0.44	−0.50	0.20	−0.62	0.31

[a] Negative in the base. A negative percentage change indicates that the variable increased (i.e., became closer to zero or positive) from the negative base. A value in excess of −1 indicates that the variable turned positive. A positive percentage indicates that the variable decreased from the negative base.
[b] Trade = net imports.

The effects of the transfers on household real incomes naturally favor the group to which the direct transfer is made. The real incomes of the original recipients increase, while, because of negative production and factor demand linkages, real incomes of the other groups decline. The distribution of real incomes thus shifts in favor of the direct recipients of the transfers. It cannot be predicted a priori whether the negative indirect effects of the transfer on village incomes dampens or intensifies the direct impact of the transfer on village income inequality. This depends critically on how value-added from village production is distributed across household groups.

In our experiments, the shift in the income distribution tends to be largest (and equalizing) in the first transfer experiment (Table 9.9), in which the transfer is made to subsistence farmers. Real incomes for subsistence farmers increase by a low of 4.3 percent in India to a high of 9.9 percent in Senegal. The negative income effects for other household groups range from -0.02 percent (the Indian nonfarm group) to -1.09 percent (the Javanese largeholder group). Transfers to mediumholder and largeholder households result in much smaller relative income gains for the recipient group (between 1 and 5 percent; see Tables 9.10 and 9.11). Subsistence-household incomes decline by 0.05 to 0.9 percent as a result of income transfers to largeholders.

The trade linkage effects of income transfers vary across villages, but with one exception they do not change sign across experiments. Intermediate imports fall or, in the case of Senegal, are unchanged. The Senegalese, Mexican, and Javan villages become less self-sufficient in final goods as increases in total income increase the demand for final goods while the higher shadow value of family time depresses output of these goods. In India and Kenya, however, negative cross-household effects of income transfers dampen final-good imports. Migration decreases, from 0.07 percent (Kenya) to 1.18 percent (India). The impacts on imports are quantitatively similar within each village, regardless of which household group receives the transfer.

Overall, our income experiments suggest that direct income transfers to rural households benefit the households that receive these transfers but may have negative implications for village production, and hence on other household groups. In theory, if the negative effects are large for some groups, income transfers could increase migration. In our four villages and in the Kenyan village-town, however, the migration effect is negative, although generally very small. Trade linkage effects of income transfers are very sensitive both to village production effects and to the distribution of income effects across household groups.

Labor market experiments

Our labor market experiments explore the villagewide impacts of changes in the institutional specification of the market for hired labor, from an exogenous to an endogenous-wage specification; of exogenous increases in the demand for family labor, through the implementation of a public works program; and of an exogenous increase in wages for hired labor. The first experiment was discussed in the production experiment section, in conjunction with the staple-price increase experiments, the effects of which were dampened by wage increases resulting from a higher staple price.

Both of the other two labor market experiments result in changes in the shadow prices of labor, but they differ in incidence and in magnitude. The wage-rate experiment increases exogenously the price of hired labor, by 10 percent. The public works program exogenously increases the demand for family labor (for a hypothetical public works project), raising the shadow price of family labor. These changes in shadow prices induce reallocations of labor to activities that are less intensive in the factor whose relative price increases, and they encourage substitution between family and hired labor where possible. By altering the shadow value of labor in the village, both experiments affect rural-to-urban and/or international migration. These migration effects cannot be signed theoretically. Nevertheless, in all five villages, an exogenous increase in rural wages *increases* out-migration, as the negative effect on household-farm profits outweighs the positive effect on incomes of wage-earner households.

Experiment 12: Wage rate experiment

An increase in the cost of hired labor (Table 9.12) leads to a change in cropping and production patterns – a reallocation of production from hired-labor-intensive sectors to family-labor-intensive sectors. It also leads to an overall decline in production, since in our model, family and hired labor are not perfectly substitutable. Which sectors are hired-labor-intensive varies by village. The production effects, therefore, differ from one village to another. In Java, there is a large reduction in staples and nonagricultural production and an increase in livestock and agricultural exports. In Kenya, the largest reductions in output are in nonagricultural production and in export agriculture; there is a small reduction in staple production and an increase in the livestock sector. In India, where all sectors use some hired labor, staple and nonagricultural production decline. In Senegal, there is a pronounced increase in nonagricultural production, which uses no hired labor, coupled with a significant decline in livestock and small declines in the other sectors. Finally, in Mexico there is a small increase in livestock, a significant decline in nonagricultural production, and a smaller decrease in staple production.

The increased cost of hired labor lowers the shadow price of family labor, despite the reallocation of production to family-labor-intensive sectors. The overall reduction in output decreases the aggregate demand for family labor, though by considerably less than the decrease in aggregate demand for hired

Table 9.12. *Wage experiment*

	Percentage changes				
	Senegal	India	Mexico	Kenya	Java
Household-farm production					
Staple	−0.48	−1.64	−0.88	−0.52	−35.92
Agricultural exports	−0.14			−2.39	16.36
Livestock	−2.25	0.10	0.04	0.02	5.76
Nonagricultural	1.94	−0.22	−2.96	−5.09	−31.66
Labor demand					
Family	−0.17	−0.03	−1.26	−2.60	−1.51
Hired	−1.44	−5.29	−12.31	−19.08	−33.27
Total	−0.60	−0.33	−2.12	−5.68	−11.78
Shadow prices					
Family labor	−0.16	−1.20	−0.33	−0.06	−1.53
Hired labor					
Physical capital		−1.36	−0.35	−3.93	−20.17
Land	−0.33		−0.25	−0.74	−5.88
Household-farm incomes					
Nominal	−0.15	0.15	−0.34	−3.49	−8.87
Real	−0.15	0.15	0.34	−3.49	−8.87
Income by household group (real)					
Subsistence	−0.29	2.08	−0.21	−2.96	−17.07
Mediumholder	−0.23	0.80	−0.32		−9.68
Largeholder	−0.08	−0.87	−0.37	−3.54	−4.34
Nonfarm		0.24		−4.59	
Household consumption					
Leisure	0.01	0.13	0.07	0.02	0.10
Staples	−0.18	0.51	−0.32	−3.44	−9.51
Manufactures	−0.13	0.49	−0.34	−3.49	−8.44
External linkages					
Migration	0.16	0.01	0.82	0.14	3.92
Marketed surplus	−35.64	−5.74	−1.36	4.87	12.87[a]
Intermediate trade[b]	0.00	−0.87	0.37	−2.90	−26.63
Final trade	−0.33	−1.70	0.57	7.60	87.48
Total trade	−0.14	−0.93	0.46	−1.53	−17.99

[a] Negative in the base. A negative percentage change indicates that the variable increased (i.e., became closer to zero or positive) from the negative base. A value in excess of −1 indicates that the variable turned positive. A positive percentage indicates that the variable decreased from the negative base.
[b] Trade = net imports.

labor. The decreases in demand for family labor range from 0.2 percent in Senegal to 2.6 percent in Java, while the decreases in hired-labor demand range from 1.4 percent in Senegal to 33 percent in Java. A lower shadow price of family labor increases migration by a low of 0.2 percent in Senegal to a high of about 4 percent in Java. It also increases the amount of leisure time in our villages, although quantitatively this effect is quite small, ranging between 0.01 percent in Senegal to 0.13 percent in India.

The increase in the price of hired labor reduces household incomes in all cases except India, both because the net income from farming falls and because the imputed value of family labor decreases. A countervailing effect on household income results from the fact that much of the hired labor comes from village households and therefore appears as a component of household income. The general fall in household incomes thus reflects that a larger share of household income originates from family-labor value-added than from wages or migration. In the exception, India, the hiring out of labor is a large component of income for subsistence, medium, and nonfarm households; these groups' incomes actually increase as a result of higher wages. The relative income loss in Senegal and Java is most pronounced for subsistence households and decreases as holdings increase.

Trade linkages between the village and the outside economy decrease, except in Mexico. Exports of goods and services and intermediate imports generally fall because of the decline in village production, and final demand imports generally decrease as a result of reduced household incomes.

Overall, the findings of this experiment reveal the difficulty of using wage policy as a means to increase incomes and welfare or to decrease migration pressures in rural economies that are characterized by a high degree of family production.

Experiment 13: Public works experiment

Rural public works projects offer a potential means to increase rural incomes and reduce migration pressures in the short run while creating an infrastructure base for higher productivity of family resources in the long run. The villagewide effects of productivity gains were explored previously. In the short run, the public works project absorbs village labor, increasing the shadow value of family labor and decreasing migration. It also competes with village production for scarce family labor. This dampens the positive effect of the public works project on rural incomes in our experiments.

The scale of the public works program is set in each village so that the income injection it represents equals 10 percent of the total income of the subsistence household group. The increased demand for family labor is then calculated as this injection divided by the (shadow) wage rate of family labor in the base. Thus, the absolute scale of the public works program differs across villages, as does the significance of the program for the demand for labor. What is comparable across villages is the relative scale of the program relative to the incomes of the poorest households.

Results of the public works experiment are summarized in Table 9.13. The public works program increases the shadow price of family labor and therefore almost always leads to a decrease in village production. This production impact is small, and is positive or zero in some cases where sectors rely little on family labor: livestock and nonagricultural production in Senegal and Kenya. The increase in the shadow price of labor is most pronounced in Senegal (7.2 percent) and least pronounced in India (1.7 percent). Naturally, the most labor-intensive activities contract the most, for example, staple and agricultural export production in Java.

Even though there is some substitution of hired for family labor, the decline in production leads to a small drop in the demand for hired labor in all villages and in the village-town. The reduction in hired-labor demand is most pronounced in Java and Mexico (0.73 and 0.67 percent, respectively). It is very small, on the order of 0.02 to 0.08 percent, in the rest of the villages.

There is an increase in the local supply (equals demand) of family labor in response to the increase in its shadow price. The elasticity of family-labor supply with respect to the family wage (the family-labor demand row divided by the shadow price of family-labor row in Table 9.13) ranges from a low of 0.24 in Java to a high of 1.00 in Senegal. Part of the increase in the supply of family labor to village activities comes from a decrease in migration and a shift away from family-labor-intensive production, and part of it is due to a decrease in leisure time.

Village incomes increase as a result of the works project, but the income changes for specific household groups, as in our other experiments, are unevenly distributed. In a few cases, for subsistence households in Mexico and Java and nonfarm households in India, it is negative. Higher incomes increase the demand for staples and manufactures. Marketed surplus decreases. As village production contracts, however, the demand for imported intermediate inputs decreases (or, in the Senegalese case, is unchanged). The impacts on the demand for final-good imports are positive in Senegal, Mexico, and Java and negative in India and Kenya.

Migrant remittance and exchange rate experiments

These experiments explore the villagewide impacts of changes in the economic returns to migration. In the case of internal migration, such a change might result, for example, from employment or wage growth in urban labor markets or from improvements in village families' "migration capital" or "migration networks" over time. In the case of international migration, changes can result either from these wage, employment, or migration capital

Table 9.13. *Public works experiment*

| | Percentage changes | | | | |
	Senegal	India	Mexico	Kenya	Java
Household-farm production					
Staple	−0.11	−0.17	−0.23	−0.03	−4.61
Agricultural exports	−0.09			−0.15	−1.46
Livestock	0.00	0.01	−0.05	−0.01	−0.15
Nonagricultural	0.00		−0.81	−0.07	−0.18
Labor demand					
Family	7.17	0.25	2.00	3.88	0.67
Hired	−0.02	−0.08	−0.67	−0.04	−0.73
Total	−0.26	−0.03		−0.11	−1.61
Shadow prices					
Family labor	7.16	1.66	3.30	4.05	2.80
Hired labor					
Physical capital		−0.14	−0.20	−0.07	−0.13
Land	−0.10		−0.10	−0.05	−0.62
Household-farm incomes					
Nominal	0.67	0.72	0.12	1.87	0.17
Real	0.67	0.72	0.12	1.87	0.17
Income by household group (real)					
Subsistence	2.41	0.10	−0.19	1.72	−0.23
Mediumholder	0.80	0.83	0.15		0.19
Largeholder	0.23	0.99	0.12	1.87	0.31
Nonfarm		−0.09		1.80	
Household consumption					
Leisure	−0.64	−0.97	−0.40	−0.03	−0.07
Staples	0.96	0.68	0.08	1.83	0.13
Manufactures	0.51	0.69	0.13	1.89	0.17
External linkages					
Migration	−1.25	−4.53	−1.01	−0.07	−0.10
Marketed surplus	−125.73	−1.78	−0.50	−3.47	5.28[a]
Intermediate trade[b]	0.00	−0.08	−0.50	−0.09	−0.20
Final trade	0.58	−8.74	0.45	−3.53	1.69
Total trade	0.23	−0.72	−0.04	−0.54	−0.03

[a] Negative in the base. A negative percentage change indicates that the variable increased (i.e., became closer to zero or positive) from the negative base. A value in excess of −1 indicates that the variable turned positive. A positive percentage indicates that the variable decreased from the negative base.
[b] Trade = net imports.

effects or from changes in the international exchange rate, which translate foreign-denominated remittances into local currencies. By linking villages with the global economy, international migration potentially makes the village economy sensitive to this unlikely, macroeconomic variable.

The direct effect of an increase in the expected returns to migration usually is to stimulate out-migration, as in the well-known Todaro (1969) migration model. (An exception is international migration in Java, for which there is evidence of a backward-bending migration supply curve.) This, however, generates secondary-income and production effects in the village that are beyond the purview of Todaro. Income gains to village households from migration raise the marginal utility of leisure and the shadow value of family labor in the village. Migration competes with village production for scarce family labor. The negative production effects in our migration experiments are generally greater than those in the previous income transfer experiments, because of the direct effect of the remittance change on village factor markets. The effects of the remittance change on the level and distribution of village income are also more complex than in most remittance studies, which ignore indirect effects of migration and remittances on village production and incomes. (An exception is Taylor, 1992.)

Experiment 14: Internal migration experiment

In this experiment (Table 9.14), the returns to internal migration (expected per migrant remittances) were increased by 10 percent. In Kenya, migrants were not disaggregated between domestic and international migrants. Kenya is therefore omitted from the discussion of this experiment.

The impacts on the village economy result from the interplay of two effects. First, the increase in remittance rates increases the attractiveness of domestic migration to the migrant-originating households. As a result, domestic migration increases by between 4 and 24 percent in our villages. Part of the increase is at the expense of foreign migration, in those cases where there is foreign migration in the base. Most of the increase in migration comes from decreasing staple and export production within the village. As a result of the increase in migration, total remittances from domestic migrants rise by much more than 10 percent: about 40 percent in Java, 35 percent in Mexico and India, and 29 percent in Senegal.

Second, village incomes increase. The combination of increases in remittances and increases in household incomes raises the opportunity cost of family labor. The increase in opportunity cost is smallest in Java (.02 percent), where domestic remittances account for only one-eighth of household income and where income from hiring out of family labor, which declines, is about one-half of total household income. It is highest in Senegal (1.8 percent) and in Mexico, where migration is the principal form of income diversification

Table 9.14. *Internal migration experiment*

	Percentage changes			
	Senegal	India	Mexico	Java
Household-farm production				
Staple	−0.72	−0.10	−0.90	−2.04
Agricultural exports	−0.58			−0.62
Livestock	0.00	0.01	−0.18	−0.06
Nonagricultural	0.00		−3.09	−0.08
Labor demand				
Family	−2.41	−0.93	−3.28	−0.88
Hired	−0.10	−0.02	−2.55	−0.32
Total	−1.62	−0.39	−3.22	−0.70
Shadow prices				
Family labor	1.80	−0.84	1.58	0.02
Hired labor				
Physical capital		−0.08	−0.79	−0.06
Land	−0.62		−0.37	−0.26
Household-farm income				
Nominal	8.73	1.33	0.22	0.10
Real	8.73	1.33	0.22	0.10
Income by household group (real)				
Subsistence	−0.36	1.19	2.40	−0.21
Mediumholder	2.61	−0.05	−1.52	−0.21
Largeholder	14.32	1.91	1.68	0.67
Nonfarm		0.61		
Household consumption				
Leisure	0.08	−0.09	−1.76	0.00
Staples	6.39	1.24	0.42	0.13
Manufactures	10.01	1.23	−0.10	0.22
External linkages				
Migration	17.24	23.92	4.19	5.93
Marketed surplus	−832.82	−2.67	−2.01	2.44[a]
Intermediate trade[b]	−0.03	−0.05	−1.93	−0.09
Final trade	11.17	8.75	0.93	1.40
Total trade	4.45	0.60	−0.54	0.05

[a] Negative in the base. A negative percentage change indicates that the variable increased (i.e., became closer to zero or positive) from the negative base. A value in excess of −1 indicates that the variable turned positive. A positive percentage indicates that the variable decreased from the negative base.
[b] Trade = net imports.

(1.6 percent). Although domestic migration accounts for less than 5 percent of total income in the Mexican village, it competes with relatively high-paying international migration for scarce family labor. The possibility of substituting hired labor for family labor to alleviate the family-labor constraint is limited in the Mexican case; hired-labor value-added accounts for only one-eighth of village household income. The increase in the opportunity cost of family labor leads to reductions in production within the villages, especially in staples and export crops. The decreases in production are most pronounced in Mexico and Java, least pronounced in India, and intermediate in Senegal.

The impact of increased migration on village incomes depends on the importance of remittances relative to village value-added for subsistence, medium-income, and high-income households. In Java, remittances from internal migrants account for a small share of total income in all but the high-income households. The negative income effect of decreases in village production dominates the positive effect of higher remittances for low-income and medium-income households. In these households, income declines as a consequence of the increased economic returns to internal migration. In India and Mexico, both subsistence and high-income households gain as a result of the increase in remittances, while in Senegal, subsistence producers, whose income is most dependent on staple production, lose, and all other households gain.

Both exports and intermediate imports decline because of the decrease in village production induced by the greater profitability of migration. Net final-demand imports increase. Total trade linkages, as measured by net imports, increase in all but the Mexican case, where the decrease in demand linkages on the production side outweighs the increase on the final-demand side.

Experiment 15: International migration experiment: Exchange rate devaluation

As migration links villages with the global economy, villages become more sensitive to changes in international as well as domestic variables. Our final simulation explores the villagewide impact of a 10 percent exchange rate devaluation. In effect, this is an international migration experiment, because labor is the only export for which our villages receive income denominated in foreign currency.

The exchange rate devaluation increases the returns to international migration in local currency. This has two immediate effects. First, it increases remittance income in households with migrants abroad. This is essentially an income transfer effect, where the transfer is distributed across household groups in proportion to their initial levels of remittance income. Second, it increases the opportunity cost (shadow price) of family labor in village production and consumption activities and in internal migration. The interplay of these two effects in theory leads to an unambiguous (negative) impact on village production but an ambiguous impact on international migration. The higher returns to migration and higher opportunity cost of family time create incentives to allocate more time to international migration. Higher income, however, increases the demand for leisure, a normal good, which competes with income activities, including migration, for scarce family time. If the income elasticity of leisure demand is sufficiently large, an increase in expected remittances from migrants abroad paradoxically may *decrease* international migration, in a manner analogous to the backward-bending labor supply curve in microeconomics.

Our exchange rate experiments reveal a positive migration response to devaluation in two of the three villages that send migrants abroad. The responsiveness of migration (elasticity) with respect to the exchange rate is 2.7 in the Kenyan village-town and 0.8 in Mexico. In Java, by contrast, the simulation reveals evidence of a backward-bending labor supply for international migration. The elasticity is negative, although small in absolute value (-0.01). The finding of a negative migration elasticity for Java, although inconsistent with the Todaro hypothesis, is not unreasonable. In a relatively high-income village, as in a high-income household, the marginal utility of leisure is likely to be high. The Javan case is arguably the most developed of the five villages. In this village, migration opportunities appear to be concentrated at the upper end of the household income spectrum (see Chapter 8, Table 8.5). A disutility of migration would reinforce the negative effect of income changes on the migration supply response.

The increased shadow value of family time leads to a contraction of all village production activities, a village version of the "Dutch disease." This is especially evident in Mexico. Staple output falls by 2.2 percent, and nonagricultural production tumbles by 7.4 percent. Livestock, the least labor-intensive production activity, is almost unchanged. The negative production effects are small in Kenya and, with the exception of staples, in Java.

The exchange rate devaluation has a regressive effect on the household income distribution in Java, but a relatively equalizing effect in Mexico and Kenya. In Java, subsistence households do not benefit much from higher remittance income, but they are hurt by lost income (especially wage labor) opportunities in the village. Subsistence and smallholder incomes decline, while largeholder incomes rise by 1.2 percent. By contrast, although production and employment fall substantially in the Mexican village, subsistence and smallholder households benefit from migration. Higher remittances from migrants in the United States more than compensate these groups for lower income from village production. In Mexico, as in Kenya, all groups gain from the devaluation, and the smallest gains accrue to the largeholder group.

Total village income increases as a result of the devaluation in all three villages.

The unequal gains (losses) from the devaluation across households and interhousehold differences in expenditure patterns lead to markedly different impacts on consumption and on trade linkages. Leisure demand increases in Java but decreases (due to a rising opportunity cost of leisure) in Kenya and especially in Mexico. As production contracts, village imports of intermediate goods decline. The patchwork of income gains and losses across household groups produces a modest increase in net final-good imports in Java. More broad-based income gains result in sharp increases in net final-good imports in the Kenyan village-town and in Mexico. The contraction of village production contributes to these final-import demand effects. In all three cases, higher remittances increase the level of integration with outside product markets on the consumption side.

Our exchange rate experiments reveal the complexity of migration responses and villagewide impacts, including the possibility of backward-bending migration supply curves. They also highlight the sensitivity of village economies to what may appear to be an unlikely macroeconomic variable in an environment of economic globalization. It is particularly noteworthy that in the Mexican village income effects are nearly three times larger in the exchange rate experiment than in the staple price experiment. That is, the Mexican village economy is more sensitive to the international exchange rate than to corn prices.

Experiment 16: Migration development

The previous two experiments captured direct remittance and lost-labor effects of internal and international migration on village economies. Stark (1982) and others argue that migration and remittances also have indirect effects, which result from migrants' role as financial intermediaries who provide rural households with capital and a means to reduce risk by diversifying income sources. Lacking access to credit and income insurance outside the household, households can self-finance a new production technology or activity and self-insure against perceived or real income risks by first investing in migration by one or more family members. Microeconometric findings by Lucas (1987) and Taylor (1992) offer empirical evidence that migrants contribute positively to productivity and incomes in nonmigration activities over time. Where rural credit and insurance markets are missing or imperfect, migration can play an important development role that is not captured by our remittance and exchange rate experiments.

Our final policy experiment explores one aspect of this migration and development hypothesis: the villagewide impact of investments in productive assets stimulated by migration. In the village models, the savings-investment constraint requires that villages self-finance capital investments. This constraint, in the absence of capital inflows from outside the village, corresponds to a context of missing or imperfect rural capital markets. In each of our migration experiments, increases in the returns to migration stimulate village savings and investment by positively affecting total income. For example, in the international migration (exchange rate) experiment, total investment increases by 1.7 and 0.4 percent in the Mexican and Javan villages and by 3.6 percent in the Kenyan village-town (not shown).

We explore the indirect asset-accumulation effects of migration by allocating the increased investment that results from higher returns to migration across village production activities in the form of increases in physical capital stocks. The increase in village investment is spread across activities in proportion to the activities' initial share in the village's total physical capital. The results of the international migration experiment reported in Table 9.15 are used as the starting point for this experiment.

Increases in sectoral capital stocks raise the marginal productivities of complementary (land and labor) factors. This induces households to channel more of their resources into physical capital-using production activities, increasing village value-added, incomes, and leisure demand. Increased demand for family time in village production and leisure activities, however, creates a scarcity of family time, which raises the family wage (as in our technological-change experiment). This results in negative factor-market feedbacks on village production, leisure, and migration.

The results of the migration and development experiment appear in Table 9.16. They are reported as percentage changes from the premigration base. The impacts of migration-induced asset accumulation are best seen by comparing the findings in Table 9.16 with those reported in Table 9.15, which include only the short-term, remittance, and lost-labor effects of international migration.

Asset accumulation positively affects production in all sectors in the Mexican village and in the Kenyan village-town. In Mexico, staple and nonagricultural production still contract as a result of migration, but by less than in the previous experiment. The 10 percent exchange rate devaluation reduces staple output by 1.7 percent, compared with 2.2 percent when only remittance and lost-labor effects are considered. Nonagricultural production decreases by 6.5 percent, compared with 7.4 percent before. In these sectors, the positive effect of migration on capital accumulation is not sufficient to reverse the negative direct effects of lost labor and the migration-induced increase in the family wage. The village "Dutch disease" effect persists but is diminished.

Production now *increases* as a result of international migration in the capital-intensive Mexican livestock sector and in all sectors of the Kenyan village-town. The slight increase in livestock output in Mexico (from a 0.5

Table 9.15. *International migration experiment: Exchange rate devaluation*

	Percentage changes		
	Mexico	Kenya	Java
Household-farm production			
Staple	−2.19	−0.07	−2.83
Agricultural exports		−0.33	−0.87
Livestock	−0.45	−0.02	−0.09
Nonagricultural	−7.43	−0.16	−0.11
Labor demand			
Family	−7.84	−0.28	−1.23
Hired	−6.13	−0.09	−0.44
Total	−7.71	−0.25	−0.97
Shadow prices			
Family labor	3.93	0.07	0.02
Hired labor			
Physical capital	−1.90	−0.14	−0.08
Land	−0.91	−0.10	−0.37
Household-farm incomes			
Nominal	2.98	4.26	0.27
Real	2.98	4.26	0.27
Income by household group (real)			
Subsistence	1.88	6.87	−0.24
Mediumholder	4.41		−0.22
Largeholder	1.69	3.30	1.17
Nonfarm		4.67	
Household consumption			
Leisure	−1.96	−0.01	0.13
Staples	2.89	4.40	0.31
Manufactures	3.23	4.21	0.46
External linkages			
Migration	7.65	26.70	−0.06
Marketed surplus	−6.50	−8.34	3.60[a]
Intermediate trade[b]	−4.66	−0.20	−0.12
Final trade	6.91	34.02	2.69
Total trade	0.95	4.26	0.14

[a] Negative in the base. A negative percentage change indicates that the variable increased (i.e., became closer to zero or positive) from the negative base. A value in excess of −1 indicates that the variable turned positive. A positive percentage indicates that the variable decreased from the negative base.
[b] Trade = net imports.

Table 9.16. *Migration and development*

	Percentage changes		
	Mexico	Kenya	Java
Household-farm production			
Staple	−1.74	1.12	−3.04
Agricultural exports		5.64	−1.13
Livestock	0.02	3.36	0.34
Nonagricultural	−6.53	2.31	0.50
Labor demand			
Family	−7.36	3.32	−1.31
Hired	−5.67		
Total	−7.22	2.70	−0.89
Shadow prices			
Family labor	4.10	0.11	0.04
Hired labor			
Physical capital	−2.95	−0.57	−0.05
Land	−0.45	1.93	−0.25
Household-farm incomes			
Nominal	3.28	7.08	0.35
Real	3.28	7.08	0.35
Income by household group (real)			
Subsistence	2.15	9.52	−0.02
Mediumholder	4.71		−0.13
Largeholder	1.99	6.18	1.19
Nonfarm		7.28	
Household consumption			
Leisure	−1.87	−0.03	0.14
Staples	3.19	7.21	0.40
Manufactures	3.53	7.04	0.54
External linkages			
Migration	7.21	26.56	−0.09
Marketed surplus	−5.92	−10.12	4.18[a]
Intermediate trade[b]	−3.46	2.85	0.44
Final trade	7.01	39.43	0.63
Total trade	1.61	7.62	0.46

[a] Negative in the base. A negative percentage change indicates that the variable increased (i.e., became closer to zero or positive) from the negative base. A value in excess of −1 indicates that the variable turned positive. A positive percentage indicates that the variable decreased from the negative base.
[b] Trade = net imports.

percent decrease in the previous experiment) is consistent with the positive effect of migration on livestock accumulation reported in Chapter 5. Asset-accumulation effects are particularly striking in the Kenyan village-town, where sectoral outputs increase by between 1 and 5.6 percent as a result of international migration, compared with *decreases* of 0.02 to 0.3 percent reported in Table 9.15.

The sign of the exchange rate effect on production also turns positive in the Javan livestock and nonagricultural sectors, which are relatively capital-intensive. Increases in these two sectors' output comes at the expense of the staple and agricultural export sectors, however: The negative impact of the exchange rate on those sectors is larger than before. Higher capital stocks reduce the shadow value of capital and increase the family wage in both the Mexican and Javan villages and in the Kenyan village-town.

Migration-induced asset accumulation increases village cash incomes in all three cases. In Mexico, total income now increases by 3.3 percent as a result of the exchange rate devaluation (compared with 3 percent before). In relative terms, subsistence households benefit the most from this asset accumulation: The (positive) impact of the devaluation on their incomes is 20 percent higher than in the earlier experiment. The effect of the devaluation on consumption demand for staples and manufactures increases, and the effects on marketed surplus and leisure, while still negative, become smaller in absolute value.

In Java, where total income increases by only 0.35 percent (compared with 0.27 percent before), asset accumulation makes the impacts of international migration less regressive. Subsistence household incomes, instead of decreasing by 0.25 percent, are now almost unchanged as a result of the devaluation. The negative income effect also declines for mediumholder households (from -0.22 to -0.13). Meanwhile, the positive effect of international migration on largeholder household incomes is almost the same with or without asset accumulation (1.19 percent, compared with 1.17 percent). These findings make sense in a village where most of the direct benefits of migration accrue to largeholder households, and where the livelihood of subsistence and smallholder households depends almost entirely on receiving value-added from village production. The Javan case illustrates nicely how vil-lagewide linkages transfer indirect effects of migration to nonmigrant house-holds. The higher family wage induced by capital accumulation discourages households from demanding more leisure than in the previous experiment.

The implications of asset accumulation for total income are dramatically higher in Kenya, where income increases by 7.1 percent as a result of the devaluation, compared with 4.3 percent before. The effect on incomes of subsistence and nonfarm households increases by 38 to 55 percent, and the effect on largeholder incomes nearly doubles, from 3.3 to 6.2 percent. A higher family wage induces Kenyan households to demand less leisure, but the positive effects of the devaluation on the demand for staples and manufactures increase from just over 4 percent in the last experiment to more than 7 percent when asset accumulation is taken into account.

Migration-induced asset accumulation has a slight negative effect on migration propensities, but this effect is not large enough to substantially change the high migration elasticities with respect to expected remittances in Mexico and Kenya. It makes the migrant-labor supply curve more backward-bending in the Javan village. Trade linkages with the outside world increase substantially in the villages and in the village-town. This is partly due to a positive effect of asset accumulation on the demand for intermediate imports in all three cases.

Overall, the results of this experiment provide support for the migration-and-development hypothesis, but with a villagewide twist. The impacts of migration-induced capital accumulation are uneven across production sectors and household groups. General-equilibrium feedbacks through village factor markets tend to dampen the positive effects of investments on production and incomes. However, they also transfer many of the indirect benefits of migration to nonmigrant households. The positive asset-accumulation effects of international migration on village incomes make our villages more sensitive to the international economic environment in an era of increasingly global village economies.

10

Conclusions

Income linkages among agricultural households are instrumental in shaping the impacts of policy, market, and environmental changes on production, incomes, and migration in LDC rural economies. Microeconomic household-farm models, the cornerstone of microeconomic policy analysis over the past decade, do not take these linkages into account. Fixed-price village multiplier (SAM) models generally exaggerate them. The villagewide economic modeling approach presented in this book was designed to capture linkages among household-farms while taking into account resource constraints and the diversity of production, market, and institutional structures that characterize rural economies in developing countries.

Our findings from village and village-town models illustrate the influence local factor and product market linkages exert on shaping policy, market, and environmental impacts. At the same time, our studies dispel any notion one might have that villages are isolated, closed economies. Although situated in vastly different economic, cultural, and environmental settings, the villages we studied are integrated into regional, national, and, in the case of international migration, global markets. All are affected by changes in external markets and government policies. Linkages with the outside world are more important to village economies than they are to the most open national economies. Even in Senegal, the least developed of the five villages we studied, village imports are 42 percent higher than village production, and migrant remittances constitute more than 31 percent of total household income. Not only are these villages not isolated economically; they are not isolated in terms of information about the outside world. For example, Mexican villagers are acutely aware of exchange rates, wages, and the prices of VCRs in the United States. Nevertheless, the degree of integration with outside markets differs markedly from village to village and also from sector to sector and household to household within villages.

The combination of integration with outside markets and internal economic linkages is the reason we need villagewide economic modeling. The villages in this book lie somewhere in the middle of a spectrum ranging from a neoclassical world of complete and well-functioning markets to a subsistence household economy. At either extreme of this spectrum there is little reason to perform villagewide economic modeling. In a pure neoclassical world, all income linkages are between village households and the outside world. In a pure subsistence economy, there are no local market interactions; households supply their own inputs and consume their own output.

The case for villagewide modeling turns on the existence of local market interactions among households together with the presence of local nontradables, that is, goods or factors whose prices are determined in local markets. Exogenous influences on the supply or demand for such goods and factors affect local prices and unleash a complex set of income, production, and migration effects. In a world where some goods and factors are tradable and others are not, and where some households interact with outside markets and others do not, analytical models lose their usefulness for policy analysis; they are generally incapable of reliably predicting the magnitude or even the direction of policy and market impacts on local economies. Incorporating microeconomic household-farm modeling into a local computable economywide modeling framework offers a means to explore both the qualitative and quantitative impacts of exogenous shocks on rural production, incomes, and migration.

Village economic linkages

Villages exhibit strong factor market linkages that transmit production changes affecting one class of household-farms to others. This results in villagewide production, income, and expenditure effects that are not picked up by microeconomic household-farm models. Openness to outside markets dampens multiplier effects of policy, market, and environmental changes within villages. Nevertheless, our simulation findings indicate that intravillage linkages are important in determining both the sign and magnitude of impacts of exogenous changes on income, production, and an array of other variables.

The magnitudes of the villagewide effects of policy, market, and environmental shocks, and in many cases the sign of these effects as well, vary greatly from village to village. They are shaped by village institutional structures, production technologies, the economic diversity and income levels of household-farms, and village resource constraints.

Many of these variables are closely related to the development level of the village or village-town, which may or may not reflect the development level of the country in which the village is located. The poorest of the five villages (Senegal and India) are also the least economically diversified, relying disproportionately on staple production, with low levels of technology and sharply decreasing returns to family labor. The highest-income and most diversified cases (Java, Mexico, and the Kenyan village-town) are more commercialized and utilize purchased inputs, including hired labor and machinery, as substitutes for family labor in a number of different production activities.

Diversification, commercialization, and use of modern technologies are associated with high production-response elasticities in these villages. This means that the initial (first-round) effects of price changes on production tend to be greater in the relatively developed villages. However, because these villages are diversified on the production side, a given percentage change in a sector's output translates into a smaller percentage change in household-farm incomes. Because households are heterogeneous (ranging from subsistence to largeholder and surplus-producing to nonagricultural), nominal income changes often are unequally distributed and deviate from real income changes, which reflect consumer prices and expenditure patterns. In our experiments, it is not uncommon for some household groups to gain while others lose, or for some to gain in nominal terms while losing in real terms. Researchers who ignore the diversity of village economies and village institutions can easily misrepresent the impacts of agricultural price policies on rural production, incomes, marketed surplus, and other variables of interest.

Village CGEs, SAMs, and agricultural household models

Village CGE models offer an advance beyond both microeconomic household-farm models and SAM-based village models for studying the impacts of policies, market changes, and ecological shocks on rural economies. Our experiments reveal a larger and more complex set of effects than are captured by microeconomic household-farm models. For example, in a household-farm model, the marketed-surplus effect of a change in staple prices is the difference between changes in staple output and consumption on a representative staple-producing farm. In a villagewide model, the price change generates production and consumption effects on farms that produce staples, but it also generates income (e.g., hired-labor value-added) and consumption effects on nonstaple-producing households. The net impact on marketed surplus from the village is the difference between these villagewide impacts on output and consumption. The village model provides a more accurate picture of the effects of price policies on the availability of staples for urban consumers. It also captures income effects across all household groups.

Moreover, in cases where prices are endogenous (e.g., family labor, hired labor, staples, and other local nontradables), the villagewide model identifies general-equilibrium feedbacks that have important effects on supply and demand elasticities. Endogenous shadow prices in our models reflect village resource constraints that limit household-farm responses to exogenous shocks. They are a villagewide analogue to shadow prices in microeconomic household-farm models with missing or incomplete markets, which do not capture interhousehold-farm linkages. Our simulation findings reported in Chapter 9 demonstrate the importance of these linkages and village price effects in shaping the impacts of exogenous policy, market, and ecological changes.

SAM multiplier models of village economies have the advantage over microeconomic household-farm models of capturing interhousehold income linkages. They have the disadvantages, however, of assuming linearity on both the production and consumption sides and of ignoring prices and family resource constraints on production response. Because of this, village SAM multipliers overstate the village income effects of exogenous shocks whenever there are diminishing returns to factor inputs or resource constraints on village production. Constrained SAM multipliers (Lewis and Thorbecke, 1992; Subramanian and Sadoulet, 1990; Parikh and Thorbecke, 1996) are more realistic for villagewide economic analysis. However, they do not provide a way to incorporate price effects into a village model. Both of these are precluded by the SAM framework.

When nonlinearities, resource constraints, and endogenous prices are incorporated into villagewide models, the impacts of exogenous changes on production, incomes, and expenditures become more complex. Theory is of limited use in predicting the sign of these impacts.

Paradoxes and policy lessons

Several of our policy experiments yield seemingly paradoxical findings. Income elasticities with respect to output price changes are negative in some household groups. Income transfers to some households negatively affect others. Agricultural price supports sometimes reduce family wages and labor demand. Increasing remittances resulted in a decrease in migration in one case, contrary to conventional migration theory. Upon close analysis, these paradoxes are easily explained by the nonlinearities, endogenous prices, and intravillage income linkages unique to village CGEs.

Despite striking differences among villages with respect to economic structures, institutions, and environments, a number of policy lessons emerge from our simulations. Our experiments uncover some robust findings about villagewide responses and impacts in different socioeconomic, cultural, market, and environmental settings. A sampling of these findings includes:

1. The limited effectiveness of staple price policy without technological and market reforms, especially in poor villages characterized by sharply diminishing returns to family inputs and high transactions costs.

2. The high cost, in terms of lost production, of environmental degradation, yet the potentially large opportunity cost of investing in environmental conservation where families engage in activities that do not depend heavily on environmental quality (e.g., migration or nonagricultural production).

3. The inadequacy of "quick fix" income transfer and consumer subsidy policies to increase real incomes and alleviate rural poverty. Our experiments suggest that sustained, broad-based development requires coupling policies to ensure basic needs with targeted efforts to increase the productivity of family resources in poor households.

4. The paramount role of income distribution in shaping villagewide impacts of policy and market changes.

5. A sometimes weak link between village income and migration. Migration effects depend critically on the way in which policies affect the distribution and level of village incomes, as well as on the distribution of access to migrant labor markets across households. Policies that increase average per capita incomes in rural areas may stimulate migration if they widen income inequalities.

6. A robust, positive effect of increases in village income on the demand for manufactured commodities. Village development ipso facto contributes to development of the urban manufacturing sector and to urban incomes. Conversely, policy biases against rural economic activities limit domestic markets for manufactures. These experiments provide new evidence for agricultural-development-led industrialization (ADLI). (See Adelman, 1984.)

7. The sensitivity of village economies to changes in the international economy. The extreme case is that of the Mexican village, where incomes are more sensitive to changes in the international exchange rate than to corn prices. Economic integration undoubtedly will increase the openness of village economies and their linkages with the global economy in the future.

New applications and the limits of villagewide modeling

As we completed this book, new villagewide modeling efforts were underway. The villagewide modeling approach is increasingly being used to model economies extending beyond the village. The Kenyan village-town model in this book is one example. Others include regional village-town economies in Mexico (Fredericks and Taylor, in progress) and Zambia (Holden, Hampton, and Taylor, in progress). The limits of villagewide modeling are not set by political borders. A joint effort by researchers at the Economic Development Foundation (FUNDE) in San Salvador, El Colegio de Mexico in Mexico City, and the University of California is employing the techniques in this book to model an economy consisting of villages and towns in El Salvador and their communities of migrants in California – that is, a transnational economic space. Because this modeling is no longer confined to villages, some researchers prefer to call it "micro economywide modeling" rather than "villagewide modeling." Micro economywide modeling is potentially applicable to developed as well as to developing economies. Perhaps more than any other feature, this modeling is distinguished by its micro, bottom-up approach to economywide modeling.

Clearly, there are trade-offs between villagewide modeling and microeconomic household-farm modeling, on the one hand, and "macro" CGE modeling, on the other. Our village and village-town study focus sacrifices geographical scope in favor of local economic detail. To date, no national survey of agricultural households to our knowledge is capable of supporting the data requirements of our models. This means that villagewide modelers presently must collect their own data, supplemented in some cases by data collection by government or international development agencies (e.g., ICRISAT in the Indian case). Until now, most of this data collection has taken the form of surveys of individual villages or small groups of villages and towns. The chief advantage of this modus operandi is to support modeling of local economies at a level of detail not available elsewhere. Village researchers in the field also acquire a "feel" for the structure and workings of village economies usually not possible from secondary data analysis. This, we believe, contributed to the unique insights that emerge from Chapters 3 through 7.

The major disadvantage of studies of individual villages or groups of villages is that they naturally raise questions about the generalizability of findings to other local economies, to regions, and to nations at large. The robustness of some of our qualitative findings across very different village and village-town settings is somewhat reassuring in this regard. However, many of our findings exhibit striking diversity across the villages and village-town. Villagewide impacts and responses to policy, market, and environmental changes are shaped by technologies, local institutional structures, and especially market development.

Two broad approaches are available to test the generalizability of villagewide economic models in specific country settings. The first is to replicate village and village-town economywide studies in a series of carefully selected sites. We are currently adopting this approach to test our Mexican village findings in other regions of Mexico and to create a basis for tracking impacts of NAFTA and market reforms on the Mexican rural economy over time.

An alternative – and we feel the most promising – approach is to incorporate micro economywide modeling data needs into the design of agricultural household surveys. The technology for extending villagewide models regionwide exists. The data requirements for micro economywide modeling are not significantly greater than for agricultural household models. Usually they can be met by adding only a few questions to household-farm surveys, by scoping out local economies for activities missed by random samples, and by stratifying where necessary to include these activities. Often, the "additional" data needed to support micro economywide modeling are also critical for microeconomic modeling. Agricultural household surveys' frequent neglect of family migration activities and nonfarm production – both of which can profoundly affect agricultural production – is a case in point.

Concluding remarks

We hope that this book serves two purposes. The first is to contribute to our understanding of the structure of village economies and the villagewide effects of policy, market, and environmental changes. In this sense, we hope it is useful for designing and implementing rural development policies. The second is to underline the importance of village-level economic research and to encourage more village economic studies in the future. Given sufficiently detailed household-farm data, it is relatively easy to construct a village SAM with the aid of spreadsheets. Recent advances in computer technology, economic modeling, and software for nonlinear programming bring applied general-equilibrium analysis within reach of researchers with graduate economics training. As rural economies become more complex and villages become increasingly integrated with outside markets, new insights can be gained by linking villages and towns together into regional CGEs as a basis for understanding the implications of economic integration for rural economies. The village-level CGEs presented in this book will, we hope, serve as a starting point for this endeavor.

BIBLIOGRAPHY

Adelman, I. (1984). "Beyond Export-Led Growth." *World Development* 12(9):937–49.

Adelman, I., and J. E. Taylor (1990). "Is Structured Adjustment with a Human Face Possible? The Case of Mexico." *Journal of Development Studies* 26(3):387–407.

Adelman, I., J. E. Taylor, and S. Vogel. (1988). "Life in a Mexican Village: A SAM Perspective." *Journal of Development Studies* 25:5–24.

Bardhan, P. (1988). "Alternative Approaches to Development Economics." In H. Chenery and T. N. Srinivasan, eds., *Handbook of Development Economics, Volume I.* Elsevier Science Publishers.

Barnum, H. N., and L. Squire. (1979). "An Econometric Application of the Theory of the Farm-Household." *Journal of Development Economics* 6:79–102.

Bendavid-Val, Avrom, et. al. (1988). *Rural-Urban Exchange in Kutus Town and Its Hinterland,* Report prepared under USAID Cooperative Agreement on Settlement and Resource Systems Analysis with Clark University (Worcester, MA) and Institute for Development Anthropology (Binghamton, NY).

Berar. (1870). *Gazetteer for the Haidarabad Assigned Districts (Commonly Called Berar).* Bombay.

Berar. (1881). *Census of India, 1881. Report on the Census of Berar.* Bombay, 1882.

Berar. (1901). *Report on the Famine in the Hyderabad Assigned Districts in the Years 1899 and 1900.* Nagpur, India.

Braverman, A., and J. S. Hammer. (1986). "Multimarket Analysis of Agricultural Pricing Policies in Senegal." In I. Singh, L. Squire, and J. Strauss, eds., *Agricultural Household Models, Extensions, Applications and Policy,* pp. 233–254. Baltimore: World Bank and Johns Hopkins University Press.

Census of India. (1941). *Central Provinces and Berar. Census of India, 1941.* Vol. 8.

Census of India. (1951a). *Akola District Census Handbook, Census of India, 1951, Madhya Pradesh.*

Census of India. (1951b). *General Population, Economic, Age and Social Tables (A, B, C, D and E series) Census of India, 1951. Vindhya Pradesh, part II.*

Census of India. (1961a) *Akola District Census Handbook, Census of India, 1961, Moharashtra.*

Census of India. (1961b). *General Population Tables, Census of India, 1961. Maharashtra, part II-A.*

Census of India. (1971a). *Akola District Census Handbook, Census of India, 1971, Maharashtra.*
Census of India. (1971b). *General Population Tables, Census of India, 1971. Maharashtra, part II-A.*
Census of India. (1981). *Akola District Census Handbook, Census of India, 1981, Moharashtra.*
Chambers, R. G. (1988). *Applied Production Analysis.* Cambridge: Cambridge University Press.
Collier, William, L. Gunawan Wirodi, Soentoro Makali, and Kabul Santoso. (1988). "Employment Trends in Lowland Javanese Villages," Report prepared for USAID/Indonesia.
Cornelius, W. (1976). "Outmigration from Rural Mexican Communities." In *The Dynamics of Migration: International Migration.* Interdisciplinary Communications Program Occasional Monograph Series 5. Washington, DC: Smithsonian Institution.
de Janvry, A., M. Fafchamps, and E. Sadoulet. (1991). "Peasant Household Behavior with Missing Markets: Some Paradoxes Explained." *Economic Journal* 101:1400–1417.
Dearon, A., and J. Muellbauer. (1980). *Economics and Consumer Behavior.* Cambridge: Cambridge University Press.
Devarajan, S., Jeffrey D. Lewis, and S. Robinson. (forthcoming). *Getting the Model Right: The General Equilibrium Approach to Adjustment Policy.* Cambridge: Cambridge University Press.
Dhawan, B. D. (1986). *Economics of Groundwater Irrigation in Hard Rock Regions.* Agricole, New Delhi.
Fletcher, P. (1994). "Casa de Mis Suenos: Consumption and Identity in a Transnational Village." Paper presented at the Annual meetings of the American Anthropological Association, Atlanta, GA, November.
Fletcher, P. (1996). Building from Migration: Imported Design and Everyday Use of Migrant Houses in Mexico. Forthcoming in B. S. Orlove, ed., *The allure of the Foreign: Foreign Goods in Post-Colonial Latin America.* Ann Arbor, MI: University of Michigan Press.
Fletcher, P., and , J. E. Taylor. (1992). "Migration and the Transformation of a Mexican Village House Economy." Paper presented at the conference *New Perspectives on Mexico–U.S. Migration,* University of Chicago, October 22–23.
Fredericks, C., and J. E. Taylor. (In progress). "The Impact of NAFT on Incomes and Migration in rural Mexico in the Context of Market Failure."
Fukuzawa, H. (1982). "Maharashtra and the Deccan: A Note," and "The Medieval Deccan and Maharashtra." *In Cambridge Economic History of India.* Cambridge: Cambridge University Press.
Gaile, Gary. (1987). "Discussion Paper No. 5: RTPCs." Mimeograph, Kenyan Ministry of Planning.
Golan, E. H. (1990). "Land Tenure Reform in Senegal: An Economic Study From the Peanut Basin." Land Tenure Center Research Paper No. 101, University of Wisconsin, Madison.
Habib, I. (1982). "Agrarian Relations and Land Revenue." In Tapan Raychaudhuri and Irfan Habibi (eds.), *Cambridge Economic History of India, vol. 1: c. 1200–c. 1750,* pp. 235–248. Cambridge: Cambridge University Press.
Haggblade, S. P. B. Hazell, and J. Brown. (1988). "Farm–Nonfarm Linkages in Rural Sub-Shaharan Africa." Policy, Planning, and Research Working Paper No. WPS 6. Washington, DC: World Bank.
Hardjono, J. M. (1987). *Land, Labour and Livelihood in a West Java Village.* Yogyakarta: Gadjah Mada University Press.
Harnetty, P. (1971). "Cotton Exports and Indian Agriculture: 1861–1870." *Economic History Review* 24:414–429.
Hart, Gillian. (1986). *Power, Labor, and Livelihood: Processes of Change in Rural Java.* Berkeley: University of California Press.
Hayami, Yujiro, and Masao Kikuchi. (1982). *Asian Village Economy at the Crossroads.* Baltimore: Johns Hopkins Press.

Hazell, P. B. S., and A. Roell. (1983). "Rural Growth Linkages: Household Expenditure Patterns in Malaysia and Nigeria." International Food Policy Research Institute (IFPRI) Research Report 41. Washington, DC: IFPRI.

Heathfield, D. F., and S. Wibe. 1987. *An Introduction to Cost and Production Analysis.* Atlantic Highlands, NJ: Humanities Press International.

Holden, S., S. Hampton, and J. E. Taylor. (In progress). "Structural Adjustment under Transactions Costs: A Micro Economywide Model for Rural Zambia."

ICAR. (1954). "Estimation of the Cost of Production of Crops: Report on the Pilot Scheme for the Estimation of Costs of Production of Cotton and Rotation Crops in Akola District, Madhya Pradesh, 1952–53." Indian Council for Agricultural Research, New Delhi.

Jodha, N. S. (1981). "Agricultural Tenancy in Semi-arid Tropical Villages of India." In H. P. Binswanger and M. Rosenzweig, eds., *Rural Labor Markets in Asia: Contractual Arrangements, Employment and Wages,* New Haven: Yale University Press.

Jodha, N. S., M. Asokan, and J. G. Ryan. (1977). *Village Study Methodology and Resource Endowments of Selected Villages in ICRISAT's Village Level Studies.* International Crops Research Institute for the Semi-arid Tropics, Patancheru.

Johnston, Bruce F., and John W. Mellor. (1961). "The Role of Agriculture in Economic Development." *American Economic Review* 51(4).

Kulkarni, A. R. (1966). "Village Life in Deccan in the 17th Century." *Indian Economic and Social History Review* 4.

Latham, Michael. (1984). "Strategies for the Control of Malnutrition and the Influence of the Nutritional Sciences." *Food and Nutrition* 10(1).

Lewis, W. A. (1954). "Economic Development with Unlimited Supplies of Labour." *Manchester School of Economic and Social Studies* 22: 129–191.

Lewis, B. D., and E. Thorbecke (1992). "District-Level Economic Linkages in Kenya: Evidence Based on a Small Regional Social Accounting Matrix." *World Development* 20(6):881–897.

Lluch, C., A. A. Powell, and R. A. Williams. (1977). *Patterns in Household Demand and Saving.* Oxford: Oxford University Press.

Lopez, R. E. (1986). Structural Models of the Farm Household that Allow for Interdependent Utility and Profit-Maximization Decisions." In I. L. Singh, L. Squire, and J. Strauss, eds. *Agricultural Household Models, Extensions, Applications and Policy,* pp. 306–326. Baltimore: World Bank and Johns Hopkins University Press.

Lucas, R. E. B. (1987). "Emigration to South Africa's Mines." *American Economic Review,* 77(3):313–330.

Madhya Pradesh. (1954). *Crop Estimating Survey on Cotton in Madhya Pradesh, 1954–55.* Nagpur.

Massey, D. S. (1984). "The Settlement Process among Mexican Migrants in the United States: New Methods and Findings." In D. Levine, K. Hill, and R. Warren, eds., *Immigration Statistics: A Story of Neglect,* Washington, DC: National Academy Press.

Massey, D. S., J. Arango, G. Hugo, A. Kouaouci, A. Pellegrino, and J. E. Taylor. (1994). "International Migration: The North American Case." *Population and Development Review* 19 (3): 431–466.

McAlpin, M. B. (1983). *Subject to Famine: Food Crises and Economic Change in Western India, 1860–1920.* Princeton: Princeton University Press.

McElroy, M. B. (1990). "The Empirical Content of Nash-Bargained Household Behavior." *Journal of Human Resources* 25(4):559–583.

McElroy, M. B., and M. J. Horney. (1981). "Nash-Bargained Household Decisions: Toward a Generalization of the Theory of Demand." *International Economic Review* 22(2):333–349.

Mellor, John. (1976). *The New Economics of Growth.* Ithaca, NY: Cornell University Press.

Miernyk, William H. (1979). "Comment on 'Reconciling Reconciliation Procedures in Regional Input–Output Analysis.' " *International Regional Science Review* 4(1):36–38.

Morris, Cynthia T., and Irma Adelman. (1988). *Comparative Patterns of Economic Development: 1850–1914*. Baltimore: Johns Hopkins University Press.

Murtagh, Bruce A., and Michael A. Sanders. (1983). "MINOS 5.1 User's Guide." Report SOL 83–20R, Stanford University (revised January 1987).

North, D. S., and M. F. Houstoun. (1976). *The Characteristics and Role of Illegal Aliens in the United States Labor Market: An Exploratory Study*. Washington, DC: Linton.

Parikh, A., and E. Thorbecke. (1996). "Impact of Rural Industrialization on Village Life and Economy: A SAM Approach." *Economic Development and Cultural Change* 44(2):351–377.

Pyatt, G. (1985). "Commodity Balances and National Accounts: A SAM Perspective." *Review of Income and Wealth* 4.

Pyatt, G., and J. I. Round. (1979). "Accounting and Fixed-Price Multipliers in a Social Accounting Matrix Framework." *Economic Journal* 89:850–873.

Ralston, Katherine. (1992). *An Economic Analysis of Factors Affecting Nutritional Status of Households in Rural West Java, Indonesia*. Ph.D. dissertation, University of California, Berkeley.

Ranney, S., and S. Kossoudji. (1983). "Profiles of Temporary Mexican Labor Migrants in the United States." *Population and Development Review* 9:475–493.

Reardon, T., C. Delgado, and P. Matlan. (1992). "Determinants and Food Security Effects of Household Income Diversification by Agroecological Zone in the West African Semi-arid Tropics." *Journal of Development Studies* 28(2):264–296.

Republic of Kenya. (1984). *Kirinyaga District Development Plan, 1984–1988*. Nairobi: Ministry of Planning.

Republic of Kenya. (1988). *Economic Survey, 1988*. Nairobi: Central Bureau of Statistics.

Russell, S. S., and M. S. Teitelbaum. (1992). "International Migration and International Trade." World Bank Discussion Paper No. 160.

Simpson, S. Rowton. (1976). *Land Law and Registration*. Cambridge: Cambridge University Press.

Singh, I., L. Squire, and J. Strauss. (1986). "An Overview of Agricultural Household Models – The Basic Model: Theory, Empirical Results, and Policy Conclusions." In I. Singh, L. Squire, and J. Strauss, eds., *Agricultural Household Models, Extensions, Applications and Policy*. Baltimore: World Bank and Johns Hopkins University Press.

SR. (1931). Draft report on the Revision Settlement for Murtizapur Taluka. August 20 at the Collectorate, Akola.

Stark, O. (1982). "Research on Rural-to-Urban Migration in LDCS: The Confusion Frontier and Why We Should Pause to Rethink Afresh." *World Development* 10: 63–70.

Stone, J. R. N. (1978). "The Disaggregation of the Household Sector in the National Accounts." Paper presented at the World Bank conference on Social Accounting Methods in Development Planning, Cambridge, April 16–21.

Subramanian, S. (1988). *Production and Distribution in a Dry-land Village Economy*. Ph.D. dissertation, University of California, Berkeley.

Subramanian, S., and E. Sadoulet. (1990). "The Transmission of Production Fluctuations and Technical Change in a Village Economy: A Social Accounting Matrix Approach." *Economic Development and Cultural Change* 39(1):131–173.

Taylor, J. E. (1986). "Differential Migration, Networks, Information and Risk." In Oded Stark, ed., *Migration, Human Capital and Development*. Greenwich, CT: JAI Press.

Taylor, J. E. (1987). "Undocumented Mexico–U.S. Migration and the Returns to Households in Rural Mexico." *American Journal of Agricultural Economics* 69:626–638.

Taylor, J. E. (1992). "Remittances and Inequality Reconsidered: Direct, Indirect and Intertemporal Effects." *Journal of Policy Modelling* 14(2):187–208.

Taylor, J. E. (1995). *Micro Economywide Models for Migration and Policy Analysis: An Application to Mexico.* Paris: Organization for Economic Cooperation and Development.

Taylor, J. E. and T. J. Wyatt. (1993). "Migration, Assets and Income Inequality in a Diversified Household-Farm Economy." University of California, Davis, Department of Agricultural Economics Working Paper No. 92–13 (December), presented at the 1993 AAEA Annual Meetings, Orlando, August 1–4.

Taylor, J. E., I. Adelman, and S. Vogel. (1988). "Life in a Mexican Village: A SAM Perspective." *Journal of Development Studies* 25:5–24.

Timmer, C. Peter. (1988). "The Agricultural Revolution." In H. Chenery and T. N. Srinivasan, eds., *Handbook of Development Economics, Volume I.* Elsevier Science Publishers.

Todaro, M. P. (1969). "A Model of Migration and Urban Unemployment in Less-developed Countries." *American Economic Review* 59: 138–148.

Todaro, Michael P. (1980). "Internal Migration in Developing Countries: A Survey." In R. A. Easterlin, ed., *Population and Economic Change in Developing Countries.* Chicago: University of Chicago Press.

Walker, T., and J. Kshirsagar. (1985). "The Village Impact of Machine Threshing and Implications for Technology Development in the Semi-arid Tropics of Peninsular India." *Journal of Development Studies* 21.

Walker, T. S., and J. G. Ryan. (1990). *Village and Household Economies in India's Semi-arid tropics.* Baltimore: Johns Hopkins University Press.

World Bank. (1986). *World Development Report, 1986.* New York: Oxford University Press.

World Health Organization. (1973). *Energy and Protein Requirements: Report of a Joint FAO/WHO Ad Hoc Expert Committee.* Geneva: WHO.

World Health Organization. (1985). *Energy and Protein Requirements,* Report of Joint FAO/WHO/UNU Expert Consultation, Technical Report Series 724. Geneva: WHO.

Yanagisako, S. (1979). "Family and Household: The Analysis of Domestic Groups." *Annual Review of Anthropology* 8:161–205.

AUTHOR INDEX

SUBJECT INDEX

261